A Wife on Gorge River

Sue and Alan
Best wishes,

Catherine Stewart

February 2015

A Wife on Gorge River

CATHERINE STEWART

RANDOM HOUSE
NEW ZEALAND

A catalogue record for this book is available from the National Library of New Zealand

Random House New Zealand is part of the Random House Group

New York   London   Sydney   Auckland   Delhi   Johannesburg

First published 2012, reprinted 2013.

© 2012 Catherine Stewart

The moral rights of the author have been asserted

ISBN 978 1 86979 923 6

eISBN 978 1 86979 924 3

Text and cover design: Megan van Staden

All photographs are from the author's personal collection

This publication is printed on paper pulp sourced from sustainably grown and managed forests, using Elemental Chlorine Free (ECF) bleaching, and printed with 100% vegetable-based inks

Printed in New Zealand by Printlink

Also available as an eBook

For Robert, without whom there would have been no story. Without him to fix the roof, deal with plumbing, and talk, cajole and wheedle me through the tough times, I would not have stayed long.

*And for Christan and Robin,
who have made it so much more fun.*

With love.

Persevering and faithful

The motto of the House Family

Contents

Author's Note
NO LIGHT-HOUSE

I once thought that if I ever wrote a book I should call it 'No Lighthouse', since having the word 'lighthouse' in the title seemed like a guarantee of sales. Starting with Mabel Pollock's *The Children from the Lighthouse*, I have read out loud in the evenings all the lighthouse books I could get hold of: *Birdie's Lighthouse, As Darker Grows the Night, The Red Rocks of Eddystone*. I was a bit slow when I heard about Jeanette Aplin's *The Lighthouse Keeper's Wife*, as I thought it might be like *The Lighthouse Keeper's Lunch* which we had outgrown, but we enjoyed it and *The Lighthouse Children's Mother*, and look forward to the rest of the story.

Since visiting the lighthouses at Cape Leeuwin and Cape Naturaliste in Western Australia as a child, I had always wanted to live in a lighthouse. (Doesn't everyone at some stage?) Admittedly, I was somewhat deflated to find that lighthouse keepers didn't actually get to live in the round towers with furniture built to fit the curving walls, instead preferring to live in 'normal' houses nearby.

As it was, I came to live with Robert Long, also known as Beansprout, at the mouth of the Gorge River on the west coast of New Zealand's South Island. Our home is about halfway between Jackson Bay, at the end of the road south of Haast, and Milford Sound. A two-day walk north would bring us to the end of the road into the Cascade Valley, and it could be another day to walk from there to the main road if no one came along and gave us a ride. To the south, we would follow the coast as far as Martins Bay, where the Hollyford Track leads out to Gunn's Camp on the Hollyford Road just below the road into Milford Sound. Robert's record for this tramp was two-and-a-half days, but once I came along, particularly later with babies and growing children, it took us at least seven days and anything up to 12.

At Gorge River we have the isolation and the exposure to storm and gale, the constant sound of the sea for company, and the exhilarating awareness of the weather and sea conditions like an inbuilt marine forecast. When we stay with the Mitchells, our next-door neighbours 30 kilometres south at Big Bay, where the house is tucked away up the Awarua River a few hundred metres behind the sand dunes and nicely sheltered, I always feel a bit out of touch with the weather. It takes a walk to the river mouth to get the same feeling, and as you tend to always be busy it can be easy to get stuck in the house and miss whatever is going on outside. At Gorge River, even in the house, you are right amongst it.

Unlike lighthouse keepers, we don't have a monthly supply-drop from the government steamer, a back-up service, a salary or any materials provided. Nor do we have to wind the lantern every 30 minutes, stand nightshifts, scrub the house spotless in preparation for the next tenants,

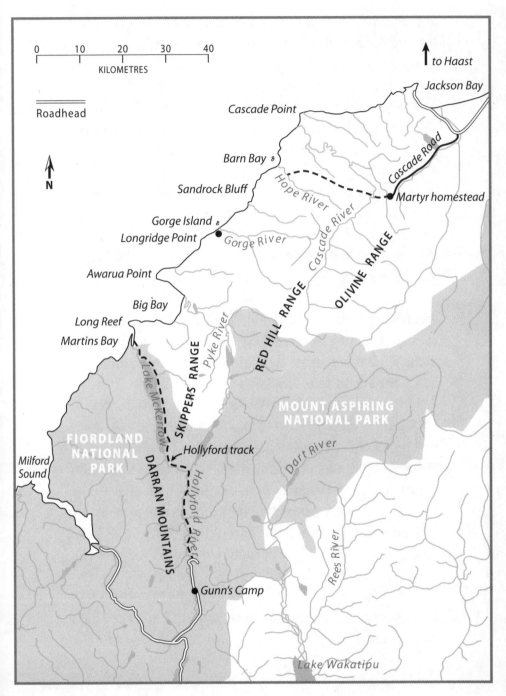

South Westland, showing Gorge River and surrounds

and board the ship on schedule regardless of how dreadful the weather is or how seasick the children are.

Although not circular, our house has many attributes of a lighthouse. It shakes in high winds or with a big sea running, and the windows are always covered in salt spray. When I left Christchurch, a friend wrote in a card *Enjoy the silence of the wilderness*, but living beside the ocean it is never silent. Our windows look directly out to sea, and we keep an eye on passing boats, planes and helicopters, often knowing already where they are going, what they are doing and whether they are likely to call in on their way back. We used to fly a flag to show that we were at home, until the sea took the flagpole away one too many times, and at night if we saw the lights of a boat we'd light the kerosene lantern and hang it in the window where they could see it. When our first child was big enough to climb a ladder safely, Robert built one for him up to the windowsill where he could stand on his lookout and watch fishing boats and seabirds passing by.

I first tramped along the Big Bay and Cascade coastline in 1987, but it wasn't until 1990 that I returned to Gorge River, staying two or three weeks at a time for most of that year. Robert and I came home from a visit to my sister in Canada in January 1991, pregnant with our first child, after Gorge River had been my permanent home for several months.

Lighthouses or otherwise, I would probably never have written a book if Robert hadn't done it first and so successfully. I resisted a bit longer, but with so many people asking to hear my side of the story, and the amazing feedback we have had from everyone, it simply had to be done, like most of what I do around here.

Preface

WHAT THE TUI SEES

Take a peek through the skylight onto a typical day in our house.

Most days we aren't out of bed very early. The summer sun doesn't get to us over the hill until nearly 9.00, although it is light much earlier. The days are long, with an hour or more of twilight after sunset. It isn't dark until about 10.30 and we tend to work late. After getting up at 8.00 or 8.30, we have lunch at 3.00, tea at 9.00, and the kids might get to bed by 11.00. Being so far west, it seems to me that if we put our clocks back an hour instead of forwards for daylight saving, I'd spend less time feeling guilty. With no school bus to catch or official working hours to meet, who cares anyway?

Either Robert or I gets up to light the fire, and the other gets a cup of lemon-balm tea, half an orange and half an apple in bed. If it is my morning in bed, I stay a while where the light is good beside the front windows to mend Robert's favourite jersey, which is just about on its last legs. Robin needs new slippers for the winter, and I'm knitting a pair of black possum/merino gloves for Christan. Since he spends so much time plucking possums, he might as well wear the product.

Over in the far corner, Robin reads for an hour or more before she gets out of bed. It is a job to keep up a supply of decent reading material for her, and I must write a letter to the Hokitika Library to ask for some more books. Christan is reading Ken Tustin's *A Wild Moose Chase* which will be a good one for his Level 2 reading log. He also needs one by a Maori author; perhaps the Correspondence School can send something.

I open the window to throw a rotten bit of apple onto the garden and three young blackbirds fly off, startled. They've been digging holes again in the lettuce patch and burying the pathetic seedlings in piles of mulch behind them. A bellbird calls from the rata tree:

♫ *Christi boy* ♫♪ *Christi boy* ♫♪

They started singing that song the first time Christan went away by himself to a school camp at Boyle River in the Lewis Pass, when he was 16. For Robin they say:

♫ *Bob Job* ♫ *ppppttt!* ♫♪

At the river mouth, a young spotted shag dries its feathers on a rock, one leg pulled up under its belly. *Flick, flick, flick* go its wings. And *kick, kick* go its feet when the bugs bite. Beyond the bar, two adults fish just outside the waves, while their younger chicks sit waiting for the next meal on the calm water between the islands.

Christan climbs out of bed, pulls on a pair of pants and

scratches his hair into place. After hanging half a dozen possum skins tacked onto boards on the deer fence around the garden, he heads down the airstrip for a look at the day. Returning, he opens the cupboard and loads up a large bowl with rolled oats, peanuts and sultanas, leaving behind him oats and half a spoonful of milk powder on the bench.

Robert sits in his seat with the half-finished painting of Lake Alabaster on his easel before him. He gazes out the window through a haze of salt spray and spider's webs, and flicks through a pile of photographs and pamphlets, psyching himself up to paint the trees in the left-hand middle ground.

'Hey Robin, would you clean the windows today, please?'

Christan will take the boat up the river through the gorge, then climb up a ridge leading to the top of the hill behind us, checking his traps. If any of the skins look good, he hangs the possum in a tree to skin tomorrow. Otherwise he plucks the fur while it is still warm. It is good money, and he probably has more in his bank account than most kids of his age.

'Right, see ya.' He reaches for his hat, with his pack on his back.

'Have you got the beacon?' I ask.

'Yep, bye.'

With the jersey mended, it is time I got up to put more wood on the fire. We need a loaf of bread today, and I want hot water to deal to a load of Christan's stinky possum clothes. Robin gets dressed in her corner, spends some time brushing her hair and comes out via the bathroom. She looks into both cupboards before settling for the last of the apple crumble for breakfast.

'There's a bit of fish there for Chooky,' I say as she picks up the jar of wheat and rejected peanuts that I sorted out of the packet yesterday for our pet chicken.

Three cups wholemeal, one cup stoneground and one cup of high-grade white flour go into the big stainless-steel bowl. I measure salt into my hand and find the jar of yeast. Now, where is my spoon? It's the only one with a handle strong enough to mix bread dough. I find it in the workshop where Christan has been ladling flour into jars for possum bait.

Two spoons of yeast and the pint cup full of warm water, then I sit down on Robin's driftwood stool to stir the whole lot in one go. I'll stand it by the stove for 15 or 20 minutes before I give it a quick knead with the spoon in the bowl. No doubt 20 minutes of vigorous kneading would make a finer loaf, but this is adequate and everyone likes my bread.

Next, there are six fish to fillet. Robert has been down earlier to rescue the yellow-eyed mullet from the net before the eels make too much of a mess. I see that two of the fish have already been gutted — the bit that eels like best before they head out to sea to breed — and one looks a bit mangled.

'There had been three more and the net was in a big tangle,' Robert says.

I leave the frames in the bucket for Christan to bury in the garden when he digs a hole for the possums he skinned last night. I cover the bucket to keep the flies out, particularly after last year when a stoat kept sneaking in through a hole under the front door to pinch the fish. When Christan has filled that empty patch of ground with carcasses, I will plant rocket and mizuna on it for the winter. The broad beans have finished there already.

Southern Legend can be heard crayfishing up at Brown's Refuge. They'll be heading south to Milford today having camped at Jackson Bay last night.

It is going to be hot in the house today with the fire going all morning. Usually I let it go out as soon as I can on a hot day, if there is enough to eat, then just get it going again for tea. I'll have to get a few bags of wood off the beach later. If I fill them the kids will carry them home for me, as my fingers are suffering from too many years of carting heavy loads and probably have a few years in front of them yet.

'Helicopter!' Robert calls, and half a second later I hear it, too. We all troop out for a look as the Robinson R44 flies by, too high to see what colour it is. We haven't seen anyone for almost two weeks.

The day goes on. Robin gets stuck into schoolwork, as will Christan when he gets back. They have both started early in January so we don't need to worry about taking time off when we want to later in the year. I try to get them to do at least some work when we are away, but it never happens, and they may as well do it here without all the distractions. Nor do they take weekends off, but that means if someone arrives or something more exciting is happening they have days to spare. I only have the occasional nag to make sure they get plenty done in the first half of the year, as invariably there is a rush towards the end once the whitebait season starts.

Throughout the day everyone helps themselves to food as it suits them, and my job is to be sure that something is available when they get hungry. I spend a lot of time in the garden, weeding, thinning carrots, digging the first potatoes. We have beans and peas through a lot of the summer, while the other things take a bit longer to grow big enough to start on. Tomatoes, lettuces and zucchini are hardly ever ready before February, but there is usually plenty of green leafy stuff for salads.

In the afternoon the kids dress in their wetsuits, grab boogie boards and flippers, and head to the river mouth. I stand up to straighten my back as they go by, and decide that the weeds can wait until tomorrow. I'm hot, grubby and sick of swatting sandflies, and even Chooky has retired to rest in the shade of the koromiko. She likes gardening with me, as I loosen up the soil and disturb the worms, but it rapidly becomes a battle of wills when she decides that *I'm* in *her* way. Her idea of the pecking order is not the same as mine, but no amount of arguing about it has convinced her.

The river is actually warmer than the sea this week and, if the good weather holds, it might even warm up a bit more. Robert and I long ago perfected the technique of the U-turn dive, so that you are virtually out of the water again before you have time to realise how cold it is! Although the kids have never had much chance to swim laps and develop a good style, they are strong and confident in cold water when many people might struggle with the shock of it.

I squirm into my short wetsuit, bought from a second-hand shop just before I turned 40. Cold water wafts in around my neck and down my back because I'm five centimetres too short for it, but the difference it makes is amazing and I can now stay in the water for up to half an hour, particularly if I'm propped up on a board.

Robin sees me coming and, bored with the lack of surf, suggests that we take the boogie boards up through the gorge. The river is about 12 metres deep up there and jade green. Towering vertically above us are limestone cliffs covered in thick mosses where waterfalls drip. Tiny papery daisies, ferns, hebe and toetoe grow in the moss, and curtains of orchids hang from bigger branches of tutu. Rangiora, mahoe and rata cling to the steep rock higher up the cliff.

We climb out to walk around the rapid and scoot down it, banging our knees on partially-submerged rocks before re-entering the deep water where we drift back down on the current. Robin always argues when I insist that I have had enough, but by that time I am so cold that I don't get much done for the rest of the day.

I ask Christan to fill the wood-box while I get the fire going again. The 12-gallon-drum stove has only a single hotplate, so I fry up cold potatoes with parsley and onion greens, then set them aside while I cook the fish. Robin brings in a large bunch of chickweed, watercress, mizuna and broad-bean leaves to make a salad. The kettle sits at the side, already hot, so it only takes a few more minutes to steam the bigger broad beans, but most of them we eat raw. We don't eat dessert at tea time. If I make an apple crumble, fruit/custard/cake trifle or anything like that, it gets eaten throughout the day.

With tea over and the mess cleared away, Robert sits at the table working with a rasp on a whalebone penguin. Robin disappears into her corner to read and to write secretly in her diary, and Christan has a bit more schoolwork to do before he is finished for the day. I'm making Christan's NCEA Level 1 creative writing assignment — for which he received 'Excellence' — into a book using some of his best photos. I will make a copy for his English teacher at the Correspondence School in Wellington and another for his grandparents.

But right now, if I don't go to bed I shall fall off my perch.

Chapter 1
BLOSSOM OF A GOOD ROOT STOCK

'There's rain in the western highlands,' Toddie observed from the front of his house near Arrowtown.

The Gamekeeper's House with its view over the Lake Hayes area and the Wakatipu Basin is the home of our great friends, Iain and Sue Todd. Although Toddie emigrated with his parents and brothers from Scotland at a young age, they still speak Scots whenever they get together.

I thrill at his words, as I've always felt like a Western Highland Stewart. However, although we can trace the Stewart family back to 1806, at that time they were living in Paisley and Renfrew near Glasgow, and we don't really know where they had come from before that. But when my brother spoke of the Western Highland Stewart tartan, or Old Stewart tartan, I felt that it was mine. They were all called Robert Stewart, perhaps back to the first Stewart king of Scotland, the grandson of Robert the Bruce.

Many of those early ancestors were power-loom weavers and Great-grandmother Isabella was a silk weaver. In 1990 when my cousin Jeanne was attempting to trace the family back in Scotland, she found six pages of Stewarts in the Glasgow telephone directory, so settled for the Armstrong clan — a choice of only three.

'Aunty Peggy?!' came the shriek in broad Scots, when the telephone was answered.

I never knew my paternal grandmother, Peggy Armstrong, who was a kilt-maker before her marriage. She left Scotland in 1931 with my granddad, Robert Stewart, and their two daughters, Olive and Marj. Her family lost contact with her during the war, and didn't know for 50 years that she had died in 1940. Robert had been a budding artist, and had once painted the wall of a room in Glasgow so that you appeared to be looking out through a door into the garden beyond.

The Stewarts went to Australia to get away from the Great Depression, but it soon caught up with them. My Great-uncle Jim went first to Fremantle, followed by Great-aunty Meg with her family, then ours. James and Isabella, their parents, came too.

'Bloody overstayers!' Aunty Marj decreed.

When I asked her why they had come to Australia, thinking romantically of the Clearances and things like that, she replied, 'Too bloody cold in Scotland! We couldn't afford to buy jumpers for all the kids.'

Olive and Marj were 10 and eight before Anne was born in Fremantle, with the three boys arriving every second year after that. In a letter to my dad, Aunty Marj explained that they were a normal happy family until he was two, when Anne got sick. At four years old, she was diagnosed with a cancer of the stomach and died only two weeks later in April 1937.

The birth of Neill followed in August. When Ian was asked, 'What do you think of your new brother?' he blew a mouthful of cracker crumbs over the baby.

Doug's birth was induced on New Year's Day 1940 after Peggy had been diagnosed with cervical cancer, and she died in October of that year. Once Peggy was admitted to hospital, Olive was the only one of the children over 16 and therefore allowed to visit, which 14-year-old Marj resented for the rest of her life. My dad was five; he remembers a day when his school teacher made a big fuss of him, and figures that must have been the day his mother died.

Even though Great-aunty Meg had two boys of her own, it was up to her to take in the five children. Olive helped with the cooking, and Marj had to look after the boys. She carried her resentment of this situation to her grave, too, and certainly it was a tough time for a 14-year-old girl. I always enjoyed Great-aunty Meg in her old age, with her hair-net and shortbread, but I bet she was cranky with five extra kids in the 'hoose'. Twice she presented Granddad with a possible new wife, whom he refused. He'd promised Peggy to keep the family together, and neither of these women was prepared to take on the boys but wanted to pack them off to boarding school as soon as possible.

After two years, it was time for a rearrangement. Olive went off to Teachers' College, leaving Marj with yet another lifelong resentment. She knew that Olive would give up teaching as soon as she was married, while she herself had a true calling for it. The closest she ever got to teaching, however, was managing the high-school canteen in Collie, Western Australia, for many years. When a helicopter-load of West Australian football players called in to Gorge River for a cup of tea a few years ago, they remembered her from Collie High School.

But it was Marj's job to look after the boys, so at 16 she ran the house while Granddad worked to support them. It was the Second World War, and Navy ships — rather than entering Fremantle Harbour and being easily identified — would anchor offshore in 'Gage Roads', and Granddad would be taken out to them to paint them. He couldn't tell Marj where he was going, and she'd never know when he'd be back. Nor was there any money until he did return. Eventually, she'd had enough of that and went bush, and Granddad could no longer keep his promise of keeping the family together.

Dad was 10 when, on the day the war ended, he and his brothers entered Parkerville, an Anglican boys' home in the Darling Range above Perth, and were immediately separated into three different houses according to their ages. Growing up, I always understood that this was an orphanage, and certainly Hell on Earth. They had to go to church twice a day, except Saturdays when they worked instead, and then three times on Sunday to make up for it. Dad's job every day was to chop wood for the kitchen, enough to cook for 200 people. He was also pressed into service as an altar boy, and a less angelic one would be hard to imagine. He told us stories of using a bike pump to fill oranges on the tree with kerosene, which seemed rather bizarre behaviour until I realised that the oranges belonged to the priest who ran the place: Arch Enemy No. 1. Dad ran away several times, but the only car that ever stopped in answer to his upraised thumb was that of the priest.

On the other hand, Aunty Marj always had the boys out of there for school holidays, so it was similar to being at boarding school. As I grew up, Dad repeatedly swore that he would never send us to boarding school. In time, Aunty Marj married George Bignell in Collie, inland from Bunbury in Western Australia. Uncle George worked five-and-a-half days a week in a coal mine, but sometimes on a Saturday afternoon he would drive Marj the three hours up to Perth to collect the boys for the holidays.

Granddad was working hard to pay for the boys' keep, but his art was now limited to the money-making necessity of signwriting for the government. He was also hitting the booze pretty hard. Dad said they saw him only about once a year. Also, while he was working full-time he couldn't get to the office in town, which only opened during normal working hours, to pay the bill for the boys' home. So it was that on one occasion when Aunty Marj and Uncle George arrived to collect the boys, they found that the boys were not allowed to leave. With the bill unpaid the boys were to be made wards of the state, and arrangements were already proceeding for the younger, sweeter brothers to be adopted out.

'Like Hell!' said Aunty Marj, and saw to it. And that was the end of that! I pride myself on my no-nonsense approach to life which I have inherited from Aunty Marj.

To us, Granddad was always very sweet and easy to get on with, and he often came to stay. In his Scots accent, our pet budgie was 'the wee chooky birrrrdie' or maybe 'the mud-lark'.

Sometimes he was supposed to be painting our house, which would take him weeks on end. We'd get home from school or work at four or five in the afternoon and he'd ask, 'What time is it?' When told, he would invariably say, 'Oh, the day is but young', but occasionally he would wander off and paint the entire lounge room before tea using a 20-centimetre brush, around all the window frames and everything, without dropping a spot of paint on the floor.

His creative energy bubbled out of him occasionally. When I was about five or six, we watched him scrape all the gold off the foil paper from a packet of Dad's Benson & Hedges smokes. Then he asked for some glue and drew a pattern with it onto the scraped piece of paper, before sprinkling the gold dust onto the glue. My brother, Andrew, kept that for years.

Another time, probably during one of the spells when he was painting our house, he painted a sleigh on the inside of the biggest front window, which happened to be that of the bedroom I shared with Alison. It was the most beautiful thing, and we kids painted the window, much less professionally, for the next few Christmases. As we never spent Christmas with the Stewarts, I guess he must have done it just before going back home to Collie.

He smoked until he could no longer roll his own, although for a while my brother would get a bit of pocket money for rolling up a tin full for him. Eventually Granddad came to live in the nursing home where Mum was the sister and second-in-charge, and where I worked in the kitchen a couple of evenings a week after school or a half-day shift making beds with one of the nurses on weekends or in the holidays. He was never any trouble to anyone, apart from being a danger to himself, so he had to be tied into his chair after falling over too many times. At times he had a few nasty bruises, but he never broke anything, nor did he die of anything smoking-related; he simply wound down. On the day he died in 1979 Mum was due to start work at 7am as usual. When at 6.35 the telephone rang, she immediately thought they were calling to say that Granddad had died, but it turned out the call was for some other reason. In fact, Granddad *had* died; they just hadn't found him by that stage.

We kids didn't go to his funeral, but I do remember the feeling when I saw his empty bed a couple of nights later on my next evening shift. Otherwise he passed out of our lives just as he had lived — at least for as long as I had known him: with very little fuss.

So Aunty Marj and Uncle George filled the role of grandparents. Their house in Collie was a wondrous place. The block was large and fairly steep, so you climbed a few steps up to the large verandah at the front. Underneath there was a kind of cave, walled off at the front and disappearing into dirt at the back. This was where Uncle George kept all sorts of things that he meant to get back to sometime: boxes of stuff and the insides of a piano that we thought was a harp. Having worked almost 40 years in the coal mine he was waiting to retire, and Aunty Marj had a list of jobs for him that had been waiting for a long time. Even so, the house was full of model aeroplanes, and exquisite boats and trinket boxes made out of shell sat on the mantelpiece.

The house was very old and grubby with cracked lino on the floors, and stepping out of the back door you passed Uncle George's shed, always knee-deep in sawdust, on the climb up to the outdoor dunny surrounded by fruit trees. He had one apple tree that gave five different types of apples from different grafts, and a whole tree of his particular favourite.

At 60, he retired and things started to change. Each time we visited, another room had been painted and re-floored, the verandah got a lovely pebble finish, the toilet moved into the bathroom and flushed, and all sorts of things were coming out of the shed. He was mad on inlaying, and enthusiasm bubbled out of him. He was the only person I knew with a wood lathe, and with it he would turn out lampstands made in several pieces. Many times he explained how he made a pattern of saw-cuts in the turned piece, then, taking a pale soft wood, he would squash it in the vice until he could push it into the saw-cut, then wet it so that it swelled up and filled the trench perfectly.

He made violins, guitars and a mandolin, and would play several different melody lines, dubbing on top of each other onto tape. He taught us to play the violins one weekend, too, and my brother's guitar had pieces of mother-of-pearl shell inlaid in the stem.

Aunty Olive also died of cancer before she was 40, just before I was born, and I never knew her kids. Even though Grandma Peggy's wish to keep the family together was always a very strong force throughout, mostly due to Aunty Marj — and passed on by her to at least some of us — three early deaths due to cancer plus a certain amount of alcohol stretched the family almost to breaking point.

Although my maternal grandmother's family, the Gileses, was arguably more respectable, they definitely had non-conformist attitudes of their own. Apart from my interest in writing, making, publishing and binding books, I'd have to say I inherited much of my cantankerousness from them, as it can't all be blamed on the Stewarts.

John Allen Giles, my great-great-grandfather, wanted to be a barrister but was persuaded by his parents, to his regret, to take orders as a deacon, then become a priest in the Church of England. After three years as headmaster of the City of London school, he refused to butter up any of the board, who in return failed to re-elect him for a second term. He wrote a series of translations of Greek and Latin classics, but the Bishop of Oxford insisted that he remove from the printing press his *Christian Records*, a new translation of the Bible without all the controversial bits. Giles asked the bishop to point out any areas where he had actually disagreed with Church doctrine, but the bishop refused to enter the conversation and Giles was forced to 'bow to authority but not to reason'. He had 'no wish to become a martyr', he had written to the bishop, 'even though my becoming so would probably do me more worldly good than ever the church has done me'. This disaffection with the Church led shortly afterwards to prosecution for an act of goodwill — that of marrying a couple before 8am, without the proper licence or the presence of witnesses. Not taking the matter seriously at first, he made his position worse by attempting to cover it up and was sentenced to 12 months' imprisonment in Oxford Castle prison, although he was released after three.

His son, Herbert Allen Giles, joined Her Britannic Majesty's Consulate Service in China, serving for 26 years, during which time he published a long list of works on the religions, poetry, literature, art, philosophy and political conditions of the country. His best-known works are his *Chinese–English Dictionary* (a classic of the Wade–Giles system of romanisation of Chinese characters) and *A Chinese Biographical Dictionary* — an absolute necessity for British Consular officials and merchants in China. He received the

Prix St Julien of the French Academy for each of these, in 1911 and 1897, respectively. After the death of Wade, whom Giles considered a fool, he was offered the position of Professor of Chinese at Cambridge University, a position which he held until the age of 87. With few students, he was free to devote his abundant energy to research and publication of many reference works, language textbooks, translations and miscellanea which transformed European ideas of China. Although he could be abrasive and ruthless with his pen, he was also a man of great personal charm, a loving family man, the soul of kindness to a friend in need, and one who, his obituary tells, would 'speak to anyone in the street from the Vice-Chancellor to the crossing-sweeper'.

His first wife and my namesake, Catherine Maria Fenn, had nine children in 12 years in China, at a time when few European women lived there. Having buried three of them in infancy, she left six others under the age of nine with her own death from liver cancer.

Two of the sons entered the Consulate Service and returned to China. A third son joined the Royal Engineers, serving in India, and accompanied Younghusband on his expedition into Tibet in 1904. The other brother became an eminent Orientalist at the British Museum, and when I arrived at Gorge River I found a book of the Tao Te Ching with a foreword to the particular translation by Lionel Giles.

My great-grandfather, Lancelot Giles, was a student interpreter in Peking when he was caught up in the siege and defence of the foreign legations during the Boxer Rebellion of 1900, for which he received the China medal with clasp.

Marjory Scott, my great-grandmother, was the first woman to be admitted to Cambridge University to read History. Having come to the aid of Professor Giles's second wife, who had fallen from her bicycle, she was a friend of the three Giles daughters (the third a product of the second marriage) and met Lance during his six months' leave from China in 1905. Her diary entry for 10 June that year reads: *Met Mr Giles in evening. Thought flashed through mind, 'This is the man I am going to marry.'* A footnote below reads: *[Note on 28/X/05: have done so!]*

The 24-carat gold wedding ring was very thick, because Lance said, 'I'm jolly well going to make sure that everyone knows that this woman is married to *me*!'

My sister, Alison, wears it now, but when she tried to buy something in 24 carat for her husband, Darrell Piere, in Canada, she was told that it would wear away quickly.

'Well, this has lasted a hundred years so far!' she told them.

Lancelot served for 35 years as Vice Consul, Consul and Consul General in various posts in China, receiving the Cross of St Michael and St George in the King's Birthday Honours list of 1928. During his final illness he served uncomplainingly and with a clear mind from his deathbed up to the day before he died, and he was remembered with admiration.

An obituary for Lancelot Giles in an English-language newspaper in China stated: 'The *Press* has cause to remember him with gratitude, for he usually had a copy of his remarks available: a consideration which was peculiarly valuable since Mr Giles was perhaps one of the most rapid speakers to be found in this part of the world.'

My family, teachers, professors and many friends also regularly complain that I speak too quickly for them to understand what I am saying. In my last year at high school I was approached by one of my teachers and asked whether I would represent the school in the Lions' Club 'Youth of the

Year' competition. I agreed, but it wasn't until two days before the meeting that he told me I needed to make a five-minute speech on a topic of my choice, with penalties for going over or under time.

Public speaking is not my forté — indeed it is one of my worst dreads. Two days! Any topic? As I was quite pleased with my latest essay in English Literature, on a short story, 'The Lottery', I timed myself to speak for five minutes on that.

The other four students came from private schools and were all in their dress blazers, with ties and the whole works. My uniform was clean, but we prided ourselves on our zip-up jacket with trendy stripes above the elbows, and my skirt was fairly well worn but would last until the end of the year. This didn't faze me, as I have never been ashamed of my relatively low station in society. Although quite used to having a low self-esteem, I also knew that I had a strength which I liked in myself and which brought me through most situations. With the possible exception of public speaking! I rattled off my speech in about four-and-a-half minutes, glowing red in the face; my main achievement being to make the next guy look brilliant, not that he needed me for that. Perhaps I can blame this on an inheritance from my great-grandfather?

Shortly before his death, my great-grandfather Giles officiated in the marriage of my grandmother, Marjory, to Ivor House, as he had for her older sister, Rosamond, four years earlier. His daughters had grown up in China, apart from their secondary schooling in England, and were keen to get home again to their parents and a life of parties, tennis, croquet and horse racing with servants to do all the work. My mother was born in 1940 in Tientsin, also named Rosamond, RII or Ah Too.

The Japanese had been in parts of China for much of the

1930s, but in 1941 during the Second World War, when Mum was almost a year old, the family took a ship to Bombay. Ivor's sister, Barbara, chose to stay with her husband rather than be evacuated, so her family spent three years in a prisoner-of-war camp near Shanghai, in the hands of the Japanese. Ivor's letters from China to his parents in Britain occasionally mentioned news he had received of them via the Red Cross, although it was a long time before they first heard anything at all and knew where she had been interned. When Alison and I visited Great-aunt Barbara in England in 1988, I asked her about the internment and received a staunch British reply: 'It wasn't too bad. We had plenty of notice and had time to pack a lot of tins of food to take with us.' That was all she said about it, but to take extra food for a family of five for three years would have been easier said than done, I should think.

Ivor had joined the British Army and was serving in Burma on the secret Mission 204 until, with the attack on Pearl Harbor, they passed into China to teach guerilla warfare to Chinese soldiers behind the Japanese lines. The idea was to cause trouble for the Japanese troops, and hence draw their firing power away from Singapore, but the Chinese weren't so keen on the idea. Although allies of the British and the Americans, they knew that the real fight would come with the communists after the Japanese were defeated, so, while keen to receive supplies and ammunition, they were reluctant to waste any of their own men or resources on plans the British might present to them.

At the end of the war, Major Ivor House, with Marjory and daughter Rosamond, returned to England to demobilise and to wait until he was required to take up his previous position in China. Richard was born in Devon, and in 1948 they sailed once more for Shanghai.

Great-aunt Roso was already back in Tientsin where Great-uncle Pete was a manager with the Hong Kong and Shanghai Bank, but by now Mao Tse-tung was completing his Long March with the siege of Tientsin, the last stronghold of Chiang Kai-shek. Great-aunt Roso and the children, Giles and Belinda, were evacuated and met Great-granny in New Zealand, but Great-uncle Pete was under orders to stay on to do business with the communists. It was a year before he resigned and left China to join them.

In May 1949 Mao bombed Shanghai, and three British Navy ships were lost in the Yangtse with the deaths of 21 sailors. My mother remembers attending the memorial service, at which Tyl Von Randow, whose father was in the German diplomatic corps, sang solo with the choir. Fifty years later, Mum met him living nearby in the Bethells Valley on the west coast of Auckland.

Marjory, Rosamond and Richard were evacuated to Hong Kong, then sailed to Australia where Ivor met them in Adelaide. In 1950 they settled in Albany, Western Australia, where Ivor died only five years later. Great-granny lived with them in their house, Greystones, and Great-aunt Roso's family had a farm nearby.

Mum left home at 18 to do her nursing training at Fremantle Hospital, and was married to Ian Stewart in 1961. My grandmother never approved of him, and even Mum had doubts at times.

'He knows too many rude songs,' she said one day.

'Oh, Rosamond! Surely he doesn't sing them in front of you!'

'No ... but he whistles them.'

Chapter 2

WESTERN AUSTRALIA

Mum and Dad built our house in Riverton on the Canning River south of Perth, and moved in a month before I was born. Andrew is two years older than I am, and Alison two years younger. Twice we rented the house out for a couple of years while Dad worked out of Perth: first when he was managing a farm in the Western Australian 'wheat belt', and working at the mine at Morawa, inland from Geraldton; and then working at the mine in Goldsworthy, inland from Port Hedland.

I have several memories of the farm before I was three, mainly of Kim our dog, who always jumped up on us, and of feeding the kid goat. I clearly remember the look and the feel of the rings around the bottom half of the glass Fanta bottle as I held it for the goat. I liked to rest my mouth on the bottom of the bottle and whenever the goat butted its head, the glass banged my teeth and hurt. I remember holding it like that and thinking to myself, though perhaps not in the same words, 'The goat is going to butt and it will hurt', which it did.

I also remember the feeling of the button that I pushed up my nose while I was supposed to be asleep one afternoon, although when asked about it later I had forgotten. More likely, I didn't connect the question with the event, something I remember happening many other times as a child, and even into my teens. For example, I clearly remember waiting outside the pub for Mum and Dad when I was three, because children were not allowed in pubs, and talking to a man who gave me a 20-cent piece. When I showed it to Mum — who now flatly denies ever having left me alone outside a pub — she said, 'I've told you never to talk to strangers!' and the meaning of her words sunk into my young brain.

Goldsworthy was an iron-ore mining town in the red dust of the Pilbara, and Dad worked with the big machinery as a diesel mechanic. It is many years now since the mine and town were abandoned: when the hole they had dug was as deep as Mt Goldsworthy had been high to start with, it was no longer economic to pump the water out of it. A siren would sound to warn the workers of an impending blast, and also served to warn any wives at home to get their washing off the line before the red dust-cloud reached them. I had a white shirt that I wore a lot, but eventually Mum dyed it purple. Sheets and underwear gradually turned a rusty shade of red.

As well as having a free swimming pool and drive-in movie theatre provided, the houses and school were all air-conditioned. We were promised to be allowed to go home if the thermometer reached 105°F, but I suppose the logistics of that were actually quite complicated, and the teachers reneged on the day it did reach 105°F. Aboriginal poet Kath Walker who, as I discovered last year, is now the well-known activist Oodgeroo Noonuccal, spoke at our school to launch her book *My People*. Seeing it in the bookshelf every time I dusted on a Saturday morning for the next decade may be part of the reason I have never forgotten her.

At first, we flew between Port Hedland and Perth by Fokker Friendship, and to Goldsworthy in a Beechcraft Baron. If an aeroplane had to land at night, the whole town drove their cars out to mark the airstrip with headlights. On one northbound flight, we hoped that the air hostess wouldn't notice that we were carrying a brown mouse, Mickey, covered in perfumed talcum powder in an ice-cream container, to be a mate for our albino, Minnie. They got married and lived in a birdcage and had 10 babies: six brown, two white with pink eyes, and two yellow with pink eyes. All was well until the day they left the nest and crawled out between the bars of the cage. Andrew and I returned from school to find some of them vanished down the back of the washing machine, and our imaginations ran wild over what would happen if Mum turned the machine on, as we scrambled to rescue them and contain them more securely.

The town was in its early stages and, although we still collected our mail at the shop, everyone had a letter-box installed soon after we arrived. A lot of cork trees were planted along the streets, and we were amazed by how quickly they grew. We cut bark to make fence posts on the large board of our train set, let the mice loose in the long plaster tunnels, and watched out of the windows as Cyclone Sheila lashed the town, bending the young trees almost double. The surrounding desert blossomed overnight with the rain, and for a week or more the town was cut off by flooding. A two-metre-deep gravel pit by the caravan park made a wonderful swimming hole, although it was a bit of a squeeze with so many kids in at once. We drove towards Port Hedland on Dad's next days off, crossing the De Grey River on the railway bridge as the ford was not yet safe; then a little further on, unable to go any further, we stopped and swam in the road.

While hitchhiking up the Western Australian coast to Darwin during the university holidays in 1984, I returned to Goldsworthy for a look. I was surprised at how different our house was, until I remembered that the whole town had been rebuilt after it was flattened by another cyclone in the intervening years.

Several times we drove for four days the 2000 kilometres of dirt road to Perth, with all the windows open to blow the dust out. Whenever another car approached, we'd wait until the last moment to wind up the windows, then down again as soon as the dust-cloud had blown by. One evening at sunset we hit a kangaroo and broke the headlights, so until we reached the next town one light shone straight up and the other out sideways, with Dad swearing all the way. Another time, after changing a flat tyre, he started to drive off without removing the jack first, putting a hole in the petrol tank. We thought it was completely unfair of him to be mad at us for not having any chewing gum, which we were never allowed to have, but he mended it with soap so we could carry on. And on our final trip down the inland road through Meekatharra with all our possessions on top of the car, we hit a pot-hole that was two metres wide. The roof-rack collapsed and everything had to be transferred to a truck to be taken to Perth.

From the time I was seven until I was 20, we lived in our house in Riverton. There was a newly built house on either side of us, where we had previously played on the empty blocks in the tea tree and woolly bush scrub, with orange-flowering Australian Christmas trees amongst it. I remember weeding and planting the street lawn, top-dressing with yellow Western Australian sand every year, and digging our own bore and laying pipes for a reticulation system when Perth went onto water restrictions for 10 years. Before Dad had it wired properly, we'd have to hang down into the hole to plug in the extension cord, and I remember the tingle in my arm as 240 volts spread through the spilled water sitting on top of the pump. It certainly beat hand-watering every evening during the summer, even if bore water did smell like rotten eggs.

Dad was very proud of his garden and made us weed it for him as he was always too busy, although he seemed to have time to stand there watching to make sure we did it properly. We really liked the big trees — you could see forever from the top of the liquid-amber.

We lived on the corner of two quiet streets and could play tennis on the road in the evenings, just moving off occasionally if a car came by. Over two or three years, though, the traffic increased noticeably until it became a nuisance and we gave up on the idea.

Family life was fairly strict, and Andrew and I used to get the occasional belting. I'm not one of those people who say 'It never did me any harm!', but I quickly worked out that it was a good idea to do as I was told. In my case it would be for not eating my tea, and after the second (and last) time, if Dad walked down the passage for his belt, I gobbled. The most disgusting meal ever — and we had it more than once — was octopus that had been pressure-cooked into liquid slime. The only way I ever got out of eating my tea was if I was sick in it, and in this case you had to make sure they saw it happen because it looked just the same afterwards.

I guess the threat must have gone off a bit later, because there were plenty more times when I had to sit at the table until I'd finished. I remember looking at the clock one night and realising that I'd been there for an hour, so I ate up and left. There was absolutely zero chance of winning such a battle.

At 14, in an attempt to express some form of control, I would go without food all day, only drinking. My stomach was always guaranteed one decent meal at night, anyway, as there was no possibility of *not* eating at tea time. I didn't have *that* much control over my life. I lost a lot of weight over a year or two, but that was a good thing. My sister went down the throwing-up route, but I had a phobia about vomiting — enough to keep me away from alcohol later on.

We didn't have a TV, but we occasionally borrowed my grandmother's TV while she was away on a trip through the desert with my Uncle Richard and their Danish anthropologist friend, Mark De Graaf from Darwin. Usually he employed an Aboriginal tracker who led them to sacred sites and helped to find the next well. In photographs, my grandmother's white hair was red from the dust, and we heard tales of her washing it in the same water she had washed the dishes in. She sometimes slept in her bed-roll on the wheel marks, as there was nowhere else to lay it out in the spinifex country, and waking up one morning she found the tracks of a camel which had come walking along the track, veered around her, then continued on its way along the track. Despite having hardly boiled an egg before she came to Australia at the age of 36, she was a wonderful cook, even over a campfire in the desert. On one trip, Mark had told her they would take a week to get to Jigalong Station and she had brought along food for seven days.

When they were delayed and it took them 10 days, they were getting hungry and radioed ahead to the station. 'You'll have to put an extra sock in the soup' was the reply.

Later she took Alison and me along while Uncle Richard prospected for gold with his metal-detector. He and Aunty Bev slept in a minivan, and baby John had a cot under a tent that folded down off the roof of the truck, with a tin can full of water under each leg of the cot to keep the ants out. Alison and I loved sleeping under the wide, starry sky on camp stretchers and watching the sun rise in the morning. We never found a scrap of gold, though, while the nugget we needed to pay for the metal detector and all the trips grew bigger and bigger.

As a small child, I watched TV sometimes at my grandmother's house, only hearing it as a noise. I remember coming back, aged nearly four, after being away in Morawa for a year or so and being able to understand the spoken words for the first time, and I recall watching Neil Armstrong step out of *Eagle* to walk on the moon. In Goldsworthy, each house came with a TV, and there were five minutes of cartoons before the news came on at 6pm.

I was in my early teens before we bought a TV ourselves, with colour. It was only to watch the news and documentaries, and we were never allowed to eat in front of it. But as the news was on at tea time — especially if you watched it on all three channels at 6.00, 6.30 and 7.00 — it wasn't long before Dad spent most of his time in front of it drinking beer, eating pickled onions, and complaining about what a load of rubbish they showed on the bloody TV. Occasionally Mum, Alison and I would gang up and insist on watching something — Charles and Diana's wedding, BBC dramas — but it was a painful process and mostly we avoided it.

Looking back now, I can see that I learnt a lot of things that are important to me from my dad. For example, I found that having an opinion about something doesn't necessarily make you right, and that if someone has to get aggressive to defend their opinion that doesn't make it any more right. Dad had little respect for authority, and I also tend to respect people whom I think have earned that respect by their attitudes and attributes, rather than by their position. I learned to question anyone's opinion, to form my own conclusions about the world around me, and not to be swayed by what other people thought. But it is much easier to choose your own path when you live further away from those with the opinions.

From the age of 14 I never stayed home sick, and for three years at university I didn't miss a single lecture, lab or tutorial.

Willetton Senior High School opened with a minimum of buildings the year I was 13, and grew throughout the time I was there. It was new and innovative, with open-plan classrooms and 100-minute periods, often divided in half, rather than the standard 40-minute period that most schools had at the time. English and Social Studies were combined into one subject, Humanities, on the premise that we could learn how to use the language properly while reading and writing the necessary facts.

The school was rumoured to be one where you weren't expected to work unless you felt like it, and which apparently existed for kids with behavioural problems, but this was not the case. We did call most of the teachers by their first names, and that, combined with the small roll, at least at the beginning, gave us an intimacy with our teachers that was unusual in schools at the time. We were generally respected as the almost-adults we considered ourselves to be, and willingly reciprocated that respect rather than feeling impelled to buck a repressive system, which is what I mostly heard from my elder brother about his school. He had a teacher or two whom he respected highly, but for him they were the exception, while for us the opposite was true.

I was always very good at Maths without having to try very hard, but Chemistry was definitely the most exciting subject. The teacher, Gary Thomas, was entertaining, with a very dry sense of humour which I thoroughly appreciated. In one of our first classes we mixed crushed iodine with powdered zinc, then added water to make a very exciting, hot fizz — and I was hooked to the point of naughtiness. I wrapped zinc and iodine in a piece of paper and put them in my pocket to try the experiment again later at home. Had I used two bits of paper, no doubt my brother would have been impressed — although more likely, he'd have yawned and said he'd done it years ago — but my next lesson in Chemistry was now working away in my pocket: that being, 'the presence of water speeds up a reaction while its absence only slows it down to a point'. I was jumpy enough with stolen chemicals in my pocket, but by the time we'd gone outside for lunch the package was hot and pink smoke was coming out! The lesson was learnt then and there, but what was I to do with it? I couldn't throw it in the bin, and I definitely couldn't flush it down the toilet! I settled for burying it, and was left wondering what would happen when the automatic sprinklers came on later that night.

Pure sodium and potassium were also very exciting sitting in the dish under oil. The instructions said to use a piece 'no bigger than a pea', although Gary's piece looked more like a quarter of that, and when he dropped it into water it whizzed around on the surface held up by the steam produced in the rapid reaction. In our final year of school we got to do that experiment ourselves rather than just watch a demonstration. I remember the look on Gary's face when the working classroom was interrupted by a loud *BANG!*

'It was only as big as a pea!' came the oh-so-innocent voice of the boy with the dreadful haircut, good-naturedly nicknamed Helmut Schmidt.

Most of our teachers went through every question after marking any test or exam we took, to show us where we might have made mistakes, which I found a very valuable teaching exercise. However, I'm usually reluctant to back down on anything if I feel that I am in the right, and I can often push it too far. Several times I showed my teacher that I was not wrong after all, but I must have done it too many times the day Gary refused to accept my answer as correct. We had been asked to describe a property and consequent use of certain elements, one of which was chlorine. I insisted, and still do, that as it is poisonous I was right in saying that it had been used to gas soldiers during the First World War. He wanted to hear that it was used in bleaches and said that my application was out-of-date.

I was 15 when I learnt the meaning of the word 'Pathology' and knew that the study of disease would be my field of choice. It seemed more than a coincidence when I found that the University of Western Australia taught Pathology as a major subject for a maximum of 10 students each year. Later I chose Microbiology as my second major subject.

In my last year of school the teachers held a mental arithmetic test for the whole school, which must have had 600 students by then. I was hauled up in front of the school assembly and presented with a large block of chocolate for scoring the highest, which was 59/60. I was disgusted with myself for leaving the dollar sign off my otherwise correct answer, but also appalled that out of all those other kids not one had got them all right. It was only basic mental arithmetic; hardly rocket science.

There were plenty of other smart kids, particularly in the four years below mine. Another competition regularly held by the Maths teacher, Peter Shepherd, was the 'Peter's pie competition' or 'Shepherd's pie competition'. In Perth, a Peter's pie was similar to a Jimmy's pie in New Zealand. This competition was held over several weeks, and the winner was the person who could recite pi to the most decimal places. Peter Cahill rattled it off to 121 decimal places and would have had it to 125 if he hadn't mixed up the 122nd and 123rd digits. I never bothered to learn it past 20 places, although I can still remember it.

Towards the end of that last year at school I took a good look at myself and decided that I wasn't all that bad really. I was probably about to do pretty well in the final exams, I had been selected for the junior state archery team again, and, although I'd broken up with my boyfriend, I was beginning to see the benefits in that. I never managed a gold medal at the archery Nationals, but I took three silvers and one bronze over the four years I was in the state team. I won two gold medals at the state championships that year, probably due to the other girl having a bad day at the same time as I had a good one. I had also been nominated for the Coca-Cola Junior Sports Star of the Year, although as the opposition included an Olympic gold medallist this just meant that I had a fancy dinner at the Sheraton Hotel.

I also took a few state and Australian archery records, one

of which I still hold. We'd shoot a 'Perth' round or a 'Sydney' round, etc., each of which was a different combination of the number of arrows shot from various distances. The 'Australian' round involved shooting 30 arrows at each of 55 metres, 45 metres, 35 metres and 25 metres, but a year or two after I'd set a record for it the national body simplified things and scrapped anything with five-metre distances.

When the final results came out for the Tertiary Admissions Exam, the University of Western Australia had cut-off levels for each of their courses. To get into Arts or Sciences you needed only 300 (out of a possible 550), but Law, Engineering and Medicine required much higher scores. Out of 53 students who finished the final year at our school I was the only one who qualified for entrance into Medicine, and there was a certain amount of pressure to do it, not only at school but in the wider community. I aimed only for a Bachelor of Science right up to the middle of January, when I found myself sitting next to a doctor on the flight from Sydney back to Perth after the Junior National Championships. He convinced me to apply to enter the course in Medicine since I could always change my mind at the end of the first year. There followed an anxious time while I wondered whether I'd blown my chances altogether, but when I was offered a place in Medicine I knew that what I really wanted was a Bachelor of Science in Pathology, and I stuck with that.

Chapter 3

A PAINTED SHIP UPON A PAINTED OCEAN

At 21 I definitely wanted to get out of home, and anyway our house had been sold before the bank stepped in to sell it for us. Having bought an archery and sports shop, Dad wanted to incorporate, but coming up with an extra $5000 was more than he could do. An archery shop is no place to make your fortune, and Dad *really* wasn't cut out to sit politely behind a counter and say 'May I help you, Sir?'

As the accounts grew progressively worse his temper did likewise, and many customers were no doubt scared off by his 'Now buy it!' attitude. Someone owing us money declared bankruptcy, knowing that their house was in the wife's name. Today, you go bankrupt, live on the dole for a couple of years and then you can start again, but Dad was of the old school where you married if you got pregnant and bankruptcy was the ultimate shame. So in order to pay the debt, our house was sold and we moved into a house belonging to an old lady who had gone to live in a nursing home.

Towards the end of the previous year, with my BSc in sight, I'd sent off approximately 200 letters; one to every medical laboratory I could find listed in the seven states. Most of them didn't reply, many of them said 'No, thanks', and only one in Tasmania was slightly interested. One of my Microbiology lecturers, who was also a member of my archery club, had a grant for a summer research project, and so employed me as a research assistant while we tested the effects of smoking and carbon monoxide on archers. The pay was quite reasonable, but I wouldn't receive any money until after the final results were submitted. As I had moved out of home to house-sit for friends, Mum didn't feel obliged to support me either, and I had very little money to pay for food.

Professor Roger Dawkins of the Immunology Department was well known to the Pathology students — some of whom would have run in the opposite direction to avoid him. So when he approached me with regard to doing an Honours year in his department, I stuck to my original intentions. I was broke, I needed a job, and I couldn't afford — and didn't want — another year of studying. He glossed over my objections, but asked his side-kick, Brian Hoolihan, 'What is she worth on the market?'

'About $14,000,' Brian replied.

For some time, he continued to present me with the

options available before asking which field of research I would choose.

'I can't afford it. I need to get a job,' I repeated.

'We've just offered you $14,000,' he said.

'I'll take it,' I replied.

In fact, asking me to choose my field of study turned out to be merely dangling a carrot in front of my nose, as he'd already decided what he wanted done and told me when I fronted up to the Immunology Department at Royal Perth Hospital early on a Monday morning in February 1985. Nor did anyone offer me any money until I eventually approached Brian Hoolihan, wondering what the story was. They thought I would have applied for a student allowance to cover some of it, but there was no way I would qualify for that with the income they had promised me.

'Well, of course, you wouldn't tell them.'

'I'm not going to lie about it!'

We worked out an agreement whereby I'd work full-time until the end of February of the following year and they'd pay me in installments as a tax-free grant. Later I asked the tax department about that and was told that it would be their decision as to whether it would be taxed or not.

My grandmother had invested some money for me several years earlier, and it was worth $2500 by my twenty-first birthday, so I used it to buy a yacht that I could live on. I would moor it in the bay below the university and ride my bike to work. I figured at the end of the year I could sell it again and get my money back, and meanwhile it would save me paying rent.

I had started to check out boats, but I needed to sort out a mooring first. I asked around about the rules governing such things, and it seemed that I could drop a lump of concrete into the river almost anywhere I wanted to and tie my boat to it. The river was governed by a federal authority, and if they ever gave you a hard time you could tie up to the jetty whereupon you became subject to the local council. There were two or three other guys living on boats while I was there.

I had help from Dan, a friend whose father owned a hardware store. With his father's tools we stripped back my bike, then spray-painted it red, orange and yellow with leftover paint I'd begged from some panelbeaters. After that, we filled half a 44-gallon drum with concrete and set a chain into it.

Neither of us had any idea how big the lump of concrete would need to be to hold a boat, but in the year I was there it worked all right, particularly after it had buried itself in the sand. Dan's father did know how much chain I should have and how much rope, and Uncle Richard taught me to splice with a marlin spike.

Richard also helped to load the concrete block into my dinghy and, with three of us sitting in the bow to balance it, he rowed like hell until the whole thing went bilge over gunwale. We surfaced, spluttering, and agreed that it seemed like a nice spot. Later, we pulled it along the bottom with his father-in-law's power-boat to be closer to the jetty.

With the mooring in place, I could turn my attention back to buying a boat. On the Friday afternoon after my first week at work I made an early start on the weekend 'Classified' list, and found exactly what I wanted for a good price. I rang the number immediately, hoping that it had not been sold already as it looked like such a good deal. The owner, Steve Bell, said he would pick me up so I could have a look at it, and while I waited for him at the front of Royal Perth Hospital I considered the fact that no one knew where I was going.

Very considerately, though, Steve arrived with his wife, Brenda, and their little dog, Bertie, and we were immediately the best of friends.

Steve was selling *Aquillo* cheap because it was in the slipyard in bits while he was painting it, but his knees were so sore from crouching inside it that he couldn't finish the job. He'd had enough of it and was determined to buy something that he could stand up in.

I'd promised my grandmother that I wouldn't buy anything until I'd had it approved by my Great-uncle John, Commander RN (retired), who had also spent a lot of time sailing in the Mediterranean. Steve was such a nice guy that I felt awful about having another check made — it looked as though I didn't trust him — but I had promised my grandmother and so it had to be done. Uncle John was obviously pleased that I had asked him, and pronounced the boat to be seaworthy and worth the price. As it turned out, Steve is such a nice guy that I don't think he minded.

First thing on Saturday morning I met Steve back at the boatyard to get the job finished and the boat floated. Although I was getting the boat cheap, he'd brought along his friend Andy to do most of the work, and Alan Parsons' new *Eye in the Sky* album to speed us on.

The boat was a 6.4-metre Hartley, newly painted inside and out and anti-fouled. It came with a trailer at no extra charge, as this was on its very last legs and would not be given a licence if I'd tried. Steve just hoped it would stay together long enough for the drive to Poverty Bay.

There were about a dozen boats moored in the bay below the university and a lot more tied up to the wharf, so it was nicknamed the Poverty Bay Yacht Club — you tied your boat up and went to the university pub for a drink. Just around the point was the Royal Perth Yacht Club with the America's Cup in its showcase at this time.

On the morning in 1984 when Alan Bond's yacht *Australia II* had beaten Dennis Conner in *Stars and Stripes* in the final race of the series, I had been driving Mum's car to university over the Kwinana Freeway when I saw a rainbow arching down directly into the RPYC. There was a pot of gold at the end of that one!

Having finished the job on *Aquillo* and having helped me to launch her, Steve and Andy came for a sail, to literally show me the ropes. I'd been learning to sail in Mirror dinghies with a guy who knew little more than I did, which wasn't the most successful experience. One windy day when we'd tipped over about five times, he insisted on letting the pressure off the main halyard instead of the main sheet. We were trying to tack into the wind with the leading edge of the sail a series of S bends! Nor did we have anything to bail with. We had already beached it once to tip the water out, but had immediately capsized again. So there we were, sitting in a bathtub, making extremely slow progress when *Australia II* went by calling 'Starboard!' There was absolutely nothing we could do about it.

Sailing with Steve was quite a different matter, and by then I had the basics anyway. It was just a matter of doing it all on a larger scale and working out where everything went. *Aquillo* had a swing keel, and with it raised she only drew 30 centimetres of water, so if we ever hit a sandbar in the Swan River estuary I could just winch up the keel and float over the top.

Steve warned me that having a swing keel also meant that if you did capsize there was no guarantee that she'd right herself, but whenever he'd gone over in her she always had.

He'd sailed her a lot around Carnarvon and Shark Bay, and we had lots of time together for him to tell me stories about those excursions.

There was the time when he was sailing along in the dark, racing around two islands off the coast of Carnarvon. He had intended to get around the top of the second island before dark, but hadn't made it. One of his crew was sleeping below, and the other throwing up over the lee side. Steve was happily sailing along in the pitch dark with one arm casually looped over the safety rail when he realised that, looking out across the side of the boat, he couldn't see any stars. In the next second a wave hit them, huge and right out of nowhere. They were knocked flat but slowly came back up again. Steve still had his arm over the rail and the other guy was still throwing up.

Another time he'd sailed into Shark Bay in the dark and anchored. During the night the tide went out and he felt *Aquillo* rock over on her keel, and when he climbed onto the deck in the morning he was astonished to find himself sitting in the middle of a desert! The tides are so big there and the bay so shallow that he couldn't even see the sea, and it was a six-kilometre walk to Denham across the sand.

On that first trip on the Swan River he showed me how the keel tended to stick as you lowered it. If you kept winding without noticing, the cable would loop out; then if the keel dropped at that moment, it would probably break the cable. So I almost always told my crew to keep the pressure on the keel and not to let the cable out too fast.

In English Literature at school, my teacher Peter Jeans had explained the mechanics of short stories to us. Unlike a novel, he said, there isn't room for anything superfluous, so if the author describes a rifle hanging above the fireplace, for example, you know that something, probably someone, is going to be shot. In hindsight, Steve telling me about the winch cable on the swing keel was a moment like that.

He also taught me about maintaining the boat. On weekends I'd scrub off the bird poop, and whenever a crack appeared in the paint he said to seal it straight away and paint over it. I got into the water regularly to knock the barnacles off the bottom, and with my head underwater I could hear the clicking noise as they filtered food out of the brackish water.

I must have bumped my head a hundred times during my first day on the boat, but I never did again. I marvelled at the way I invariably stopped with my hair brushing up against any obstacle. I also learnt, after the first ducking, not to stop to talk with one foot on the boat and the other still in the dinghy.

I slept in the space under the starboard side of the cockpit and I could wedge myself in with my knees on rough nights, although these were rare. In the summertime in Perth's climate it was a lovely place to be and, with that as my bedroom, the whole world became my front yard. Even in the winter while my windsurfing friends complained that it was fine all week but rained every weekend, that suited me perfectly, as mostly I went home on weekends. Only once did it rain all week, and I ran out of dry clothes by the end of it. The hospital provided us with a clean overall every day to be worn in the lab, so I only needed a few T-shirts and shorts, or sweatshirts and pants in the winter, and I took my washing home on the weekends.

Sitting on the centre-board casing, my head just touched the roof of the cabin. I had a gas stove in front of my knees, and usually only had Milo, milk powder, muesli, crackers and peanut butter on board. I could get an excellent meal at

Royal Perth or QEII Hospital with a vegetarian option for $1.23, and I usually ate one meal a day there. I used the toilet on the jetty, showered at the hospital, and spent most evenings in the medical library.

Arriving back at the jetty one afternoon I met a lady painting the view in watercolours, with *Aquillo* in the centre ground. I asked her to sell it to me, and she agreed so long as she could take it home first to finish properly with pastels.

Dragging my dinghy up and down the sandy beach each day eventually wore a hole in her bottom until she was leaking quite badly. When one morning I jumped in to row ashore and found a blowfish swimming in it, I thought perhaps it was time I did something about the hole.

I often sailed out to sea with Steve and I always felt safe with him. 'Awesome' is a much over-used word these days, but I found being out on the ocean truly awesome. His new boat, *Allegro*, was more like a caravan, I thought — even the table folded down to form a double bed — but he could comfortably stand up in her. Steve wore glasses for astigmatism, so whenever he found the sea too alarming he could take them off, whereupon the waves would look smaller and he could sail on, oblivious.

One day, beating into a 25–30 knot sou'wester while I was pretending to be brave and trying hard not to be sick, he called out, 'It's going to take us all day! We might as well put on the auto-pilot and go below for a sleep.'

'I might as well throw up now,' I thought, but he knew how I was feeling without me saying and made the decision to turn back. As soon as we turned away from the wind I was fine. We spent another night in the marina we'd left a few hours before, and called Brenda to drive up and stay the night with us and bring some food.

'What do you want to eat?' he called, heading for a phone.

'Baked beans,' I replied, without hesitation. I hardly ever ate them, but they were always my first choice after extreme physical stress.

Brenda arrived bearing beans, but very little sleep was had that night, as the swell, even in the shelter of the marina, kept working the fenders up and out with an ever-increasing shriek until Steve got up to re-adjust them. Again, it was all about not complaining until Brenda said, 'It's driving me mad!'

I got up to help, and suggested tying them from both ends so they lay horizontally, and miraculously the shrieking stopped. In the morning Brenda remarked how Bertie, the dog, was looking at me. 'He's gazing admiringly at Cathy because she stopped the squeak.'

'It's driving me mad!' Steve mimicked.

The wind had changed, and after Brenda and Bertie drove away we had a lovely sail back and were inside Fremantle Harbour in about three hours.

I took *Aquillo* out to sea only once, with my scuba-diving mates. Chris had an outboard motor, John knew how to sail, and the University Underwater Club was going to Rottnest Island for the weekend. The forecast was for gale-force winds, but it was so calm inside the harbour that it was hard to take the forecast seriously and we were too silly to think about what would happen if the winds came up when we were halfway there.

Luckily, it happened much sooner than that. Visibility was only a couple of kilometres and, although we had a compass, we didn't have a bearing. Anyway, there was no choice but to sail straight into the swell. John was seasick within half an hour and I would have been five minutes later, at which point Chris said, in a squeaky voice, 'I want to go back!'

What a relief! I was so glad he'd said it, although up to that moment it hadn't occurred to me to change my mind. We flapped around for a few minutes discussing it, before I realised that we'd torn the sheets out of both sails and would have to motor back to port.

Safely back in the river and having run under all the bridges, I rang home to say that I was OK. 'Oh yes, and what else is happening?' asked Dad, as oblivious to the storm as we had been three hours earlier.

By the end of that year, when I'd already had a month's extension to submit my Honours thesis, *Aquillo* was somewhat neglected. Once, I even stayed awake for 44 hours in a stretch, working. Alone in the department on a Sunday, I'd carried on into the night trying to finish my thesis. By the time I considered knocking off it was already getting light, so I stopped for breakfast in the hospital's staff dining room and returned for a full day's work in the lab. It was pretty hard to stay awake during the boring weekly departmental meeting and progress report, but they always bribed us to attend by providing lunch and threatened dire consequences if we didn't. Back on the computer again in the evening after everyone had gone home, I gave up at about 10.30pm and wobbled home on my bike to my floating bed, hallucinating.

I couldn't believe how fast the barnacles had grown when I finally got into the water to have a look at *Aquillo*'s bottom. I beached her at high tide and came back when the tide had retreated to knock them off. When large lumps of paint came off as well, I knew I was in for a major job. She might not have been a very big boat, but she looked huge from underneath with a piece of sandpaper in my hand. Without a trailer I had to borrow an outboard motor to take her up the Swan River to the slipyard, where luckily no one else wanted the cradle for a week. After each day in the Immunology Department, I worked on her until dark, sleeping out on the back deck where the night breeze helped to keep the mozzies down a bit.

Repainted and anti-fouled, she was ready to refloat at the end of the week, and Alison, Uncle Richard, Aunty Bev and six-year-old cousin John came for a sail that afternoon. It was quite difficult up there where the river was so narrow. We had to tack every five or 10 minutes, which involved a lot of crew work, and I had neglected to warn Bev about the winch cable... So when it looped off the drum she picked it up to put back on, and at that moment the keel dropped. I heard her say 'Damn!', but was busy myself keeping the boat off the shore and shouting instructions in a disorganised fashion. Uncle Richard was a good crew, but I heard Bev say 'I've pulled my fingernail off.'

Alison, the nurse, took a look, saw that it was worse than that, and went below to find the rest of Bev's finger. With it packed in a plastic bag and Bev's hand wrapped in a towel, Richard drove her to the hospital leaving a guilt-wracked skipper waving goodbye.

With Mum working, it fell to Dad to collect Alison and to drive John home. John, who'd learned words such as 'bum' and 'fart' at preschool, was wide-eyed in astonishment, peering around the edge of his booster seat while Dad drove across town in his usual fashion, abusing every other idiot on the road. They seemed to follow him wherever he went, and, what's more, every traffic light would turn orange as he approached.

'Don't sit there with your thumb in your bum and your

mind in bloody neutral!' he'd yell.

'Come on, Stupid! It's green! Are you waiting for it to get ripe?'

It was a long drive, and he gave John the full benefit of his repertoire.

I had one last sail on *Aquillo* that evening. It was Australia Day 1986, so Linda, Brett, Amanda, Nola and Alan, friends from the Immunology Department, arrived to motor down the river before the fireworks started in the city. After the disaster of the afternoon it couldn't get worse, but the trip was still a debacle — luckily more comic than tragic. About the only thing that went right was that Brett remembered he'd left his car keys in Linda's car in time to go back for them. His car was parked at the jetty where we planned to leave the boat on my mooring, and after everything else that happened that night, being unable to get into the car would have been the last straw.

The two-horse-power Seagull outboard motor I'd borrowed from another workmate was not terribly reliable and conked out several times on our downriver run. Each time we drifted resolutely shorewards while Brett hauled on the pull cord, and eventually it would start again. There were several bridges to pass under before we could step the mast and sail the rest of the way.

We arrived in front of the city barely in time for the fireworks, so, rather than bothering with the anchor, we tied off to a spit-post until the Coast Guard boat came by to tell us we couldn't do that. While drifting we ate chicken and salad, but the champagne was something of a challenge with no corkscrew.

The river was packed with boats, but when no one seemed to be in a hurry to leave we decided to head for the Narrows

Bridge. This proved to be the wrong decision when the whole fleet of cowboys in their floating gin palaces roared by just as we were through the bridge, swamping the outboard and removing it permanently from action. We were tossed sideways in the huge wash, and, while the others did what they could to fend us off the rocks, I mucked around trying to get the mast up. A tiny yacht, smaller even than we were, threw us a rope and tried to tow us, but came to an abrupt halt when the slack was taken up. They switched tack, and this time hauled us off as I raised the mast and set the sails. As I was meaning to sell the boat by this time and get my money back, I had a few bad moments wondering what I'd do if I lost her now.

Next, the wind died. For four hours any puff of breeze there was came directly from where we were headed and it was a very slow trip. Amanda went below to pee in the bucket and found the floorboards floating, so we occupied ourselves for an hour or more with the bilge pump. We hadn't noticed that the outboard motor had pushed the stern so far down that the scuppers were underwater.

Finally, the easterly night breeze kicked in and we covered the last couple of kilometres. I had planned to motor in to the jetty to borrow a dinghy, as mine had been pinched a few weeks earlier. I hadn't replaced it as there was usually one around that I could use, but I couldn't leave it on the mooring for a week. The breeze was too tricky to try manoeuvring between the other boats, so we just grabbed the mooring on the first attempt. I swam ashore for the dinghy and swam out again, towing it as the wind was too strong to row against. It was about three o'clock in the morning by this time, and if Brett had discovered then that his car keys were 15 kilometres up the river, I think my crew would have lynched me.

I didn't dare sail *Aquillo* again after that, and I was sad but relieved to sell her a few weeks later.

Thinking back on it, I was very grateful to have been offered the chance to do an Honours year. Although I had done sufficiently well in the previous two years of my course, at the end of it I felt that I had perhaps short-changed myself by not working as hard as I might have. I worked very hard throughout this year and was surprised and thrilled to receive a first-class Honours, which I had hardly dared hope for.

Although I had agreed to stay in Perth for this extra year, I still definitely wanted to move on and see more of the world. Partway through the year, the next opportunity opened up. One day, working in the routine diagnostic laboratory of the Immunology Department, I addressed a parcel of frozen serum samples to go to the Otago Medical School in New Zealand. In the 1960s Dr Duncan Adams had discovered the long-acting thyroid-stimulating factor that was the cause of Grave's disease and, as the diagnostic test was still not performed in Australia, the samples were being sent for testing in Dunedin. I made a note of the address, as at that moment I decided I wanted a job with him in Dunedin. I wrote, and waited and waited for an answer, but none came. When I wrote again, he replied, 'The reason I have taken so long to answer your letter was that I have been applying for a grant for your salary. I have just heard that my application was successful.'

Yippee! New Zealand was where I wanted to be, and now I had a job to go to.

Chapter 4

SIGNPOSTS ALONG THE WAY

My grandmother had brought us to New Zealand for a holiday in 1970 when I was six. We had two hired cars — a Mini and a Morris 1100 — and had driven from Auckland to Wellington, flown to Christchurch, and driven around the South Island, staying in Tourist Hotel Corporation motels. The road between Haast and Paringa had only been completed in 1965, opening up this route for tourism.

My brother was nine at the time, and there and then he decided that he was coming back one day. It was so different to anything we were used to, living in the Pilbara region of Western Australia as we were at the time. We were amazed by how green everything was and by the wet rainforest full of ferns along the sides of the winding roads, with banks above us on one side and a steep drop-off on the other. Geysers, glaciers and fiords and great blocks of ice standing at the side of the Homer Tunnel etched themselves permanently in our memories, reinforced over the next few years by regular showings of Dad's slides.

And sure enough, when he turned 18, Andrew left home and took a bus across Australia to Sydney. From there he flew to Christchurch and a new life. The last verse of Neil Young's 'After the Goldrush' played in my head throughout that day. The bus was like a silver spaceship taking him to a new home and we were crying.

We came home to a quiet house that would never be the same again. Alison moved into his bedroom, and I retreated into mine just as, 30 years later, Robin would creep away into her corner of a house without Christan when he left. The world carried on, regardless.

A year or so later, Andrew returned to Perth unannounced, for a holiday. He showed us photos of the Routeburn Track where he'd spent the summer guiding. One photo taken from the Harris Saddle, looking down the Hollyford Valley to the sea, stood out for me amongst all the others. Without understanding why, I found myself unable to stop looking at it.

'See that red light in the distance?' he asked. 'That's a fish-and-chip shop on the beach at Port Moresby.'

Five years passed before I finished university in Western Australia and came to New Zealand to live. I had often studied maps looking for tramping tracks, and was fascinated by the apparent inaccessibility of the area south of Haast where the road turned inland to go back over the pass to Otago. Then one day, I found a dotted route linking up with the Hollyford track and I knew that sometime I wanted to go there.

Dire Straits played at Lancaster Park in Christchurch on

the night I arrived in March 1986. It turns out Robert Long was there, and I have met many other people since who were. I could hear the music from Halswell where I was staying with my sister-in-law, Dinah, and two-and-a-half year old nephew, Ned. I wonder if they played 'Telegraph Road', about the man with a pack on his back who walked 30 miles on a track and made his home in the wilderness.

As I headed south by train the next day, with a pack, a suitcase and a bike in a box to take up my new position in the Autoimmunity Research Unit at the Otago Medical School, Robert Long, known as Beansprout, hitchhiked back over Arthur's Pass to the West Coast.

I first heard of him sometime later that year as I hitchhiked to Haast myself. I was picked up by a man in a Morris Minor, and as we got to talking it turned out that he was going tramping into the Cascade and looking for someone who lived down there, way down and out on the coast. I don't remember what else was said, but later I was pretty sure that he had been looking for Robert.

Also that year, late one Saturday of a long weekend, wandering around south of Haast in our VW Beetle, Andrew and I came across the Cascade Road and took it, looking for a hayshed or something similar to sleep in. The road went on and on, and as the sun set we began to wonder where we'd end up, but the further it went, the more likely it seemed that it must go *somewhere*. Climbing over a spur of the Red Hills we saw for the first time the Cascade Valley and a light at the end of the road, which I later learned was the Martyr homestead. Away to the left across a paddock we found a locked hut with a couple of bed frames on the verandah, and we made ourselves comfortable for the night; at least until it began to rain.

'Kip,' I heard Andrew call in the dark, 'how are you keeping dry?'

'I've got my raincoat over my sleeping bag and my mat standing up at the side of the bed,' I replied. 'How about you?'

'I'm not!'

On Sunday morning we drove back out to the Haast motor-camp and paid for a night in a warm, dry cabin. On the side of the road we passed three men in Swanndris winching a Land Rover out of the river in the pouring rain.

'That's what real Kiwi men do on weekends,' was Andrew's comment.

In January 1987, Cathy Mountier suggested that Andrew and I come to the Towards 2000 festival at Whitecliffs in Canterbury. Andrew and Cathy had been guides together on the Routeburn Track in the first year he was in New Zealand, and later he married her sister, Dinah. I had spent a summer with Andrew and Dinah in Alexandra in 1983–84 when their son Ned was a baby, and I had picked fruit to earn some money before returning to Perth for my third year at university. No longer married to Dinah, Andrew met and fell in love with Jenny Smith at this festival, and I laid eyes on Robert for the first time. As the festival finished, I hitched a ride south as far as Oamaru with Murray Cayford in his bus. A tall, thin, long-haired man with a beard and a funny hat waved to the bus as we pulled out with Lou Brown and his kids also aboard.

Lou lived at Barn Bay, a day's walk from the end of the Cascade Road. He carried three-year-old Jennifer on the back and two-year-old Sam on the front. His wife, Liz, carried the baby, Elinor, and 12-year-old Jasmine carried the lunch. They left clothes, sleeping bags, spare nappies and anything else they needed in the car at the end of the road for the next time they came out.

My face lit up as I considered the possibilities when he suggested that I should walk in to see them some time. I'd been fascinated by Andrew's photograph looking down the Hollyford Valley to the sea, by maps of this area, and now here was someone who lived there inviting me to visit! But it absolutely never occurred to me that I might actually live there myself.

I am very glad to be able to say that the next thing I asked him was what I could bring them, as virtually everyone who lands here in an aeroplane or a helicopter asks us. And, as we now do ourselves, he answered, 'Nothing, just bring yourself.'

'Oh sure, but there must be something that you miss out on and would really like. I know — what about some fruit?'

Living like this now, too, we try to make people understand how much it means to us to have them call in to visit, and how hard it can be here at times when we haven't seen anyone else for weeks. Much as we appreciate anything they think to offer us, it is definitely secondary to our enjoyment of the people themselves.

Cathy had had more to do with the Browns at the festival than I had, and later that summer she walked through from Haast to the Hollyford Valley, spending some time at Barn Bay and also at Big Bay.

Lou was a crayfisherman, but the previous year he and Robert had wrecked the boat, *Scratch*, and the family had headed to Canada for the northern summer and a well-earned break. Several months pregnant with her fourth child, Liz didn't enjoy it so much. She was past seven months before she could persuade Lou to come home, although she didn't look it and they didn't mention it to the airline. In the winter of 1987, Lou worked on a film set in Queenstown, building a submarine and doing a lot of diving in Lake

Wakatipu. Cathy Mountier also worked on the film set and shared their house, so I met the rest of the family there on the winter solstice as they celebrated Sam's third birthday with a Christmas tree.

Cathy was keen to walk in to Big Bay again, and I jumped at the chance I had been waiting a long time for. I returned three weeks later when the Browns were all out and Cathy had gone off to work, so I was a visitor and alone in the house when there was a knock on the door. And here was that tall, thin man again, with the same funny hat which he'd made himself from thick, lumpy wool spun on a drop-spindle and dyed yellow/green with lichen. He also wore a long, homespun woollen swannie which he had just finished knitting on needles made from the wire of an oven tray. The buttons and toggles were dolphins' teeth, coral and bone. Had my fairy godmother fluttered by at that moment, waving her wand and pronouncing 'Thou shalt be married!', I probably would have swatted her. I once read an article entitled 'How to Marry a Rich Man', with 10 pointers, one of which was 'look at his shoes'. Apparently, even when casually dressed, a rich man will always wear good-quality and expensive shoes. Robert's lace-up gumboots bore hand-stitched patches cut from the inner-tube of a tyre.

He told me that he was the Browns' neighbour from the Coast, but I was a bit dubious as it was hard to imagine who might call themselves a 'neighbour'. I said they'd be home later in the day and, according to Robert, shut the door in his face; I didn't feel that I could invite him into their house when they didn't yet know that I was there. He didn't forgive me for that for years, and it certainly wasn't the last time we saw the same situation from completely different viewpoints.

Of course, he came back later or I wouldn't be writing this.

He had arranged a ride to Nelson for the next day to do a tutorial for his Diploma in Naturopathy, but when he heard that two women were tramping in to his part of the coast he thought perhaps he'd better come with us and carry on to Nelson afterwards. He found us all a ride to the Hollyford Valley instead. Having Beansprout with us meant that Cathy was keen to walk up the Pyke Valley and out to Big Bay that way. I agreed, blissfully ignorant of what I was letting myself in for.

I'd been in New Zealand for over a year by this time and fancied myself a tramper, but the truth was I'd mainly done tracks like the Routeburn and Milford, which are split up into three- to four-hour days, all nicely bridged and mostly well surfaced. I thought the best thing about tramping in New Zealand was not having to carry water as I often had in Australia, and with huts provided I didn't need a tent. Although you needed plenty of clothing, I had found it all a lot easier, and I often spent extra days in a hut to do a side trip just to be out there longer. Even climbing with Andrew and two friends, Clint and Brian, over the top from Anita Bay at the end of Milford Sound to Transit Beach in typically steep, muddy Fiordland bush, we hadn't travelled a huge distance. It was horrible enough for us to think better of coming back the same way, so we had a difficult scramble around the coast instead. My pack wasn't outrageously heavy, but quite bad enough when creeping along a 10-centimetre-wide ledge on a vertical rockface which meant I couldn't lean forward to balance the weight of it, and instead fell into the bouldery sea between waves.

This time, however, we were carrying food for about 10 days. Cathy had suggested bringing some mandarins — 'A sweet treat in a biodegradable package' — and a few apples for the first couple of days, but we hadn't had time to eat the other half of the bag as planned and they all went into the pack as well. I have carried much heavier pack-loads since, full of babies and their paraphernalia, but I'd had time to grow into it by then, mentally and also physically.

From the end of the Hollyford Road after midday, we reached the Hidden Falls hut that night. I was a bit surprised the next day, but didn't object when Beansprout and Cathy decided to carry on past the DOC hut up the side of Lake Alabaster.

'It's only another three hours or so,' they said.

There was still a track around the lake at that time, and Beansprout explained that when you got sick of clambering over mossy roots you could walk along the side of the lake for a while until you'd had enough of slippery boulders. I learnt the wisdom of this as we swapped between the two options six or eight times at shorter and shorter intervals. The track is overgrown now so there is no relief from the slippery boulders, but when the lake is high and you are wading, I guess you'd be glad of those.

It was very late in the short winter's day when we reached the Pyke River at the head of the lake. Beansprout said we'd sleep in the hut across the river then cross back higher up in the morning to avoid the Black Swamp. Hitchhiking in the North Island two years later, I was picked up by a man who began talking about the Pyke track.

'How did you get on in the Chocolate Swamp?' he asked.

'We just avoided it.'

'You what? How did you do that? My son is over six feet tall and he fell in up to his neck, pack and all!'

The sun was long gone behind the hills when we reached the far bank of the Pyke, and I commented on how warm I felt with my legs red and burning after the cold of the water.

'It's probably the last of your vital energy escaping,' was Cathy's remark.

In the morning we walked up the airstrip to the next river crossing. This one was deeper than the one the previous night and, with me being quite short, I had to be held upright by Cathy and Beansprout, as my pack floated me and all I could do was kick with my boots. Then onwards through Davey Gunn's old paddock, breaking through ice on frozen puddles to sink up to the ankles in mud beneath. I'm not sure whether I'd ever been so cold before. Along the Pyke track we waded waist-deep through a river of ferns, feeling our way along the depression, several centimetres deeper than the surrounding ground, that had been left by so many passing feet over the years, including those of Davey's horses and cattle.

It was only a short day to the Olivine hut, but by this time I was really struggling with the weight of my pack. I thought the best way to solve the problem was to eat the apples, but Cathy was making them last the distance.

'You can carry them then!' I said, almost in tears from the strain of not showing how hard I was finding it all.

The stretch from the Olivine out to Big Bay still stands as the longest day's tramping I've ever done. And again, it was very late as we forded the Awarua River waist-deep and found the hut. DOC kept half of the hut locked at that time, so there was a barbecue to cook on outside.

Beansprout was digging through his pack until he found what he was looking for.

'I thought I still had a potato in here,' he said, slicing it with his pocket knife to cook on the hotplate.

In the morning I decided that no matter how cold it was,

I couldn't go any longer without a wash. Had I put my wet boots on first perhaps it would actually have happened, but I'd forgotten how far we'd come from the river the night before. I only got about halfway before the frost on my bare feet convinced me otherwise and I had to run back to the hut. I settled for a swim in the sea later in the day after we'd walked to Dale Hunter's place at the south end of the bay.

Cathy had spent a few weeks with Dale the previous summer, so we stayed an extra day while she made two loaves of bread. It was a lovely north-facing spot looking over the bay, tucked out of the worst of the sou'westerly wind, but with a ringside seat for every dramatic northerly storm coming across the Tasman.

From Dale's hut to Ryan's Creek is about 30 kilometres, and therefore the second-longest day I'd ever had tramping up to then, and I was also coming down with a nasty cold. After the first five kilometres of lovely sandy beach, I met up with the boulders for the first time. I was to live at Gorge River for five years before I felt I'd got the hang of them.

We slept the night in Beansprout's bivvy before he led the way for the last eight kilometres to Gorge River. He was often up to half a kilometre ahead of me on my short legs, and Cathy would be somewhere in between, so I never had much idea about where we were or how far we had to go. I saw them start climbing up a bluff and thought maybe he lived up there, but it was just a high-tide track and we returned to a bit more boulder-hopping on the beach.

Climbing up onto a bank, I found 400 metres of flat green grass and moss to walk on — the Gorge River airstrip. I passed a freezer shed that was used in the 1970s to store venison and crayfish, and the New Zealand Forest Service hut. The Department of Conservation came into being that year, 1987, but it wasn't until 2001 that the Forest Service sign was taken off the hut. Beansprout had been recognised as a caretaker with the Forest Service for most of the seven years he had been living here.

Then around the next corner I saw for the first time the hut that was to become my home.

Beansprout suggested that I have a shower, as he and Cathy had already. It sounded like a wonderful idea, and I was highly amused and impressed by the detergent bottle punched with nail holes that made a perfectly adequate shower nozzle. I was less impressed by the trickle that came out when I turned the taps, but made the most of it.

'How was the shower?' he asked when I emerged clean and shining and smelling better than I had for a week.

'Great thanks.'

'Was there any water left?'

'Umm, well, it was only a trickle.'

'Oh. It must have run out. The tank has a lot of holes in it, so there's only about 30 centimetres of water in it when it isn't actually raining.'

We stayed for a week eating Beansprout's food before we walked on again, this time to Barn Bay. The potential beginnings of a relationship had been made with him, but I wasn't ready to stay anywhere just yet.

The Browns were home from Queenstown for the remainder of the winter. They still had the return half of their air tickets back to Canada from their holiday the previous year, but had decided to stick with crayfishing. In September they would shift up to Matamata to start building the new boat, *Scratch II*. I was waiting for my sister to finish her nursing training before we travelled together overseas, so Lou talked me into buying two of their tickets. Alison and I arranged to meet at Auckland airport at the end of August, where they checked us onto the plane. I didn't come back for a year and a half.

Chapter 5

OE, USA, UK, EU

T he two years that followed my introduction to the Cascade coastline was a period not so much of growing up but of refusing to until I'd done all the things I wanted to first. I'd always had a fear of getting married and moving into the next subdivision, and I'd fought against the currents that swept me along through my life, including that of the education process, right through to my time in Dunedin.

I'd taken five subjects at school, then four in the first year at university. In second year my four subjects were subsets of only two from the previous year, and in the final year we were to choose two, preferably related, subjects to major in. Having achieved a first-class Honours in Immunology, I was persuaded by Duncan Adams to enrol to do a PhD in Autoimmunity, and it seemed to me that I was learning more and more about less and less, presumably until I knew absolutely everything there was to know about nothing at all! No matter how far I went along the track, there was always an expectation that I would continue on to the next step, with less and less room for anything else in life. But I had places I wanted to go to and things I wanted to see.

Coming from Perth, it had taken me several weeks to settle into the slower pace of Dunedin. I'd have lists of things to do in my lunch break, but when cashiers stopped to talk to each customer the list would never be more than half-completed in the available time, and I was happy to adjust to my new surroundings. The job was extremely interesting, but for the first time I had the leisure to consider where I was heading. I took up badminton and transcendental meditation, attended public lectures at the university and the library, and enjoyed a wide range of reading and learning purely for the sake of it.

Most weekends I hitchhiked up to Central Otago to spend time with Andrew, building his house-truck, working on orchards or gold mining in the Clutha River. At other times I'd catch a bus to Christchurch to see Dinah and Ned, or ride my bike out onto the Otago Peninsula and camp on the beach. Having bought Andrew's old bomb VW for very little — before spending half a fortune on it for a warrant and to make it go — once again I decided to stop paying rent. I stored my small amount of gear and, although I couldn't sleep in a VW bug, I could drive out to a beach or a cliff-top on the peninsula and camp the night in my bivvy tent. Having a pillow while camping seemed like the height of luxury! I'd spend wet evenings in the library then drive out in the dark to a hidey hole in a hayshed, an abandoned house, or occasionally to a friend's place. And all the time I was saving money to travel overseas.

Alison finished her nursing training at Fremantle Hospital

and joined me in New Zealand for a month before we headed to Canada. In Vancouver we could stay with friends she had met the previous year on a trip to Rwanda where they'd climbed up a volcano to see the mountain gorillas. We had intended to work our way down to South America, but at the airport Lou convinced us to go to Alaska first.

I thought Vancouver was a beautiful city, with the sky and surrounding mountains painted the same blue as Fiordland. We crossed on the ferry to Vancouver Island and hitched a ride north with a pair of silviculturists. Their job was to go into a regenerating block of conifer forest and thin the trees to encourage them to grow more quickly. They taught us the difference between cedar, Douglas fir, spruce, pine and hemlock, which all looked like pine trees to us, and explained how they'd choose the best species in each spot and cull the others around it. We weren't so impressed when they spotted a yew sapling, the first they'd seen in years, and leapt out with the chainsaw to take it home.

From Port Hardy we took another ferry to Prince William, and then one up through the Inside Passage to Haines, Alaska. After sleeping out for a couple of nights we were headed below for a shower and missed seeing a pod of orca, but we saw humpback whales the next day. We snuggled in our sleeping bags in deck chairs hoping to see the aurora borealis for the first time. At about two in the morning, Alison woke me to what looked like a narrow band of greenish cloud across the sky, wondering whether that could be it. As we watched, it seemed to notice that we were awake and began to dance as if to greet us to Alaska for the first time.

The aurora australis (the Southern Hemisphere aurora) had also put on a display for me the night after I'd told

Duncan Adams that I was leaving my job in Dunedin. It was a big decision to make at the time, and that night, camping above Brighton beach, I felt that the aurora was confirming for me that I had indeed made the right choice. I have never met anyone else who saw it that night.

Alaska fascinated us, and it wasn't long before we decided to stay for the winter. We hitchhiked everywhere, and many people asked us to come home with them 'to let my children hear you speak'. We made many friends where we were welcome to stay, and in five months we only paid for three nights' accommodation.

One day we hitched a ride with Ray Kruckenberg, who was driving his truck all the way south to Houston, Texas. Although we didn't want to go that day, he gave us a number to call and said he was back in Alaska every four weeks. In the middle of November when it was cold, dark and miserable but not yet terribly amazing, we called him and went off to check out the 'Lower 48'. Crossing the border into British Columbia, the first night we asked whether he would stop for a bit to see whether the aurora was playing. Ray agreed to sleep there until morning if necessary, but within 10 minutes up it came and danced for us in a beautiful farewell display before gradually fading away.

'Oh well, we might as well keep going.'

The aurora knew our comings and goings and would perform on cue if we asked respectfully. I have seen it south of where I stood near Fairbanks, Alaska, and heard it whispering as if in the leaves of the trees that stood bare around me. Many times it spoke to me of joy or momentous occasion or perhaps just of good fun. And once or twice, it lent me hope in the face of despair.

We saw the Grand Canyon, saguaro cacti in Nevada, and

a giant panda at the San Diego zoo. We arrived at Yosemite as the sun was setting, but in the morning it was snowing with a cloud layer at about 50 metres, so we sat in the foyer of a warm hotel watching squirrels through the window until it was time to catch our next bus back to Mum's cousin's house near San Francisco. On our way up to Edmonton for a white Christmas, we crossed the Golden Gate Bridge and saw sequoia and Mt St Helens, which had erupted a couple of years before.

Alison met another truck driver, Darrell Piere, in Houston, and three weeks later he asked her to marry him. Of course she said no, but eventually he talked her into it and she lived in Canada and Montana for the next 10 years.

In return for a day's work in a Salvation Army shop in Fairbanks, we received two Eskimo coats and two pairs of felt-lined boots. My jacket was ex-US Army; a long down jacket with a strip of wolf fur around the hood. We sewed our own fleece or felted woollen pants, but hitchhiking from Banff to Calgary on New Year's Eve we stood on the side of the wrong road for over an hour while our socks froze to our boots. The sign pointed to Calgary that way, but every car turned off the other way, and it turned out that they were heading out to the main road rather than passing through the Indian reservation that lay straight ahead. After that, we bought brand-new Iceman boots and were equipped for whatever the winter threw at us.

Don and Curt Ward, father and son, took us back to Alaska on their return trip from Christmas in Oklahoma. It was warm enough with four of us in their pickup, but we had to nurse our bag of beansprouts to protect them from frostbite. Our water bottle froze where it rested against the side of the cab. I took a turn at driving in the middle of the night, and managed to miss a moose as well as stay on the snowy road, although I ended up pointing back the way we'd come. I 'got back on the horse' and continued to drive, but when the tyre blew shortly afterwards I called it quits.

Alaska was very much a boom-and-bust economy and mentality. Many people who worked extremely hard all summer, slept, watched TV and drank the winter away. Don and Curt were not drinkers, and we helped them cut and deliver loads of firewood. They stretched a tarpaulin over the front of the log skidder, lit a blow torch under it, then sat back in the truck for 20 minutes while the motor warmed up enough to try starting it. Deciduous birch trees only grew on hills where there was enough soil to support them above the permafrost layer. In places on the flat, stunted spruce trees stood a metre high, two or three centimetres in diameter and over 600 years old!

The winter of 1987–88 was a mild one, and often, as we hitched 30 kilometres in and out of Fairbanks, we'd pass a 60-year-old man who rode his bike into town every day of the year. The temperature only dropped to −43°F once, and as Don and Curt had been using domestic heating diesel to avoid road taxes, the truck froze up. Curt walked or hitched to a garage to buy methylated spirits to dissolve the water in the fuel tank so that it would go on through the engine. The rest of us sat and waited in the truck with the windows closed to conserve the remaining heat, while the dog farted.

The following day the temperature rose to −10°F, but the wind was blowing enough to make it equivalent to −70°F with the wind-chill factor. Dressed as I was, I was able to stand out on the two-metre-thick river ice with most of the rest of the population of Fairbanks for an hour, watching the start of the Yukon Quest, a 1600-kilometre dog-sled race.

We wanted to walk on the Arctic Ocean. On the day in question, we'd driven with Ray into Prudhoe Bay early in the morning to deliver a load of oil-field equipment from Texas. We could barely see the front of the truck for blowing snow, and so stayed on the road guided by edge markers that appeared one at a time from the gloom before vanishing into the dark behind us. We wouldn't be able to tell whether it was ocean or land, so gave up on the idea and settled for buying souvenir T-shirts, avoiding anything with penguins. Mine read: *If you think Hell never freezes over, you've never been to Prudhoe Bay.*

The following summer I was back to put my feet into the Arctic Ocean, but again it was something of an anti-climax. The sea ice still held outside the bay, so the water was shallow, dead calm and looked like nothing more than a muddy duckpond.

In the spring we flew from New York to London and had a couple of months in England, visiting Mum's House relatives and travelling with bikes on trains to the Orkneys, Skye, the Lake District, North Wales and Cornwall. We wanted to see the England we had grown up hearing about: Beatrix Potter's cottage and Devonshire teas with clotted cream, Tintagel — the supposed birthplace of King Arthur, Stonehenge, Edinburgh Castle and the Yorkshire Dales. Having bikes made it easy to get out of the towns, and we often slept in a camping ground for only 50 pence or camped in a corner of a field. Apart from a couple of days in London, we managed to live on very little money and avoided the main cities in the Midlands.

My grandfather's eldest sister, Aunt Daphne, lived in Yorkshire in what had been the dowager house of an estate.

The house was built in the 1600s around a twelfth-century fortified tower, and the panelling in the drawing room was wonky, perhaps fitted later into whatever was there after it had slumped for a hundred years or so. It was rather like the lining in our house at Gorge River where nothing sits square. Aunt Daphne died in 2011 at the age of 105.

The cheapest airline-style seats on the boat from Newcastle to Bergen were right down in the bilge, and after one look we settled in deckchairs with sleeping bags again to enjoy the crossing. We stayed in Bergen for two or three days, which was as long as we could afford when even groceries were very expensive, before taking the train to Oslo and then Bødo above the Arctic Circle. The Gulf Stream allowed deciduous trees to survive well above the circle here, and we camped out of town on a north-facing hill to watch the sun not set.

Our one-month Eurail pass took us from Norway to Greece and back to Belgium. Being limited more to the main cities was OK, as that's what we most wanted to see. As it would have taken two weeks to get a visa for France in London, we didn't go there or to Spain, but had our French experience in Geneva and Belgium. We blinked as we passed through Liechtenstein and didn't realise until later that we had missed it, but made a point of getting to Luxembourg.

We had been keen to get as far as Istanbul, but the Eurail pass didn't apply in Turkey, and in Athens we quailed at the thought of a 36-hour journey each way with rumours of up to 15 people in each six-person compartment. Six people sleeping head, tail, head, tail, head, tail like sardines was bad enough.

With little money it was becoming hard work, particularly being two girls travelling together. Calls of 'Signorina, I loo-oove you!' following us down the streets of Florence were one thing, but having my bum fondled with one leg in and one out of a pair of pants in a dressing room in Corfu while my money belt sat on the floor was starting to push it, particularly when I left my sunglasses behind and had to stalk back in and out again to get them. I was sorry to leave the pants, too.

So instead of Istanbul we enjoyed Greece before returning to the two cities we had loved most — Salzburg and Venice. With our knowledge of the Greek alphabet from Maths at school, we could spell out ΠΑΤΡΑΣ (Patras), ΚΟΡΙΝΘ (Corinth), and work out which of ΑΝΔΡΟΣ and ΓΥΝΑΙΚΟΝ was the appropriate toilet to enter. In Salzburg, people wore dirndl and lederhosen, five or more bands played in the streets in the evening, and there was any amount of chamber music, orchestra or puppet shows if we wished to pay for them. We followed a self-conducted *Sound of Music* tour past the abbey, the church, the Schloss Mirabell and the little summer house. And Venice was everything we had ever imagined and more.

I flew on a standby ticket with British Airways from Heathrow to Anchorage, directly over the Arctic. We passed to the northeast of Iceland and over the icecap of the northwest corner of Greenland. I'm afraid I refused to close my blind for the sake of everyone else watching a movie, but this flight was one of the most amazing experiences of my life. The pack ice looked like a lace tablecloth, with pressure ridges brighter white than the intervening ice. The northernmost islands of Canada were bare rock at first, and muskeg further south. The sun shone gold on one creek system after another as we passed, with all the meandering tributaries like the blood vessels in a brain.

Meanwhile Alison flew to New York, but due to a mix-up she had a return ticket. Jet-lagged and raving over the phone about my incredible flight, I urged her to use her ticket to fly straight back to London and come back over the top, but she didn't.

I spent a few more months trucking between Houston and the north coast of Alaska, but after our time in England I found it harder to deal with the American way of thinking. We had thoroughly appreciated the English sense of humour and talking to people who understood us, eating Anchor butter from New Zealand, and Vegemite from Australia House in London. In contrast, America is such a large country that they seemed very self-contained and relatively uninformed about the rest of the world. And their feeling for the environment seemed limited. For example, people told us of a proposal to divert the proposed Alaska–Canada highway around a tree with a bald eagle nesting in it — in their eyes, evidence of how crazy greenies were. Moreover, if a whale did $40,000 worth of damage to a net in Nova Scotia, they'd argue that the whale should be shot. 'That's the fisherman's livelihood!'

Even being vegetarian was seen as a sign of protest and would arouse their defensive natures.

'How do you get your protein and the all-important vitamin A?' someone asked, as if it was any business of his.

'Carrots,' I replied, which silenced him momentarily.

'You can't survive a winter in Alaska without eating animal fat!' many people told us, and we just shrugged.

'We eat butter.'

Actually, in an Alaskan winter you almost never get cold. If you do you are probably going to die, so you always have to plan not to. Houses and shopping malls are kept warm, and as long as you had suitable clothing to walk from one to the other you'd be fine. People even heated their garages, and car parks at the malls provided power points to plug in your engine-block heater. I found it much colder in the winter in Christchurch where our houses are not so well-insulated. We were most amused by the occasional person we met in Alaska with an outdoor toilet and Styrofoam toilet seat!

And I missed the ocean. In Australia, 98 per cent of the population lives around the coast, and even though I grew up 30 kilometres away from it there was always an awareness of it. You waited each afternoon in the summertime for the sea breeze. You could always go for a swim without too much effort. Even in winter we often went fishing or just walking on the beach rugged up against the wind. The prairies of America have their own beauty, and I also love the emptiness of central Australia, but to be a thousand kilometres or more from the ocean for months at a time left me feeling as if something fundamental was missing in my life.

Chapter 6

PEASANTS BY CHOICE

Back in New Zealand, in February 1989 I walked into Barn Bay with Alison. Although I wasn't conscious that I was showing her that this was what I was choosing to do next, I guess at a deep level that was part of the reason for going there. In fact, I didn't know *what* I was doing next. Certainly my fascination with the area had not diminished and I wanted to show her that, at least. At the Martyr homestead at the end of the Cascade Road we met up with Maurice Nolan who owned the farm on the south side of the river. There was room for only one of us in the truck, but Maurice said, 'I'll take the four-wheeler', as he jumped onto his horse.

He had a spare horse to take down, too, and as Alison was the rider in our family I climbed into the truck with Simon Williamson from Birchwood Station who was helping Maurice with the mustering. We travelled much more slowly than a horse could over that rough and muddy track. Alison crossed the Cascade River and reached the hut well ahead of us, but she was having so much fun that she carried on with Maurice to bring the cattle up from the swamp. That night, after Maurice and Simon had departed for Haast, she described crossing streams in the swamp that were so deep that while she sat on the highest point at the back of the saddle with her feet up on the front of it, the water flowed between. She had also enjoyed Maurice's way of cursing while simply stating the facts.

'Come on, you dog-fighting bitches!' he'd shout to shift the cows.

From Barn Bay we fished with Lou on his new boat, *Scratch II*, down to Gorge River. I hadn't really figured out what I'd say to Robert when I saw him, but as it turned out he wasn't home anyway. I left a note on his table with a telephone number in case he wanted to get in touch sometime.

He called me two or three months later when he was next by a phone, and we arranged to meet in Queenstown in June to tramp through the Greenstone track. It was a wickedly cold but stunningly beautiful trip in a hoar frost, and I can still smell the moisture in the air ahead of an approaching northerly storm on the wet West Coast as we stood on the highest point at the Greenstone Saddle. In the morning it was raining.

At the Divide, Robert turned north to walk down the Hollyford Valley, and I hitchhiked back to Christchurch where he came to visit a few times over the rest of that year.

During 1990 I spent about half my time at Gorge River, and Robert was keen for me to live there permanently.

'It seems like a dream,' I answered.

The Lady Poverty

I met her on the Umbrian hills,
Her hair unbound, her feet unshod:
As one whom secret glory fills
She walked, alone with God.

I met her in the city street:
Oh, changed was all her aspect then!
With heavy eyes and weary feet
She walked alone, with men.

— Evelyn Underhill

Here was a place I could live with the basic necessities of life; a piece of ground that was big enough to grow what I needed to eat, and whatever I put into it would come back to me. I wouldn't have to work for a salary for years in order to first buy the piece of land, while the chances of ever living the lifestyle potentially grew more remote. To work towards a distant goal risks being diverted from it by the meanderings of the path itself. If I was to save money it would be silly not to do it in the field in which I was trained, but it hardly made sense to go further along the track of specialising and gaining a PhD with the goal of one day being a peasant. Here, I could walk straight out the door and pick up the shovel. It didn't seem such a difficult decision after all.

You can watch the sea for hours and never grow tired of it while it fills you with energy and vitality. It becomes a part of your fabric, so that often you are hardly aware of it, although it is disturbingly noisy on a stormy night or when you first arrive home after being away for a few weeks.

Robert could hear music coming off the sea and the mountains and river valleys of the wilderness. He spoke of the 'Persistent Piper', 'the Canadian accordions', 'the bass drone' and 'the all-encompassing OM'. Sometimes I could hear it, too, although never as clearly as he described it. He could even play the melody on his guitar. Certainly, I could hear the kettledrums of the orchestra.

We were happy to eat like peasants. A bag of rice went a long way with a few potatoes and root vegetables from the garden. Swedes, turnips and parsnips came up by themselves every spring, as they had before Robert arrived in 1980. Comfrey and watercress gave us all the greens we needed. He had grown cabbages throughout the 1980s, but at this time the rabbits were giving the garden a hiding.

I didn't much like the ground kelp powder which Robert sprinkled on every meal, but it was a great source of minerals and quite edible when thrown into the rice and vegetable 'stew' which we ate every second night throughout the autumn and winter, with mung bean and lentil sprouts and a salad of comfrey, watercress, parsley and chives, sometimes with turnip or swede flowers. On the other nights we added a bit of flour, usually hand-ground, to thicken the leftover rice, and fried it in patties. If there was no oil, we rolled it into chapattis in flour, cooked them on top of the stove and spread them with butter, if we had it, and Marmite, which was often left behind in the DOC hut and never ran out. We made bread from hand-ground wheat and rye flour, and sometimes fine flour, and in autumn we picked sedge grass seed to dry and grind and I made 'bran muffins'. Robert cooked buns or scones or biscuits, which were all much the same thing, changing only with the ingredients available. If we had peanuts he'd put a few in and call them 'peanut brownies'. Visitors often asked me for the recipe of the 'scone' and I'd say, 'It's only flour and water [plus salt and baking powder].'

'There's something else... a flavour...?'

That was the hand-ground flour, which, although hard work, has a freshness that makes it well worthwhile. We enjoyed freshly ground grains in porridge, too.

At first when I came to visit I carried in Swiss rye bread, milk powder, butter and sweet wholemeal biscuits which Robert seemed to enjoy, but they didn't go very far and as I was putting such a hole in the stock of rice, I had to start bringing rice instead.

'These are white man's biscuits!' Lou Brown said when we offered him the packet when he called in for a cup of tea while fishing.

'Eat them up so I can make some real ones,' Robert answered.

I've always had a sweet tooth, but after living here for a while I didn't find it hard to go without, and even enjoyed it. It made me appreciate things so much more whenever I did have them. We used to dream about eating apple crumble when we got out to town.

Apart from bull kelp which washed up on the beach after a storm, Robert collected Neptune's necklace seaweed in the rock pools and boiled it with a spoonful of oil and a few peanuts and sultanas before adding a handful or two of rolled oats to make porridge. We ate it with salad and sprouts. In summer we occasionally collected karengo off the rocks. You had to be careful to remove all the periwinkle snails, though, or you risked losing or cracking a tooth, but dried and toasted on top of the stove, karengo was a rare and favourite treat, like a salty cracker.

Without milk, Robert would put a couple of teaspoons of Creamoata into a tin cup with water and butter or oil, and sit it at the back of the stove to cook slowly before adding tea. At first I thought it looked awful, but it wasn't long before I was hungry enough to enjoy it. Other ground grains could also be used, and they always tasted better after the Creamoata was finished. Robert still has rolled oats and sultanas in his cup of tea, although I stopped doing that when I finished nursing babies except maybe for a quick meal when arriving hungry at a hut.

A major part of coming to live here meant adjusting to the way Robert did things. He dreamed of his soul-mate, but when she didn't turn up he had to settle for me banging pots and burning the bottom of every loaf of bread. It was all very well for me to waltz in here with my own ideas, but Robert had already spent nine years working out the best way of doing most things. Any ideas of mine had to wait some time before they were accepted, even if they were better.

One day he would be offended if I thought something should be improved on, and the next he'd be wondering why I wasn't cleaning something that would still be dirty afterwards if I did. While I practised turning a blind eye to some things that couldn't be fixed, he'd wonder why I wasn't washing it. I guess most relationships go through that stage.

I still had money saved from the two years that I had worked for a salary, even after travelling overseas for 18 months, but, knowing that it was only there so long as I didn't spend it, I was accustomed to living on very little. Robert could always crew for Dale Hunter or Lou Brown when he needed money, but in between he concentrated on spending as little as possible to delay the time when he'd have to work again. He had been able to live for the whole year on what he could earn in just a few weeks' fishing, up until the last four years when he had needed a lot more money to pay for his correspondence diploma course from the New Zealand Naturopathy College.

He was studying hard in his final year and slept with a pile of textbooks on the bottom corner of the bed. I tried to fill in time and make myself useful by grinding flour, until it bothered him too much and I understood the degree of quiet that he was accustomed to. Next I tried gardening.

'What's this?' I asked as he walked by.

'That's a potato,' he informed me and I guiltily took another look.

'Oh well, it's too late now.'

Many apparently dead stalks were meant to stay there for the sake of their seed, and so my 'rip, tear and bust' technique needed some refining.

Gradually, the house did get cleaner. I swept the floor in the morning, knowing that in half an hour it would probably look as though I hadn't. Often I swept around Robert as he sat filing a piece of whalebone, and the falling dust would begin the layer for the next day. I thought of it as the 24-hour cut-off point.

In Heather Heberley's book *Riding with Whales*, Ida Seymour tells of nearly being caught out sitting around the table reading after a Sunday dinner, dishes forgotten, when a boat came around the point heading to their beach in the Marlborough Sounds. We get about five minutes' notice of visitors arriving by aeroplane and about two minutes' by helicopter. We *always* have dishes in the sink, the table half-covered in junk and the other half piled with whatever is being done at present. It isn't a very big house, so if I clean under the beds and into damp corners, everything stored under there has to be stacked up in the more central areas and we squeeze around it for several days while the corners dry out sufficiently. I usually apologise for the mess when people arrive, but I don't bother feeling guilty as I would have in 1950. As the aeroplane circles, the scramble is on. A quick tidy of the table or floor, sweep the worst of the dirt under the wood-box, change my filthy gardening pants for something slightly better, or tidy away some of the food and dirty dishes on the bench. Oh, and put some wood on the fire so the kettle can get started.

Some problems were not solvable with a logical brain, so it was better to learn to live with them. Robert's logic is usually quite different to mine, and this has often been a source of confusion. When I have asked him to explain his rationale to me I usually find that it makes sense, so mostly I have learned to accept it at face value or ignore it if it is too exasperating.

I've watched his mum clearly understanding him in such conversations, while his dad and I sit there shaking our heads, saying 'Huh?' It is definitely a case of alternative realities, and although I have learned that I am not always wrong, it doesn't mean that he is either. Still, sometimes things seem so important, and later, looking back, you wonder what all the fuss was about.

We share this house with mice, particularly in the autumn and winter, when quite reasonably they are looking for a warm, dry spot to be. In the early years, we'd nearly always get up in the morning to mouse poop on the kitchen bench. One morning as I wiped it down it suddenly appalled Robert that I was using the same cloth as I used to wipe the table. As

I'd probably been doing this for about three years by this time, I was somewhat surprised and exasperated by his reaction.

'But we have food on the bench, too.'

'But they poop on the cloth anyway.'

'What do you expect me to do?'

Next morning we had one cloth for mouse poop and one for food areas, colour-coded to tell the difference.

'OK, so which one do I use to wipe mouse poop off the table?'

The subject was dropped.

Later, when the three boards that made up the table were needed for the new floor, Robert built us a bigger and much nicer table out of the stained and varnished head- and foot-boards from the spare double bed. With the legs set well back from the corners, mice were no longer able to climb up onto the table.

Before I moved to Gorge River, I wrote to an old friend explaining where I was living and how we collected the mail from the Haast post office whenever we were passing. I mentioned that sometimes an aeroplane flew over and dropped it with a rock tied to it. Sometime later I received his reply with a * in one corner of the envelope and the written instruction: *Please attach rock here!*

I wrote a letter to Robert from Wellington once to tell him that Tsehai Tiffin from the *Holmes* show would be arriving on a certain day in August and sent the letter c/o Geoff Robson, a fisherman from Neil's Beach, hoping that it might reach Robert sooner. I knew that Geoff would probably be fishing past Gorge River on his boat *Oregon*, or that he might give the letter to Lou Brown to deliver.

Robert saw Geoff signalling as he tied a message to a buoy

TOP My parents, Ian Stewart and Rosamond House, on their wedding day. They married on 9 June 1961.

BOTTOM I retrieve my arrows from the gold at the State Indoor Target Championships, 1980. Unfortunately, this was just a practice end. For the rest of the day, I shot like a hairy goat and 'couldn't hit the wide wall of a barn from the inside' as my dad would say.

LEFT *Aquillo* on a lovely summer's day with the University of Western Australia behind.

BELOW Inside *Aquillo*. I could sit up on the centreboard casing with my knees in the galley. The head of my bed is at the lower right of the photo and I could reach over to put the kettle on the gas stove.

TOP Robert at the end of 1989 — quite good-looking really, without the funny hat.

MIDDLE Knitting Robert a new jersey. We worked by candlelight until we bought our first solar panel in 1998, and even after that on cloudy days or late at night in the winter.

BOTTOM The house and garden when I first started living here in 1990. The front verandah was useful for drying firewood but made it very dark inside.

TOP And then there were three. This was the first time anyone came along to take a photo of all three of us.

BOTTOM Christan accompanied me everywhere. I remember working out where to cut legholes in my pack so that I could still carry a reasonable load as well.

We held our wedding at Whisky Corner on the road to the Cascade River with a view of the valley and out to the coast. Although the Catholic Church recognised that Robert had baptised Christan in the Cascade River, he hadn't used any oil so Father Foote wanted to finish it off.

LEFT Robert extended the little front pack with green canvas inserts, as Christan was soon too big for it, especially when he wore at least three layers of clothing. We carried him everywhere in it for the first couple of years.

BOTTOM Checking the net was Robert and Christan's first job nearly every day.

TOP Life was more fun once Robin was big enough to play.

BOTTOM LEFT When bathing in the sink became too dangerous, the children graduated to the bucket, where they could sit or stand for as long as they wanted to with less supervision. Christan fell asleep in there once.

BOTTOM RIGHT Both kids loved the bouncer made from a pair of jeans, a piece of wood, rope and a bungee cord.

TOP With a hat, long sleeves and pants for the sake of sandflies, we never had to worry about sunscreen.

BOTTOM The Gorge River ferryman.

on one of his craypots and, despite the not-particularly-calm sea, rowed out to collect it. Geoff had left his own note in a plastic bag with my letter, asking Robert whether he had seen the West Coast tramper, a Californian guy who was attempting to walk right around the South Island, and including in the plastic bag a pencil for him to write an answer.

The sou'westerly wind suddenly picked up as Robert rowed back into the beach, blowing him north of the safe landing spot and up to the stretch we call 'Hungry Beach'. When he saw one huge wave approaching he dived off the bow of the dinghy and left it to find its own way to shore. Grabbing the rope, he dug his heels in, trying to hold it as the waves sucked back out.

It was still upside down and full of the weight of the water, but each time a wave pushed it up the beach Robert would run ahead of it and try to hold it against the retreating water as the oars were ground off in the rowlocks. When the biggest wave pushed it far up the beach he was able to hold it. My letter was sodden, but he had a moment to read it before it fell apart in the wind.

We weren't the first people to have lived in this remote part of the world. Mary Trayes, an avid historian who works with the Westland Regional Council, typed the following excerpt from a photocopied handwritten manuscript found in the Department of Conservation Archives at Hokitika on 4 May 2009. In many places the writer, Charles Douglas, did not use a capital letter after a full stop, which she has corrected. Otherwise she has left the punctuation and spelling as it was in the original.

*Survey: Westland from the Hollyford to the
Arahura, 1899,
Part II by Charles Douglas
Gorge to Barn Bay*

*It is certainly an out of the way place to live in
no mail no steamers, and a difficulty to get stores.
Boating stores down the Coast if continued long
enough has only one ending 'Davy Jones Locker'
but a party with sufficient means to lay in twelve
months stores could always get them landed by
Government Steamer.*

*Round the bluff the route is open travelling to
the Hope river it can't be called good walking
by any means. The beaches are steep slopes of
boulders about the size of a sixty four poundshot
and move down in an aggravating way when
walking along the slope is direct from the scrub
so there is no get(ting) away. However the boots
suffer much more than the man in them.*

During my first two years at Gorge River, I clomped along in Ashford lace-up gumboots. My brother said that they were what people wore on the Routeburn Track and in Fiordland. Some people even put holes in them to let the water out, as inevitably it would get in. I didn't go that far, but I would hold my leg up behind me to tip the water out after crossing a river or a deep puddle. With soft rubber soles they were perfect for walking over rounded boulders, where a tramping boot was too rigid, although boots have come a long way over the past 20 years. Robert would have considered giving his eye teeth for a pair large enough for him, whereas I had the opposite problem.

The smallest size available was still two sizes too big for me, so I filled them with sheepskin inner soles and two pairs of thick socks — a great weight at the end of my leg. I'd often stop to pour half a cupful of bloodstained water out of each boot after crossing the Cascade, and would barely be out in town long enough for the gouged-out blisters to heal before walking in again. Since then I've never bothered too much about the pressure Kiwi trampers put on you to walk straight through a puddle rather than attempting to keep your boots dry for a bit longer. It seems to me that your feet are what is going to get you there, and taking care of them makes as much sense as servicing your car regularly. Mostly I can keep my shoes dry for the first day on the coast to Barn Bay, and from there, through all the creeks and muddy puddles, wet feet can survive one day without too much damage.

Whenever I walked behind Robert I had to concentrate on where I was putting my feet and also on going as fast as I could, and there was no time to look around. So the first time I came in on my own I lost the track in the last kilometre before Barn Bay where the meanderings of the Hope River often take out a stretch of it. Having spent some time trying to find it again, I decided to follow the water-pipe which I knew would lead me to the house, but it only took a hundred metres or so of that to realise my mistake. Robert had laid it out four or five years before on a compass bearing, straight through the swamp or whatever obstacle he found, and following it was all but impossible. I also missed the sharp left-turn in the track near the top of Sandrock Bluff the next day, and rather than climbing back up to find it I sallied forth through my first and worst-ever kiekie thicket, where you have the option of crawling underneath or climbing along two metres off the ground on the long and sinuous stems. A steep learning curve indeed. By the next trip I knew the way.

If I had to wait out a northerly storm at Barn Bay, the next day would often bring sou'west squalls, which tend to set in about 10 o'clock in the morning. In a trick of the light the sun usually shines most brightly just before a squall hits, so often having had an early start I'd be skipping along thinking what a nice day it was turning into, then look up to find the sky black and bearing down on me. I'd retreat to the shelter of the flaxes for the hailstones, and once the shower was over there would probably be a half-hour break before the next squall. After a while I learned to smell them coming.

Leaving too early after a northerly storm was also not a good plan, with the Hope River being the first obstacle. I quickly learned my limitations there, too, after washing downstream for a couple of hundred metres with my pack on my back.

At the end of the year, wearing a ring on my left hand that Robert had carved from deer antler, we flew to Canada where my sister was now married and having her first baby. I really wanted to be there to help her, but I didn't feel that I should be away from Robert for such a long time at that stage of our relationship. Despite warnings from her midwife of the dangers of a home birth, we came back with Christan on board.

Chapter 7

A JOEY IN THE POUCH

hristan was a 'blue moon' baby. A full moon is called a blue moon when it occurs for the second time in the same calendar month, and Christan was conceived on a blue moon on 31 December 1990 in Canada when it was already 1 January 1991 in New Zealand. Consequently, the day we landed back in Auckland, 30 January, was another blue moon and with February being a short month, 1 and 31 March also had full moons. I hadn't exactly planned to be pregnant just yet, but with all that going on I guess I didn't stand much chance against fate.

Robert was absolutely delighted, but at first I struggled with it, bitching and complaining. Although I'd looked forward to having babies for most of my life, it had always been in some mythical future and I waited for the time to come when I would feel ready for it. In hindsight, I think perhaps it never would have until I was faced with it. The reality of it seeped in gradually as my belly expanded, but even at seven or eight months I described it to Robert as the feeling you have when watching the colour creeping into the sky in the early morning. Although your brain tells you that the sun will rise and nothing can stop it happening, the glory of the sun as it springs above the horizon in that first shaft of light is completely new every day and you can't really *know* or even quite imagine it until it happens.

While Robert was away in Australia for three weeks in March, where his sister was dying of cancer, I had a chance to stand back and take a good look at myself. I accepted then that although life might be a whole lot easier on my own, it was also pointless. I couldn't take Robert's child away from him, and I certainly would never leave it. Just as Grandma Peggy Stewart made my granddad promise to keep the family together before she died, I believe that nothing else matters as much as that. From the day that Christan was conceived there has never been any other option for either of us, and although we didn't get around to having a wedding for a couple of years, we were effectively married at that moment, for better or for worse. Lying in bed, I curled around this wee dot, and Robert curled around me, protecting us both.

Heading home on a morning in April, the Cascade was fairly high but not such that we couldn't cross. At the deepest point, holding Robert with one hand and trying to keep my pack high behind me, the water reached my brisket, and now that we were well into autumn it was just about cold enough. My swelling belly seemed particularly vulnerable and, as we tramped on, on the south side, I felt cold to the depths of my being. Or perhaps it was to the depths of wee Joey's being, as shortly afterwards I felt him move for the first time. He was probably doing star jumps, trying to warm up. It was several more days before I felt him move again, and after that he did it every day.

In the sixth month we walked out via the Hollyford Valley to find a midwife and check that everything was progressing properly. Denise Black from Alexandra was happy to help us, and she gave us an ear-trumpet to take home as well as urinalysis sticks to keep a track of my protein and sugar levels. Robert had already been taking my blood pressure, so when he had to go to Barn Bay and I was to be alone here for the first time he wanted to listen to Joey's heartbeat before he left. He poked about trying to hear it, but the main beat he could hear was at a rate of about 15 per minute.

'I think he's got the hiccups,' I said, when he got too frustrated.

I'd always known that my first child would be a boy. It was only in the last couple of weeks before he was born that I had any doubts, or could even imagine having a girl. After his birth I knew that the next one would be a girl, though perhaps not with quite the same conviction.

During that winter, a particularly friendly fantail flew over to squeak at me whenever I stepped out the door. It flitted about when I was gardening, landing on my head, my shoulder, and once on my hand, and getting under my feet as I walked. Of course, it was only chasing the sandflies I'd accumulated, but after that many of the other fantails also seemed more tame than usual. Even in the Hollyford, the fantails seemed to have heard the exciting news.

Dale Hunter asked Robert to fish for him in July and August, and we badly needed the money. I looked forward to it as a chance to get away from Gorge River for a while and meet a few other people. At Big Bay, the fishermen often rowed in to the sheltered shore as they very rarely can at Gorge River. Dale had said that he would collect us in his boat, which sounded good to me, but, not for the first time, I was overruled by Robert's idea of the way things worked around here. He said the sea could turn rough just at the wrong time and Dale might be unable to get up here for three weeks. We'd walk to Big Bay, although we could split it into two short days and one long one, stopping at Ryan's Creek and the Awarua River on the way. I was seven months pregnant and not exactly happy about it, but I agreed when he pointed out that the boat ride could be far worse. He said I should only carry a day-pack, although I loaded it up with compact, heavy stuff to make the remainder more manageable for him. I took my first attempts at homespun wool and a pair of knitting needles Robert had made from No. 8 wire to knit a few pairs of thick, woollen, over-nappy pants during the next few weeks, but anything else I needed for the baby had to wait until I got out to town.

Whenever I caught up to Robert sitting, waiting and getting cold, he asked how I was going and I'd say 'I'm fine, I'm going to make it, I'll be OK.' It was so much more productive than bursting into tears and declaring that I couldn't possibly go another step, although that was equally true.

At Big Bay, the radio aerial had blown down, and even after Robert fixed it we never had an answer from Dale out in Queenstown. Nor could we get through on the portable radio he'd loaned us, and we realised how little an improvement it was to have one if there was nobody listening at the other end. Finally, on the prescribed day, we watched Dale zoom by in a cloud of spray, heading north to Gorge River. We had been looking out, hoping that he would come to his place first and see us there, but he was too far away to do anything about it. He arrived back at his place about two hours later, frozen and furious.

Dale mostly communicated with a minimum of words, and Robert told me that a certain amount of telepathy was required. I wasn't playing that game, so I appointed him as official translator, relying on him to let me know if anything mattered. Dale declared that he could eat soup every day of the year so, with permanently black, sooty hands, I dutifully had soup waiting over the open fire whenever they got in from fishing. Even the day when they almost lost the boat on the Hollyford bar I made soup, unaware of how close I had come to being a single mother. With just a few ingredients available, apart from almost unlimited Jerusalem artichokes, they must have grown sick of it. Finally, Dale told me to write a list of anything we needed and flew out to Queenstown for a break, but when he arrived back with less than a third of what was on the list, which included many things he'd written himself, we went back to soup. But I did appreciate it when he told Robert that I was to stop chopping wood and that they would do it between them. After that I only carried it back from the beach, but often felt that I wasn't really earning my keep.

In September, with two weeks to go to our due date, it was time for us to get out of there. The whitebait season had begun and aeroplanes flew in and out from the far end of Big Bay beach most days when the weather allowed, but to fly out was an expensive option. When Darren King-Turner offered to take us to Milford Sound on his boat after he'd finished his pots the next day, we accepted gratefully. The planes flew away, the weather began to come in with the approaching storm, and Darren forgot. OK, so what was Plan C?

Luckily the weather held off a bit longer, and the following morning Robert rowed me out to Dale's shark cat, *Sika*. I tried to keep out of the way on the tiny deck as they worked the pots around to Martins Bay, where we crossed the bar and went ashore at Jerusalem Creek.

Neil Drysdale had arranged for Russell Baker from Air Fiordland to fly us out to the Upper Hollyford strip on a back flight. He handed us about 50 grams of whitebait in the bottom of a wee pottle to give to Murray Gunn, as there had been hardly any appearing up the river so far.

Wee Joey did several backflips and was definitely not happy as Russell flew circles over Gunn's Camp as a signal to Murray. If Murray didn't get the message, we'd have to walk about eight kilometres up the road, but he was at home and shortly afterwards arrived to collect us at the airstrip.

He seemed a bit surprised when he looked into the pottle of whitebait, and clearly hoped we wouldn't want to share it with him! Next, he bought nearly all of Robert's carvings, which was a great boost, not just to our finances but also to our confidence that Robert could support us with his art and craftwork in the future. All the time we'd been at Big Bay he had been hesitant about working on them, as he thought Dale wouldn't like the noise, but actually he made more money that day selling his work to Murray than Dale paid him for the previous eight weeks' work crayfishing, particularly as they had caught so little.

After a cup of tea and a 'fistful' of biscuits which we hadn't seen in a long time, Murray drove us up to Cascade Creek on the Milford Road where we met the managers, Owen and Doreen Payne, who arranged a ride for us on a bus to Te Anau.

'Stay there,' Murray said, climbing down from the van. I didn't hear the rest of it, which turned out to be 'I'll go and tell them you're having it.'

As I waddled in a couple of minutes later, Owen, red in

the face, was directing, 'I'll make up a room and you get on the phone…'

'Do you know what he told us?' he asked me, both amused and outraged, when he realised that he'd had his leg pulled. They were not very busy at the time, so we sat down to a lovely meal and Owen asked me, 'Seriously, how long have you got?'

'Oh, ages yet! I'll have time to finish my soup.'

'I deserved that,' he conceded.

Our son was born at the Toddies' house near Arrowtown, just before first light on 26 September 1991 while they were away at Big Bay whitebaiting. Seven pounds of boy! That is, approximately three-and-a-half pounds of joy, and the rest, sheer hard work.

'Hello, Joey.'

'Is that a name?' asked midwife Denise.

'Well, it's one name,' I said.

'His name is Christan Robert Long!' Robert announced, and from that moment our son wasn't Joey anymore. We had agreed on the names a couple of months earlier. I had assumed that we'd call a boy Robert Long, as the previous five generations of his family had been. I was happy to do so, as long as we called him Robert Stewart Long for all those generations of my family as well, so I was surprised to find that Robert didn't want to. Instead, he wanted to name him after Christ, who was the best person he could think of to name someone for.

I clutched Christan and gazed dutifully into his enormous eyes above the wee receding chin, thinking that he looked rather like a squirrel, and waited for the magical bonding process to happen. I was very surprised by the dimple in his chin, as I hadn't realised that babies were actually born with them. Maybe I should have expected it considering his father, both grandfathers and at least one great-grandfather had them, but two of them covered it with a beard and I'd never met the other. Christan gazed back at me, but, having been awake for well over 24 hours, I fell asleep before he did. I didn't notice any thunderclaps or anything, but by the time I woke, the magic had happened and I was devoted to this child forever. I felt like I'd had a brain transplant! I'd done an awful lot of complaining about being pregnant, but now, rather than just realising that it was all worth it, I couldn't even remember what all the fuss had been about.

Anne Mitchell, our neighbour from Big Bay, was the first person to see him, after ourselves and Denise. I woke up, still lying in all the gore, as she stepped into the room. Christan, sleeping on me, had added his own contribution to the mess.

'Oh! When Robert said it was born I didn't realise he meant it was *just* born,' she said.

By the end of the first week Christan had developed a pattern of crying to be fed, then crying and arching his back away from it, which I was finding quite distressing. When I asked Denise about it, she replied, 'Oh, these things sort themselves out in time.'

At the time, I found her answer offhand and unsatisfying in my state of total absorption in my baby, but in the long term it was the best piece of advice I ever received and I have offered it in my turn, although with some apology. It can be applied to many different situations, and it reminded me that sometimes all you need to do is stand back a bit and see the problem from a wider angle. Things that can seem so important, so all-consuming at the time, are often completely forgotten a week, a month or a year later, and one needs to keep things in their proper perspective. Another mother a few months later asked me, 'Does it get easier?'

'Ummm . . . it gets different' was the most encouraging thing I could come up with.

Almost a month had passed before we could fly home after the birth, and, as happened every trip from this time on, we had accumulated quite a bit of paraphernalia, ranging from 'vitally important' through to 'might come in handy sometime'. Discussion ensued as to what was most important.

'You don't need clothes pegs do you? They could wait until next time.'

Guess who ended up chasing nappies all over the landscape every time the wind blew? And guess how much time it took to tie them onto the line with bits of string?

Robert had looked forward to having me keep up with him better again, but on our first walk up the river for a day out I was slower than ever! Although I was no longer pregnant and awkward, I carried a tiny, sleeping baby on my back in his little pack. It is tricky enough walking unhampered over boulders, but up the river, at any time, you can be suddenly skating on thin slime.

Unlike Bambi on the frozen pond, my legs can only go in two directions, but gravity has the final say as to which way the rest of me goes, and dumps my pack down on top in a final flourish. And now, here I was with this precious scrap on my back, his head like an eggshell. One slip could ruin the rest of our lives.

So Robert carried him over any tricky parts and I took him when the going was easier. It became a standard procedure to change over at certain points whenever we travelled out to the Cascade River or south to Big Bay and

Martins Bay, and despite the increasing weight, it was always a joy to carry the kids in our packs.

Tramping in sandshoes for the first time, through Christan's first summer, was such a wonderful relief. With a huge load off the front and two lead-weighted gumboots off the ends of my legs, I was fairly skipping down the beach for the first time ever. At the end of March I reluctantly returned to boots, thinking I'd have to for the winter. I dragged them to Barn Bay and, with this on top of nursing a voracious six-month-old baby, I was thoroughly stretched. Although I was actually carrying sandshoes to wear when I got out, the thought of packing boots instead was enough to keep me persevering. From the next day forwards, I never wore boots again. The occasional winter's morning at Maurice Nolan's hut in the Cascade Valley in a wicked frost, having to run frozen socks and shoes under the tap to thaw them enough to put on has been a small price to pay for the joy of skipping over boulders with lightweight feet, regardless of all the bits that hurt.

For the first year or so Christan slept most of the time, but later as he stayed awake more he always had a lot to tell us about his view of the world. In a mast year when every flax had one or more flowering stalks, Christan demonstrated his understanding of the mechanics of counting, though lacking the words.

'There's another one ... and another one.'

By the next trip 'two' meant any number greater than one.

'Two bellbird. Two rain.'

A friend, Morag McAulay, had given us a net which I used occasionally over his pram bed if I could ever get him to sleep in it. Usually by the time I got him tucked in and sandfly-proofed and picked up the gardening fork, he'd be awake. Most of the gardening was done with him asleep on my back in the wee pack, and I'd come back inside to a telling off for getting him sunburnt when his head had flopped over so that his hat was no longer covering his face. Then one day Robert got him sunburnt worse than I ever had and stopped hassling me over it.

I hadn't yet learned how to avoid mastitis, so had several episodes with Christan. One hot evening, slaving over the stove, it seemed to me that I kept momentarily pinging out of consciousness, but otherwise I felt fine. With the meal on the table I measured my temperature and found it to be 39.6°C! I told Robert, who thought there must be something wrong with the thermometer as I looked all right, and after he'd eaten he disappeared next-door to visit a couple of trampers! I had an energetic four-month-old baby to keep happy and about a million sandflies up on the bed, so I hung up the net which Christan found very entertaining. He played with it happily until he fell asleep, and finally I could, too.

For our first Christmas dinner when Christan was tiny, we had smoked herrings that had been hanging for a few days and tasted 'just like a Christmas ham', and something that could loosely be called a 'cake' iced with ground-up rolled oats and vanilla instant-pudding mix with two raspberries on top. I dressed Christan in a wee red sunsuit I had bought at Zermatt in Switzerland and took a photo of him with the cake on his beautiful circular shawl, hand-knitted by his nana. When the radio played Billy T James singing 'When a Child is Born', we figured we had everything we wanted for Christmas.

The boulders around Awarua Point, which Robert speaks of so fondly in his book, were invisible under half a metre of foam as I passed Christan over to him to carry. Within 10 minutes I'd fallen. A boulder mid-thigh acted as a fulcrum, while my pack shot forward and ground my face into the next rock. Christan was usually well packed in with blankets, clothes, etc., so perhaps he wouldn't have actually shot out of the pack, but he would have had an awful fright. I did, even without him on board.

At Big Bay, Dale got on the radio to Angus Tapper at the Hollyford Tourist Company, and next thing we had a choice of a flight to the Upper Hollyford strip or to Milford Sound. We set out to Martins Bay, hoping to have time to call in on Neil Drysdale first, to thank him again for arranging the flight for us four months earlier.

Between Dale's place and Penguin Rock is a stretch of salt marsh with layers of rock tilted at about 70°. Picking my way over slimy rocks between puddles, it was slow-going. Robert zoomed along happily, so much better at it than I was and in a hurry to get there. I felt awful having to drag him back to earth, but we'd both be there sooner if he'd slow down a bit and let me follow him instead of having to pick my own route through a tricky part.

In 2011, walking through that particular stretch I was sure that it was only about a third of the distance and it was hardly slimy at all. Perhaps some of it has been sanded in or maybe it changes with the level of the tide, but I was left wondering how much my memory had magnified it all.

We stopped at Cascade Creek to introduce our baby to Owen and Doreen Payne after their kindness on the previous trip, and that was the night that threw Christan's sleeping pattern out permanently. I guess I could have gone to the room with him at 7pm while Robert had all the fun in the lounge, but instead I brought him back with me and laid him in the corner asleep. When he woke to noise and electric lights he assumed it was daytime, and at four months old he was up and dancing with the barmaid until 10pm! Big mistake. He woke up about every hour for the rest of the night, and by the time we got home several days later the pattern was set.

On our next visit to Queenstown, the Plunket nurse was talking about some poor woman whose baby wanted to nurse every two hours around the clock. I mentally calculated that to mean four times in the night, whereas a night when Christan only woke up five times was a good one. Often it was five times before I even got to bed, and 15 times was not unusual.

The time came when I was really struggling with it and something was going to have to change — which turned out to be my attitude. After all, with him in bed with us, all I had to do was roll over and plug him in; none of this sitting up in the middle of the night in the far bedroom, trying not to fall asleep, then having to get him settled before you could get back to bed. I couldn't have done that, but nor could I do the 'just let him scream' method.

We think there is nothing nicer than all snuggling into bed together on a cold night, and when they were tiny I couldn't sleep without knowing that they were right there, warm and breathing.

Christan slept through the night once at two months and once at two years. It was only at about two-and-a-half, staying with Robert's parents in Mooloolaba where he had a camp stretcher beside our bed that he began to sleep through and I realised that I had been waking *him* every time I moved.

After visiting my sister and one-year-old Elena in Montana, Mum flew home with us to stay for a couple of weeks when Christan was four months old. Looking down from a hundred metres at the thin strip of grass between the Tasman Sea and the South Westland forest that she was to land on, she exclaimed, 'What, that?!'

She found it a most amusing contrast when Robert went to Martins Bay to play in Jules Tapper's golf match on the Hollyford Tourist Company's airstrip. Whereas Darrell, her American son-in-law, could pick up his golf bag and walk through the back gate onto the course, Robert hefted his hand-sewn canvas pack, picked up his driftwood golf club and paddled out on his surfboard to *Scratch II* as Lou Brown and crewman Jonathon Larrivee stood offshore. The following afternoon they returned, Robert paddling in again from the boat as the sandbar at the river mouth made it unsuitable for Lou to attempt to come up the river at the time. He was wearing a shiny, white Mt Cook Airlines T-shirt which was the prize for the best team result. Robert explained that the main reason they had won was that they had arrived quite late, by which time nearly everyone else was too drunk to hit the ball straight.

When I first visited Gorge River in 1987, Robert was still managing with the old Shacklock coal range which hadn't seen coal in 15 years and was somewhat the worse for wear after a long diet of salty driftwood. In winter, he'd light it long enough to cook a meal, then jump back into bed to eat because the house was so cold. By 1990 he had pulled it out piece-by-piece and replaced it with a much more useable 12-gallon drum, leaving the wetback and hot-water cylinder untouched, but the ceiling above the stove was still perforated with holes to let the smoke out, and the cobwebs were sucked inwards in the draught as most of the heat disappeared upwards to warm the Great Outdoors. With a piece of plywood to seal it off, the cobwebs blew outwards instead and the house gained several degrees.

Sitting in bed one frosty morning, I complained in a letter to my sister in Montana about how cold it was. In her reply, a month or two later, she suggested that I needed a bed-jacket. A bed-jacket! She probably had in mind something pretty and diaphanous, whereas I already wore a T-shirt, a woollen singlet, a sweatshirt and a jersey.

Before the beginning of Christan's first winter Robert closed in the verandah, which was really only useful for storing firewood. Sitting out there in the evenings was not an attractive option with sandflies joining you for cocktails. The new front wall was almost completely made up of windows and we now had a wonderful sunroom, while the light reached right to the back wall for a few weeks either side of the winter solstice. Later we had a piece of carpet on the floor and a ground-level shelf for kids' books, and it was a lovely place to play. Even so, Christan wore a woollen singlet, a cotton fleece suit, a jersey with a hood, and a full woolly suit over the top. In addition, once he was crawling I added a pair of jeans to protect the wool, and sheepskin slippers. Like the nuns at the Holy Cross convent Robert had attended in Papatoetoe, all we saw of him were his hands and face. With all that lot, changing his nappy was a major drama.

We'd heard reports of friends, Morag McAulay and Phillip Hancock, whose daughter Brogan objected to nappy changes so much that they held her down with one leg to free both hands for the job. We called it 'The Brogan Hold' and I tried it on Christan one particularly bad day, but Robert didn't really like the idea. A year passed before I had the opportunity to discuss this with Morag, and she replied, 'Phillip didn't like the idea either, so I said *he* could change her and he ended up doing it, too.'

Their second child, Tobias, seemed much more amenable, but by that time they did it out of habit.

Before Christan was two I had given up putting a night nappy on him until after he was asleep to avoid the drama. In contrast, three years further down the track our daughter Robin would want to nurse before going to sleep, and if I wasn't ready to come she'd lie on the nappy and wrap it around herself.

Robert was very proud of the fact that he always changed Christan's nappy first thing in the morning. As he usually did it up on the bed, he'd ask me to pass a flannel and a bowl of warm water ... and a clean nappy ... and I could take the dirty one away now, thanks ... and here's the bowl and the flannel. Then I'd scrub it, rub soap into it and drop it into the soaking bucket until I came back after breakfast to add them all to a bucket of soapy water, let them soak for a while, wring them, rinse them, carry them down to the river for a really good rinse, wring them again, and hang them on the line, or in the hot-water cupboard on a rainy day.

One day, Lou Brown came down from Barn Bay on his boat bringing us a hand-wringer. Liz was a bit put-out as she'd planned on having it for the tourist lodge they were building and she was going to give me their old one. She was also unimpressed when Robert hadn't set it up for me a month or so later, but was more understanding when I explained that I couldn't really ask him to when he had been so busy building.

We had taken some time to work out where to put the wringer. There wasn't much room in the bathroom where I washed nappies in a bucket in the shower. I could fill the bucket from the cold tap on the wall with a hose, then tip the water out down the drain before carrying the nappies down to the river for the final rinse, but there was nowhere to put a wringer.

'I guess it would be most convenient to have it down at the river,' Liz suggested.

'Well, yes, but we don't want it to be washed away in the first flood,' I replied.

'No, we don't, do we?' she agreed.

Robert had been earning money all this time, since before Christan was born, but saving it was still a high priority. As Davey Gunn called it, this was 'The Land of Doing Without', and Robert was better at doing without than anyone else I have ever met. In fact, I must be better at it than anyone he has ever met, too, just not quite as good as he was and always up against my limits. It was a two-way process, so, while I learned to manage without many of the things I'd been used to having, he gradually relaxed a bit, and often in the resultant pendulum swings it would be Robert encouraging me to spend money on something that had become necessary or at least within the realm of possibility. It seems to be a basic part of human nature to always want to improve things, to make life better or easier, and we are no different to anyone else.

Early on, Robert would often say, 'You don't mind roughing it, do you?' and I'd always reply 'No', but after sleeping in a hayshed in a frost and having his bum washed in a frozen puddle in the morning it would be Christan who was sick, not me. Staying at friends' houses with a baby, complete with wet nappies and all the other gear, was one thing; but when the baby also had a fever and grizzled continuously for days, it was quite another, especially when Robert or I came down with the 'flu as well.

Christan got into a pattern of developing nondescript fevers whenever we did too much or stressed him too far (even if there wasn't any nasty bug doing the rounds), and he didn't grow out of this until well into the teenage years with the help of large doses of vitamin C. If we tried to travel any further with him at such a time, it would turn into an ear infection and/or chest infection, with antibiotics and the whole drama, which it often did. People often ask 'What do you do if you get sick?' The answer is: 'Mostly we don't — except when we come out to town.'

Chapter 8

FOR RICHER, FOR POORER

With a baby on the way, having a wedding was one of the last things we had time to worry about, but whenever Robert suggested to his parents that they should come to visit, Bob would reply, 'I'm waiting for the wedding.'

Robert told him that this wedding business was all very well, but it would leave him financially deficient and unable to support his family, so Bob offered him a thousand dollars to get started. Having been to a lot of parties in Haast, we liked the idea of giving something back, and the money would cover most of the alcohol. Bob also brought a lot of duty-free spirits when he came, and my dad bought the potato chips. We sent invitations to a few people whom we were afraid wouldn't come otherwise, and told everyone else to spread the word. It was an open invitation and perhaps they might bring a bit of food to help if they wished, which would add diversity to the feast.

We spent a week at Neil's Beach preparing for it, during which time many neighbours and friends helped, giving us fish and crayfish, whitebait and two back legs of venison. With these, we prepared large amounts of a few things. Others helped to prepare huge quantities of salads and a fruit salad, or cooked bread.

Earlier, I had asked my friends from Christchurch, Robyn and Graeme Kennerly, to come in order to feel that I had someone sitting on my side of the church, along with my parents and brother, and they drove down with a load of soft drinks. Much as I enjoyed having them there, the precaution turned out to be unnecessary. We were completely blown away by the number of people who turned up, and I was surprised to find how many of them I knew. Two hundred people in a long line of cars and two helicopters joined us at Whisky Corner on the Cascade Road where it overlooks the Cascade Valley on Beltane, 1 November 1992, as near as we could get to having it at our place. The priest from Whataroa, Father Foote, held the service and we couldn't have asked for anyone more fitted to the job. We exchanged rings which we had made for each other from mother-of-pearl.

The Catholic Church accepts baptisms by lay people, and Robert had baptised Christan in the Cascade River the first time we crossed it after he was born, but as Robert hadn't used any oil, only water, Father Foote wanted to anoint Christan at the same time as marrying us. Then on the day he forgot to bring it, and asked us whether we had any oil. We had castor oil — also called 'palma Christi' or 'the hands of Christ' — which seemed very appropriate, even if we had brought it along for nappy changes.

Christan managed the ceremony very well as people mainly stood back to watch. In his wee, white, smocked shirt, he played in the dirt at our feet with two-year-old Casey from Barn Bay, who taught him to pour handfuls of dirt onto his head. But having fallen asleep in the car on the drive back out to Okuru, he woke in the hall to find 250 people looking at him and freaked. If I'd known there was a back door to the hall from the kitchen, we probably would have managed out there with people coming and going, but as it was I spent most of the evening at the beach with a few different friends or out in the car park. By the time Christan went to sleep and I could take him inside in a pack on my back, everyone had either gone home or was drunk.

'You were conspicuous by your absence!' neighbour Liz Dibben commented in the morning.

I guess that's why you get married before you have kids.

A couple of weeks after our wedding Lou arrived on *Scratch II* at the river mouth with my brother on board and a load of wedding presents. Again, we had been astonished at everyone's generosity, and at the thought they had put into the gifts, considering toasters and electric kettles were not much use to us. Far from costing us a fortune, we were given more than we spent in money alone, which was only a small part of the kindness and goodwill we received from our huge circle of friends. Ever since, we have heartily recommended having a wedding to anyone who asks.

Having no regular transport at the time, we had wondered when we'd ever see all the wonderful things we'd been given, so it was lovely of Lou to arrange to bring them for us, and an extra bonus to have Andrew here. He stayed for a couple of days, but was conscious of not having brought much food of his own. We weren't really aware of it since we had more food than we'd ever had, almost. So with the weather changing for the worse, he decided to walk back to Barn Bay.

This was the first time for me, but there have been many others since, when we had to take responsibility for giving someone advice on the weather. We do have local knowledge to help interpret the forecast on the radio, but it is a huge decision to tell someone that they should or should not go. Once we row them across the Gorge they have a six-hour tramp and two smaller rivers to cross before the next hut at the Hope River. Depending on how wet or dry the land is already, either of those can potentially stop you with a couple of hours of rain.

Heading home ourselves once as it started to rain, before we had children, we hurried to get across the Spoon River knowing that the dinghy was on our side of the Gorge. We passed a couple of older trampers with a quick chat, and hurried on. South of the Spoon, however, the creeks were rising quickly, and when I fell over in one, barely knee-deep, I was amazed by the power of it and how difficult it was even to get up again with a big pack and a face full of water. It wasn't until the following afternoon that the other trampers arrived, calling for a row across the river. About an hour behind us, they'd come over Sandrock Bluff and been unable to continue down the creek so had climbed back up to a flat place to pitch their tent.

The creeks can go down again as quickly as they come up, but after a long spell of rainy weather it may take longer. We generally allow at least two days for the Cascade River to go down by the time we get to it.

So long as people are carrying a tent we can tell them what the forecast says and warn them that they may be stuck at a river depending on how much it rains. If the rain holds off for an extra hour or two, they may have no problem at all.

One party without a tent, or any deadline, stayed here

for a week! Late each afternoon the river would go down enough for us to row them across, knowing that the next two rivers should have dropped sufficiently to cross by the time they reached them. But by then it was too late in the day to start, so they would stay another night — to find the river flooded again in the morning. They were good company and kept our kids entertained, teaching them table soccer and playing long, loud games of Monopoly with much hilarity.

So here was Andrew wanting to go and, although the forecast was not that flash, the rain might still hold off long enough for him to get through. He was well experienced, so I didn't feel the pressure of having to advise someone who possibly didn't know what they could be up against. Robert suggested that Andrew take the dinghy across himself so that he could shelter under it if he did have to come back, although it turned out that Andrew didn't understand that Robert had said that.

After we'd seen him heading away we listened to the midday forecast and, sure enough, it had changed for the worse. It takes about two-and-a-half hours to get to the Spoon River, so we had plenty of time to get more and more worried about him. Finally I sat down with Robert for a pep talk, as there was absolutely nothing else that could be done about it and I was feeling very anxious. Yes, he might just get across it; yes, I felt better about his capabilities than anyone else who came through here; yes, I'd better just have faith because it was the only thing I could do.

Then we heard him call out. 'Thank God,' I thought, imagining him safe but wet on the other side of the river. But Robert looked out of the window to see Andrew flash by on his way out to sea. It was Friday the thirteenth, he had retraced his steps, and he had greenstone in his pockets; three strikes and the dragon got him.

'That's the last we'll see of him,' Robert said.

But I thought, 'No! He will make it.' And my faith never faltered for a moment.

Andrew had been through several life-threatening situations before this one, but standing on the shore in the rain holding my 13-month-old son, with Robert clad in a wetsuit and holding his surfboard, I had absolutely no doubt that he'd be fine. It can be hard to judge distances, and I didn't know then how much further away the island looks when seen from above, but we figured he'd been washed about halfway out to it. Luckily, the northerly swell pushed him out of the current fairly quickly, and we could see that he was swimming and making progress.

'Don't do anything stupid,' I said to Robert, knowing that with both of them out there I couldn't do anything to help if it meant leaving Christan alone.

The first thing we did was to throw the lifebuoy into the river, but Andrew never saw it. Later in the day we found it washed up at the river mouth, his pack containing Lou Brown's radio — a fat lot of good that was in the case of an emergency — at the north end of the beach, and he himself washed in at the south end. Robert was ready to get him if he hadn't made it by then, as swimming around the rocks and into the next bay would have taken a lot longer.

While I'd been freaking out and Robert was giving me the pep talk, Andrew had been watching the river for some time before deciding to try it. He knew there was no way he could cross it unaided, but thought he'd be OK in the boat. There was an eddy on his side, and he sat in it for some time getting the feel of the oars before making a quick dash across the main current. What he couldn't see was the eddy on the south side which took him straight around and back into the main current and out. That was the moment when he yelled, never thinking that we would hear him. The boat tipped up in the first wave, and he swallowed first fresh, and later salt, water. Back at home when he threw up, he said it was in the opposite order.

The following day Robert walked 15 kilometres south before he found the dinghy washed up on Awarua Point. Meanwhile, Lou arrived, heard the story and took Andrew back to Jackson Bay on the boat.

Two months and two days later, Lou's smaller dinghy was tied to a log near the spot where Robert sets the net. At about three in the morning Robert sat up, listening to the rain on the roof, then lay back down, deciding not to check on the dinghy. It was probably just as well, as it was high tide just then and if he'd seen what was happening he probably would have tried to save it amongst waves, floating logs and debris. Reading the signs in the morning, it appeared the taniwha had climbed out of the river leaving a three-metre-wide gap in the driftwood pile, grabbed the dinghy and pulled it back down what looked like a boat ramp. The log it was tied to had also gone, and being rata it wouldn't float, which may explain why we never saw the boat again. The only thing we salvaged was one oar which washed up five kilometres down the beach.

While Robert was away that day looking for it, I watched a large fishing boat, bigger than any I had seen before, apparently drifting north without power. I could see no sign of anyone on it, although it was well out to sea, and I calculated that it would come ashore at Brown's Refuge if it continued as it was. With no dinghy and Robert away, again there was absolutely nothing I could do, and maybe the crew was just having lunch or dealing with a trawl of fish. If the tide had been low enough to cross the river safely with Christan, I would have walked up the beach to keep an eye on what happened. After an hour or more I saw it sailing away towards Cascade Point, but it had all seemed quite bizarre. Nearly always when things happen around here we find out the story behind it at some later date, but so far in this case I never have, and Robert probably thought I'd imagined the whole thing.

The next trampers who arrived, a couple of girls from Nelson, had to be ferried across the river on surfboards while Robert took their packs. Lou brought Robert's sea kayak up from Big Bay so, when we next crossed the river on the way out to Haast, Robert took Christan first with a very long rope tied to the kayak for me to haul it back. Worrying about how swiftly the current was dragging it downstream, I pulled before Robert had put the paddle on board and I felt like a complete twit paddling across the river with my hands.

Shortly after that, Lou brought a dinghy down from Barn Bay and the Gorge River ferry was back in action.

In fine winter weather, cold air falls off the high slopes inland, sinking into the valley and funnelling out through the gorge. Most days, a 30-knot easterly blast can be seen blowing the tops off the waves for a kilometre or more out to sea, and it is unwise to try landing an aeroplane at least until after 10am.

One wintry morning, heading out to Haast, Robert decided that with the tide out and the river so low it would be simplest to walk across the river.

'I'm not doing that — it'll be freezing! I'll take the kayak and you'll be glad to have it on the other side when we come back.'

It was freezing all right. I jumped in one side and fell straight out the other, getting half-soaked in the process. Robert, on the far bank, stalked off with Christan on the back, and I was dry by the time he stopped long enough for me to catch up.

U p to the age of six months Christan was quite fearless. He didn't mind thunderstorms or being out in the rain. If Robert showed him a live crayfish, he reached for it. Then he learnt to crawl and it seemed that he would crawl straight off the edge of the bed if allowed to. As our bed was quite high up, Robert had already built a railing down the open side with a gate in it. Only a fortnight later, Christan could pull himself up to stand, but he was so young that he wasn't smart enough to remember to hold on yet. Several horrendous falls eventually knocked the sense into him, and was perhaps the reason why he grew up very cautious, even overly so.

As the youngest of seven boy cousins he was fair game for teasing, and the others never missed an opportunity when we met up with them in Queensland. In vain, he'd tell them to stop rocking Grandad's dinghy before demanding to be put ashore. Even we laughed at him, but caution is an attribute we like our teenaged children to have.

I was present when my nephew Ned took his first steps — one, two, fall over, up again, repeat. After the third time he was so excited that he crawled up and down, up and down like a lion in a cage, but after the next day I never saw him crawl again.

Christan, on the other hand, took one step and drew the second foot up, one step and drew it up in a super-cautious, diagonal fashion. It was six weeks before I saw the realisation flash in his eyes as to the potential of this new form of locomotion, and six weeks more before he gave up crawling altogether. But it was understandable considering that he'd been crawling for more than half his life.

We were also very glad of his cautious good sense in his early years, and figure that he learned a healthy respect for the river from the vantage point of the backpack. The one time I lost him, at about two, I didn't know where to look first. I had dashed out the door with two buckets of washing and turned left to take them to the wringer in the DOC hut next-door. He thought he was following me to the river, so had turned right instead, down the back track.

'Where's Christan?' I asked Robert as soon as I came back past the hut.

'I thought he was with you.'

Panic! The river was probably the most dangerous possibility, but the idea of having him wandering in the bush was what really scared me. I took a quick look at the riverbed from the end of the track, then went looking next-door and on the airstrip. With no sign of him, I went back to the river for a proper look and found him sitting quite happily up on the log where Robert scaled fish every morning, at least 50 metres from the water. Not knowing what to do when he didn't find me, he knew perfectly well not to go any further but chose a familiar place to sit while waiting for someone to come and sort it out for him.

Our whitebaiting friend Justine Hewer has two sons who were the complete opposite. The elder, Ziahn, once walked straight off the end of her stand and hung motionless underwater until rescued. Ethan, a few years later, spontaneously headed for water the instant Justine's back was turned, and she actually had to tie him up.

At 16 months Christan was 'Captain Havoc', but now on his feet. Dale arrived on the summer solstice to ask Robert to crew for him over Christmas. We hadn't planned on fishing anymore, but Robert could never say no to anyone who asked him for something, so within an hour or so we were all on board the shark cat *Sika*, heading south. I carried Christan strapped to my back and wore a lifejacket over the top. It was only later that we considered how it would have been if I had ended up in the water. Christan's head was below the cushion at the back of my neck, and would therefore be underwater, and I couldn't have reached him without first getting out of the lifejacket.

Dale and Robert headed out to do the pots, leaving me in a house full of infinite possibilities for a 16-month-old walking disaster. A bottle of diesel stood by the hearth of the open fire and, needless to say, in Dale's house it didn't have a lid. So Christan's first trick with my back turned was to tip it upside down to see what would happen. As I turned in response to the splash, he stepped into the diesel, slipped over backwards and was covered from head to toe. I washed his hair seven times with soap in lukewarm water before I'd got it all out, and he screamed blue murder throughout. Even at home hair-washing was a huge drama. Usually I wrapped him up tightly in a towel, then quickly turned him upside down. By the time he'd recovered from the shock of it and gathered breath to yell, I'd be half-finished.

During Christan's second year, a couple of Geology students stayed in the DOC hut while collecting data for their PhD theses. We'd met one of them, Rupert, and his partner as we'd walked out of Big Bay when I was nearly six months pregnant, at a time when we hadn't spoken to anyone else for five weeks. His partner was a kindergarten teacher and she had sent me a recipe for playdough. For a year or more, Christan had scraps of mosquito netting stretched all over the kitchen with playdough fish in it that could be taken out, cut up, smoked in a billy with sticks under it or cooked in his frying pan, while the playdough skeleton would be put into the 'fire'. He spent hours in a cardboard box, row, row, rowing the boat merrily, merrily. And at three, after Peter Bowmar had been here with his inflatable boat and little outboard motor, Christan used Robert's retractable tape-measure for an outboard motor, as he could pull it out and have it snap back in like a pull-start cord.

Apart from boats and fishing, most of his play involved a wooden aeroplane that Robert had made him for Christmas, so for his third birthday Robert made a little helicopter. I added three 'deer' made out of sticks of various sizes for the body, head, legs and antlers. He'd hang them under the helicopter and fly it around with appropriate noises. He hardly ever played with cars until after Robert attended the Deerstalkers' Ball in Haast in 1995. Coming home with a friend late that night, the driver missed the sharp turn after the Arawhata Bridge and rolled the car into the ditch. Christan was highly impressed the next day when a large digger extracted it and set it back onto its wheels before it was driven away. For months afterwards he'd line all his cars up along the carpeted step we had in the middle of our main room, tip them all off into the 'ditch', then come along with a large serving spoon to scoop them out and set them back on their wheels.

Arriving at Neil's Beach once in 1993, my friend Henrica asked, 'So how has it been the last few months?'

'Oh, good. We had lots of food.'

There was a brief silence until Henrica, never one to sidestep an issue, said, 'You know, no one has ever said that to me before.'

I spluttered and tried to cover my tracks by saying that we never actually ran out of food, but it could be pretty lean at times.

If you came out to town behaving like a fruitcake every three or four months and that was all people ever saw of you, they would get tired of it fairly quickly, and so you just had to learn to shut up. I seriously considered going nuts several times between Christan's birth and Robin's, but never quite knew how to go about it. In my family it wasn't an option.

When you are pregnant, people say, 'You're eating for two!', but the baby is very small at that stage and the process is far more efficient. After they are born and at the breast, the food has to be digested twice, and nursing a two-year-old on lean rations can be quite hard on the mother. I nursed Christan until he was nearly three, knowing that it was the best thing I could do for him. It wasn't until after Robin was born and he was weaned that we organised for regular supplies of food to be flown in, as it became much more important to keep him fed.

We took any chance that was offered — for example, if a helicopter was coming back later to collect someone — and Lou brought things into Barn Bay for us on his boat or to Gorge River when he was fishing down this far. Otherwise, we had what we could carry home ourselves or grow and gather. We never had a gun, and didn't eat meat until my second pregnancy. So when I was grinding wheat to make a loaf of bread and we had no butter or anything but Marmite to put on it, I reckoned I spent more energy making the bread than I got from eating my share of it. People often brought us loaves of bread, but we would have swapped them for a pound of butter any time. We could usually make bread.

We always bought brown rice by choice, but occasionally when it ran out we'd have to eat white. After a bowl of millet and white rice porridge one day, I felt like I'd eaten half as much as I actually had. White rice is all very well when it comes with meat and all the trappings, but if it is all you have we reckon you could starve on it.

Pregnant again, I wallowed around for several weeks, a complete misery-guts. I'm pathetic when I'm sick, and morning sickness seems endless. Christan's toys were not picked up for five weeks but kicked under the table out of the main walkway, and the house was a mess. Robert was very helpful, but he too was wondering how long this would go on.

'Maybe *I* should be getting the cup of tea in bed for Mother's Day?' he suggested.

I silently counted to 10 while sifting through several acid comments, but settled for 'I think I'm doing my bit as far as being a mother is concerned!'

At that time I couldn't bear the smell of frying, so, while Robert cooked an evening meal that I would probably refuse to eat, I'd have to vacate our bed and try the spare bed out in the workshop, although it seemed that nearly half the smells came that way, too. Mornings were the best time, and I'd get up to light the fire each day and cook a pot of freshly ground oat porridge. Then I could start on food for the rest of the day while my stomach worked on that lot. I'd learned quickly that if I waited for Robert to get up and do it I'd be too sick to eat by the time it was ready.

During one long wet spell I cooked beans one day, split peas the next day, and lentils the day after that. Then repeat. I'd have to eat several small helpings throughout the day until, by the tenth day, I was gagging just looking at the pot. Finally I had to send Robert out to catch a fish, but he returned sometime later empty-handed.

'I only caught tiddlers, so I threw them back.'

'You threw them *back*?!'

The next day he brought home everything he'd caught and after that I was sick of fish.

At two-and-a-half, Christan walked about a third of the way out to the road-end over two days and carried a little pack. I promised him that we'd see a car but not until we'd crossed the Cascade, so after every creek or puddle he'd ask again, 'Car?'

There was one parked when we arrived at the Martyr homestead, and we sat talking with two friends from Haast for 20 minutes or more before they got up to drive us out to Neil's Beach. Christan freaked when they started the engine, and, grabbing me by the hand, took off back the way we had come.

'Home!' he insisted.

In the bush that day, just before we reached the river a robin landed in front of us on the track. Of course Christan chased it, but it kept coming back. Other than in the Hollyford Valley, we have only seen a robin three or four times around here, so this is a special memory.

'It's come to tell us to call the baby "Robin",' I said.

It has always amazed me how generous people are to us. Many times people have offered us help, but we often ended up asking for too much. Hitchhiking was easy enough with two people, and adding a baby to it didn't make a great difference, but generally Robert would walk on ahead leaving me to ask first for a ride with Christan in the front-pack. Most people who stopped for me would be happy to squeeze Robert in, too, whereas they might have gone by if faced with the whole caboodle up-front.

With Christan almost weaned it was becoming more important to get food home. My friend John Pickles, a travelling salesman for a pharmaceutical company, offered us a ride from Christchurch to Haast on his circuit of the South Island, and I suggested that we could freight some of our gear on ahead.

'It will be all right,' he said, but he probably couldn't imagine how much a family of three or four could eat in three months, and I wanted to get a large bag of milk powder for the first time. Adding a load of groceries was definitely asking too much, and we had to learn what was reasonable, regardless of whether the other person said it would be OK.

Having arrived in Haast with groceries for a couple of months and a 25-kilogram bag of milk powder from the Westland milk factory, the walk home had to be faced. During my first pregnancy I'd learned to grit my teeth and get on with it without complaining, no matter what. When my brother's partner, Jenny, pregnant with her second child, said, 'I hope you're not trying to be Iron Woman?', I'd replied 'Oh, no!', but the truth was that if I had admitted to myself that actually that *was* what was required, I couldn't have kept it up.

Robert often said, 'You never know, maybe a helicopter

will come along and give us a ride', and I'd be stumbling along, watching the sky, waiting for it. Eventually I realised that 90 per cent of walking anywhere was in the mind, and if I just focused on getting there I'd be far better off. It was so much easier to walk 25 kilometres along the beach than the same distance on the Cascade Road when I kept thinking that a car might come along at any moment and offer us a ride.

Only once did someone go by on that road without picking us up. I was four months pregnant with Christan and rain was threatening.

'We aren't going very far,' they said, and I bit my tongue rather than beg, 'Anything would make a difference.' It was an hour or more before they returned, having made it to the end of the road, surprised at how much it had improved since their previous visit 20 years earlier.

'It's going to take you all day!' they said, which it did, and it was just starting to rain.

Much later that same day a campervan stopped to offer us a ride, but as we were only about a hundred metres from the end of the road by then, this was also the only time we ever turned down the offer of a ride.

So here I was, six months pregnant again. With an almost three-year-old to carry, Robert was finding it a bit hard, too, and there wasn't likely to be much help coming from my direction. He suggested spending some money — something we hadn't done much. Our life revolved around doing whatever was necessary rather than spend money. He said we could ask the Cascade whitebaiters what it would cost to have them fly us home. Up to this point we had flown in or out only five times, usually with one or other of our parents on the flight and paying for it.

I found it hard to enter the conversation or even to let the idea into my head. I was focused on walking home and on getting there, no matter what, but in fact it was a lot harder than it had been in my first pregnancy. I'd walked to Big Bay at seven months carrying only a day-pack, and for approximately one-third of the distance those early contractions had felt like having a stitch in my side. This time round, it was more like a full contraction and I couldn't walk until it passed. Still, I would do what I had to do. But to discuss it meant allowing myself to consider that there was an alternative, and as soon as I did that, being unable to do it became a possibility, then a probability. As this wasn't something that Robert would understand, he just got annoyed with me for refusing to discuss it.

'You just let me know when you've decided,' I said, which is the way it had to be at my end, regardless of how he saw it.

After all that, it cost $120! The equivalent of one greenstone carving. Twenty minutes later we were on the ground at home with enough food to keep us going until we'd have to go out for Robin's birth. It was a milestone on the road towards learning how we would live here with children.

Shortly before Robin was born, Robert said, 'Three more years … we'd want to stay until the new baby is as big as Christan is now …'

Hearing him say it made me realise that I didn't want to go anywhere else. However, the fact that I wasn't stuck here forever made all the difference, and I've never had to promise to stay for more than the next year or two, or as long as it would take to get organised to go.

We had just been away for most of the winter, including staying with Robert's family in Australia and my mum and brother in Auckland, and I realised that I hadn't seen anywhere I'd rather be or anything I'd prefer to be doing. Admittedly, I'd had a bad few moments on arriving back in Haast in the middle of winter, cooking greasy chips and pancakes that smelled exactly the same as ever on a coal range. Liz Dibben said, 'I know how you feel, and I don't have to go any further down there', but as it turned out it was just Haast that was the problem. Once we got home it wasn't like that at all. We tended to avoid Haast during the winter, but as the days grew longer and the whitebait season got started, the mood of the whole community was different. Since the road to Wanaka has been sealed and so many people have bought baches to spend time by the beach, Haast is now the place where everyone wants to be.

Chapter 9
A NEW BALANCE

'They've got *another* baby at Gorge River!' Doreen Miller of Lumsden announced to her husband, Ron, one morning soon after 22 November 1994. The birth notice read:

> BEANSPROUT — *To Catherine Stewart and Robert Long of Gorge River, South Westland, a daughter (Robin Grace Long).*

'We'll have to tramp down there this summer.'

At the Balfour playgroup, someone commented, 'That poor child! Imagine being called Robin Grace Long Beansprout!'

Robin was born in the married couple's cottage at Peter and Celia Bowmar's Waikaia Plains Station. We flew out to Haast a bit sooner this time, as I felt that she wasn't going to stay in there much longer. At Neil's Beach everyone was mostly interested in hustling us along and safely over the hill as soon as possible. They had not yet forgotten that Chloe Monachan had been born in an ambulance at the Karangarua River, south of Fox.

It took us a few days to settle into the cottage and meet Terryl Muir, our midwife. I'd only spoken to her on the phone so far, although I had been to see a doctor in Queenstown in July. Terryl was lovely, very relaxed, and all appeared to be fine.

Returning late one night after having dinner with friends we found that a possum had paid us a visit. We never worked out whether it had come in through the cat door or down the chimney, which seemed impossible, but there was no doubt that it was covered in soot as it had climbed up, along and down the other side of every curtain and doorway in the living room and kitchen. I retired to bed with Christan and hardly a guilty twinge, and left Robert to it.

One of the good things about having a home birth is that you are living in your own germs and therefore shouldn't have to worry too much about infection. But giving birth in anyone else's home is not much different to being in a hospital as far as that goes, so I bleached the bath and the old sheets and towels we'd brought with us, scrubbed and cleaned and got it all shipshape.

Early the next morning I rang Terryl with a progress report, and she called in for a second visit since she was in the area visiting another lady. As she was leaving she said she wouldn't be surprised to see me again later in the day.

The Bowmars had promised us a cellphone, as the telephone in the cottage had recently flown across the kitchen and through the window during a thunderstorm, scattering digits across the floor along the way. The window had been repaired but the phone was not yet reconnected, so late in the afternoon Christan and I took the Bowmars' spare car, which they'd also given us, to the woolshed to find Robert and to collect the phone. That turned out to be up at the main house, so I called Terryl from there and was keen to get back to our cottage.

'When do you think it will be born?' Robert asked as we ate a meal.

'I'd say by this time tomorrow things will be different.'

Indeed, by then we had a daughter, a nana and a washing machine, and the first load of nappies already dry.

Terryl had arrived as I was trying to settle Christan into bed, and she sat talking quietly with me until he fell asleep. I was having to sit up for contractions by then, and he was aware that something was going on but the timing could hardly have been better. Although we'd planned to have Robert's mother, Ngaire, there to look after him, I was not entirely comfortable about all the messy bits. With him asleep the problem was solved, at least so long as he didn't wake up.

We adjourned to the living room, then the bath, and eventually back to the living room, where Christan met his wee sister by candle- and fire-light about half an hour after her arrival.

Diagnosing me with mastitis a few days later, Terryl insisted that I have 24 hours in bed.

'Really?'

'It won't do you any harm,' she insisted.

This was a new experience. With Ngaire there, at least it was a possibility, and when I got up to go to the toilet she even popped in and made the bed for me! I felt pampered and cared for and, when I thanked her later in a letter, she really valued it too. I made it to 23½ hours until, with Christan jumping off the chair onto the bed, I figured it would be more restful to get up.

You often hear·tales of kids being violent after playing video games or PlayStation. Without TV Christan found his inspiration in nursery rhymes and stories. He learned to sing 'Rock-a-bye baby', and when Robin was sleeping in her bassinette he wanted me to put her up in the tree.

The afternoon of the day before Peter Bowmar flew us home in his Cessna 185, the Plunket nurse visited Diane Smith and her six-week-old son, Andrew, who lived across the road from where we were staying. As I was there, she suggested having a wee look at Robin, too, now four weeks old, and told me that the nappy rash that had been such a plague was, in fact, thrush.

Well, it was a bit late then, wasn't it? I phoned Terryl and asked her to bring something from town the next day, but we were already in the air by the time she could have got there with it. Nor did I have Napisan, having relied on vinegar, washing soda and sunshine to deal to any nasties. Christan had had the same rash and, after consulting Robert's naturopathy notes, we'd eventually dealt to it with a wicked concoction of essential oils — peppermint, eucalyptus, lavender — whatever we had, apart from the citronella, which we kept for other purposes. On occasions, Christan would go to bed with a comfrey and plantain salad in his nappy; a poultice, that is. We sunned his bum regularly, and once I even got it sunburnt! That sure fixed the nappy rash, but only briefly.

Now, finally, I knew that it was thrush, but what was I to do about it? Robin had it in her mouth occasionally, too, but baking soda helped there. It didn't seem to bother her much either, which made it easier for her guilty mother.

A friend from Haast came tramping down the coast with a message from the district nurse asking whether we needed anything, so I sent back a request for gentian violet. I also sent a letter to a friend at Hannah's Clearing, Heather Abel, asking her to send me some more castor oil which I used for nappy changes. Although they both obliged happily, our mail languished at the Haast post office for several months, and when the castor oil ran out I resorted to a large jar of Vaseline which I had preferred not to use. Suddenly, the thrush was suffocated! Only then did I realise that it was feeding on the castor oil. Vaseline was nasty stuff to be washing out of a nappy, though, without the help of a washing machine, hot water and fancy detergents. Robin was six months old before we walked out to Haast and collected the bottle of gentian violet from the nurse. She continued to get thrush intermittently, and we often had a row of violent violet nappies hanging on the line. But this was easier once we had hot water to wash in.

Although I was prepared to go without things myself, I would insist that the kids did not have to all the time, particularly at Christmas. Christan's first introduction to Father Christmas came at the Balfour playgroup in the weeks after Robin was born. We had arranged to go with Diane Smith, and as I got into the car she asked, 'Have you got a gift to go under the tree?'

'Umm, OK. Hold on a minute.'

We'd been given a pile of board-books, one of which was almost new. I wrapped it up with a packet of chalk I'd bought for Christan and which I could replace the next time I got to the local shop. It was the best I could do, and I hoped whichever child received it wouldn't be so sophisticated as to be disappointed by their gift.

Back in the car on the way to Balfour, Diane said, 'I've just got a couple of little cars for my son. Some people put some ridiculous things in that are quite over the top,' whereupon I realised that the recipient of the gift would be Christan himself.

'Rats!' I thought, and could only hope that he wouldn't notice. I could have wrapped up the rainbow-striped, extra-bouncy ball and he would have been absolutely thrilled, but that was to be for Christmas Day and the real Father Christmas.

As it happened, he didn't think much of the book and handed it to me to hold, but he was thrilled to bits with the chalk and didn't let go of the packet until we got home and he could try them out. He paid no attention whatsoever to what anyone else had, and everyone was happy.

We flew home with some exciting Christmas presents from Nana. Robert gave me one of the four sapphires he'd found at Tomahawk Creek in Queensland, which his father had sent to Thailand to be cut. He tied it and a smaller one for Robin into a tiny piece of silk, sat the bundle in the corner of a small yellow-foot paua shell and covered it with another smaller paua shell. As the mother of a tiny daughter, it looked very symbolic and maternal and moved me to tears. He gave a third one to Christan but kept it for him in the box with his own one.

We also brought home a small piece of carpet which was Robin's gift from us. With that on the floor in the sunniest spot we had a lovely place for the kids to play for the next 10 years or more, from stacking blocks right through to games of cribbage and Monopoly. The house was five degrees warmer by this time, so Robin only wore three layers of clothing inside.

With the birth of a daughter, life was very different around here. Although I always knew she'd be a girl, I thought I'd be quite happy to have another boy, not realising the difference it would make in such a male-dominated society as we have here south of Jackson Bay. Fishermen often have a female crew, and at Haast Jenny Barrett skippered for her husband for some time. I have met one woman hunting, three piloting a helicopter and several aeroplane pilots, while trampers and passengers in aircraft might be up to one-quarter female.

Our lives became so much more balanced after Robin's birth. We now had two adults and two children (although it took Christan a while to accept the truth of that), two females and two males, two Cs and two Rs, two air signs (Aquarius and Libra) and two water signs (both Scorpio).

Like me, Robin was born on a Tuesday and her middle name is Grace. ('Tuesday's child is full of grace…') I discovered later that my middle name, Anne, also means 'grace'.

Robert and Christan were both born on a Thursday. ('Thursday's child has far to go…') Also appropriate.

Robert had built Christan's new bed along the wall at right-angles to ours, meeting at the head ends. I'd bought him a pillowcase as a special incentive to sleep in his own bed. A fence went right around the whole thing because we were quite high up. When Robert spent several nights sleeping in Christan's bed I figured I'd make the most of the space, as it wouldn't be long before we had someone else in with us as well.

At the Bowmars' cottage, Robin had been sleeping on one mattress with me where I could see that she was warm and breathing, while Christan slept on the far side on Robert's mattress. After nearly a month of that, when we got back home we had three people in one bed and Christan in the other by himself, and you can probably guess how long that lasted. So it was rebuilt again with three single mattresses next to each other and each of the kids under their own separate eiderdowns. We all enjoyed that until they chose to get out themselves.

After five months at home settling into the routine of a new baby, we were ready for a trip out to town. With Robin riding in the pack, Christan at three-and-a-half would have to walk. Carrying one baby still allows you to go almost anywhere, although we did have to alter a few things in order to take fewer risks. But with two children we were a travelling circus, and we discovered several more things in our packs that we could do without. Travelling was limited to the speed of a small child, and there was no picking him up to race a coming storm. To get across the Cascade, Robert would have to ford it three times.

I held Christan's hand and found myself having to watch his feet, to put each one onto the next rock. He was having a lovely time looking around at the sky, the trees, the waves, and chirping away about everything he could see. When Robert took his hand I found myself looking at the trees and the shape of the hills. Walking at Christan's pace, this was the first time I'd had a chance to look at the view apart from when I stopped for a break. It happened again when Robin first walked out at three-and-a-half, but they soon picked up speed and I was the slow one, as ever.

Arriving at a hut or someone's house at the end of a long day could be a real challenge. I remember sitting before the stove at Barn Bay waiting for Robert to come back from wherever he'd disappeared to. I thought he'd be bringing some wood so I could get the fire going. Christan was worn out after walking all the way, while Robin had been sleeping in the pack all day and was ready for mischief. She wasn't quite crawling yet, but she could get around. I'd already moved any mouse-traps or rat poison I could find, but who knew what else might be hiding in corners, and I would have to keep a sharp eye on her if I put her down on the floor. Late in autumn the day was all but over when we arrived, and right now we needed a fire, a meal and a bed to sleep in. When I couldn't wait any longer, I took the kids out to see what Robert was doing and found him happily cleaning up a stoat nest in the wee hut out the back.

'You didn't see how bad it was!' he argued, which was quite true; I didn't want to know about it.

'Don't worry. It will still be there tomorrow,' I assured him.

We had aimed to reach Maurice Nolan's hut on the south side of the Cascade River and stay there the night, but arriving at around three in the afternoon we found it locked. In May in the Cascade Valley the sun drops behind the plateau quite early, and it was getting cold and felt much later. There seemed to be no alternative but to push on.

'You'll have to carry Christan,' I said to Robert, but could he? Even if I took Robin, his pack was full.

'Yes,' he replied, and his matter-of-fact tone reassured me as we headed back to the gate. We were closing it behind us when our ears pricked up at the sound of an approaching vehicle. It came into view shortly afterwards, sloshing through a muddy puddle on the far side of the river. With packs off again, we sat down to wait as it crossed the river and came along the track towards us. This was the second well-timed rescue Maurice had provided.

'You've locked the hut,' Robert said, in greeting.

'Some bastard took my shotgun so I'm keeping it locked. But you fellas would just have to break a window!'

This was often Maurice's method of entering a hut, particularly when it was one of his own that someone had taken over, done up, and then locked. In an emergency I suppose we would have had to consider it, but it certainly hadn't occurred to us that day. It would have been tough to carry on to the road-end that evening, but it could have been done.

As it turned out, we spent a night with Maurice and Peter Stephens with plenty of entertainment. We discussed how heavy our load was with two kids on board, but also how lucky we were that we had small, lightweight children. 'You don't get a big calf from a heifer,' Maurice concluded.

He had a couple of army ration packs and handed Christan a cracker with a bit of cheese on it. Next he pulled out a tube of jam and squirted some onto Robert's cracker, so Christan held his out for a bit of jam, too. Anything like that was scrupulously shared in our house.

'You finish what you've got there first,' growled Maurice, and Christan understood that this was not someone to argue with.

'I sleep there,' said Maurice later, pointing to the bottom bunk. Peter took the top bunk, which left us the inner room where we could deal to the needs of babies with a bit of privacy.

In the morning we got a head-start to walk to the river before Maurice drove us across it and out to Haast. We wanted to baptise Robin, as we had Christan, in the Cascade before taking her back out into the big world.

Collecting rain off the roof had been perfectly adequate for Robert for the first nine years, and when I came along it was just a matter of how much storage we had and how long the fine spells lasted. With one baby, we often had to conserve water during good weather, and Robert replaced two rusted-out 44-gallon drums with the plastic inside of Eoin Wylie's freezer, which still stood in its original place in the old shed. Wylie had lived here for five years deer-hunting and crayfishing in the 1970s. It served very well for the cold-water supply. A small section of the back roof was raised in order to collect water for the hot tank and provide a bit of pressure for the shower, while the bottom half of a very rusty 44-gallon drum still held water from the bathroom roof to flush the toilet sparingly.

During Robin's first summer, Robert began rebuilding the bathroom, adding building paper for a bit of insulation. Prior to this, we'd used it as an icebox throughout the winter. Even in summer it was cool enough to store food. Robert said, 'Bring on global warming!'

With the loss of half our water catchment during the building process, I often carried eight buckets up from the river each day during any fine spell longer than a week, and the weather was particularly lovely that summer and autumn. I preferred to do it while Robin slept, as it was easier to carry a bucket to flush the indoor toilet than to get Christan over to the long-drop at the appropriate time, which couldn't be planned around the needs of a baby.

Getting out of the house in the day was a treat, even a feat, particularly as the winter set in. At least once each day I'd get to the river to rinse a load of nappies. I could have rinsed them in the sink on rainy days, but I always resisted that idea, feeling it to be real drudgery. In bad weather it was often the only time I got out and I could always expect Robert to look after the children while I went.

I took Christan with me one squally southerly day, as he needed to get out as much as I did. It was very windy down there and raining a bit, so I parked him on top of the bank, well away from the big waves pounding in up the river. He was never a worry in such a situation and always stayed where he was told to. We were both bundled up in jerseys and raincoats, and I was chasing after nappies as an extra-strong wave swept them away from the rocks that weighed them down.

'Mum!' I could hear Christan calling through the wind and rain, but it took me some time to grab everything out of the water and carry it back up above the high-water mark.

'Mum!' Perhaps I should have left him at home after all.

'What?' I asked as I reached him, over the noise of the wind flapping in the hood of my raincoat.

'The duck's coming!'

I still regularly thank Bruce Kershaw, a dairy farmer from Paeroa, for his gift of 600 metres of water-pipe. Even when we put up the first solar panel and had a light at night instead of stinky candles and a kerosene lantern, I maintained that having water was far more life-changing.

Bruce and his son, Sidney, flew in with local helicopter pilot Dave 'Sax' Saxton, for a week's hunting during the Roar in 1995. For four weeks in March and April each year, South Westland DOC issues hunting permits in a block system. Each party of hunters has an exclusive right to hunt in their allocated block for seven days, as determined by a ballot system. With them came 400 metres of pipe, plus all the fittings and taps we have needed for the next 17 years. The other 200-metre roll was left behind in Sax's hangar to come later, but unfortunately it was still there when the hangar went up in flames.

Whenever I wanted something, Robert would say, 'Maybe it will wash up on the beach', but it seemed unlikely that a 200-metre roll of 2.5-centimetre water-pipe would wash up any more than the first two rolls had. So Robert actually walked into Mitre 10 in Alexandra and bought it!

'That was pretty easy,' he said. 'All I had to do was hand over $95 and they gave it to me. I gave them another $10 to freight it to Arrowtown so we don't have to take it on the bus.'

This was a major step forward for us. Robert had found quite a good market for his paintings and carvings, and was making plenty of money for us to live on so long as we were careful. We began to spend more to make life a bit easier. After living for so long on so little, it was a new experience for Robert. For me, there was always a sense of guilt involved, as it wouldn't have happened if I hadn't been here. I haven't made much money over the past 20 years, so I have always felt that it was up to me to save money and go without. Often it is my role to rein in the big ideas, while Robert says, 'It's OK, we can afford this.' He is also quite a bit older than I am, so while he's beginning to find it all getting too hard, I'm still focused on putting up with it, not complaining and appreciating what I have. Mind you, whenever I mention a washing machine the conversation comes to a sudden halt.

The water system is gravity-fed, and requires no pump. So once Robert had laid out the pipe and connected everything, sorted out all the airlocks and other problems and got it working properly, maintenance of the water supply became my job. For the first few months I'd climb back down the waterfall, negotiate the muddy bit, follow deer trails and the creek back out to the beach, then stop and think: 'Now, did I turn the tap on?'

After climbing all the way back up to be sure several times, rather than walking the rest of the way home first, I decided not to forget anymore.

Maybe half a dozen times in the past 17 years I've climbed up the hill, fixed whatever seemed to be the problem, cleaned the silt out of the settling tank and turned the tap on, only to find on arriving back at home that the water had not. At that point, it becomes Robert's job. Once a tree fell over the line, but, although it seemed to run a bit more slowly for a while, it was still OK for a year or more until the windfall settled further and some other problem was proving difficult to fix. Robert cut and rejoined the pipe over the tree, giving us a join within 50 metres of the tank which has been handy at times.

Another time when I couldn't find anything wrong but the water refused to flow, Robert found a tiny eel jammed in the tap on the tank. Considering that it happened within the first two or three years, it is surprising that nothing has blocked it since. I got a big surprise when a 15-centimetre-long Gordian worm came, gradually, out of the kitchen tap. At first I thought it was a stick or a piece of insulation from a thin piece of copper wire, but a few years later we saw a lot of these worms in the puddles left on the riverbed by the outgoing tide in the Awarua River and understood how it could have travelled so far.

Whenever I'm up at the waterfall for maintenance I stop for a moment to give thanks to the oread of Mt Malcolm for the wonderfully pure water of the spring-fed creek that has never stopped running, even in the driest summer, and also to Bruce Kershaw for the gift of pipe that carries it to the tank in the rata tree behind the house. Most of the time the tank overflows into a pond and we don't have to bother too much if the taps drip.

Apart from the fact that I could now wash clothes in hot water, the next item on the list of new luxuries was hot baths whenever we wanted, instead of only when it was raining. We'd taken to bathing in a fish-case in front of the fire when I was pregnant with Robin, rather than braving the bathroom in the middle of winter. At three, Christan insisted on getting in at the same time as Robert, which wasn't as difficult as it sounds as Robert couldn't get his legs in anyway.

With the kids in bed I'd make a hot drink, pour a spare bowl of hot water into the fish-case, and bring a book, then steam myself into a sweat while listening to the drips landing on the pile of huhu-grub-infested compost under the floor, the last piece yet to be replaced. If I'd been eating garlic and turnips I could sometimes imagine that I was at Rotorua.

At nine months, fully clothed, including a yellow-and-white striped woollen suit, Robin stood up to watch her bath filling with a hose from the kitchen sink and 'Whoops!' There she goes, face-first like a bumblebee buzzing around a blue bucket full of water in the summertime. In such a small house there was no need to spend even a moment considering what might have happened. Instead, I laughed as I took two steps and hauled her out by the only dry bit at the scruff of her neck.

Later, when she could talk and the bath sat in the bathroom in the new shower tray, she'd step in, immediately climb out the other side and say, 'Too 'ot!' whether it was or not. Mostly I would add a bit of cold water, but she was just as happy if I added hot. Then she'd hop in, and as it overflowed she'd say, 'Look! It's upping!'

I could hardly get out of the house for several months after Robin's birth, so Robert collected most of the firewood. People always comment, 'You'd never run out of firewood!' when they see the huge pile of driftwood on the beach. But by late winter when there hasn't been a decent flood for a while, and just enough drizzle to keep everything wet and rotting, it can be hard to find much sound wood, and Robert had enough to do already without walking further and further to get it. He never used to have the fire going so much when he was here alone, but he did appreciate having a warm house.

'Mix it with some good wood,' he'd say, but, as the bulk of the wood got soggier and more rotten, it seemed to be a waste of the good wood trying to burn it. Tempers frayed as I got more and more frustrated and he felt like he was doing all the work.

'I'm not trying to hassle you, I'm trying to feed you!'

He liked to repeat the line Mitch used to say at Big Bay: 'If I bring you any firewood, you'll only burn it!'

'Fine! I won't have to cook anything then. You'd only eat it!'

As Robin was getting bigger, I decided that it would be easier to go and get the wood I wanted than to sit here any longer trying to burn soggy, rotten stuff. It was time to break loose from my indoor bondage.

I'd take Christan with me and pull him along the airstrip in the trolley. On the return trip he could ride up on top of the bags of wood, very proud of himself. I carried Robin in the backpack, but as she grew bigger I had two of them to haul along in the trolley and it got to be a bit much. The day came when Christan was kicked out to walk, but when I tried to put Robin into the trolley she insisted on walking, too. As she refused to negotiate the matter, I was stuck with hauling the loaded trolley at the pace of a toddler.

Living in a building site is never easy but, while we were pretty tolerant, Robert was also very good about making it manageable. The floor had to be rebuilt, right down to replacing the piles, before the huhu grubs finished doing it their way, and, as he worked on one section at a time, we lived around a two- or three-metre hole in the floor. We'd negotiate around him during the day, and each evening he'd leave it tidy and approximately safe until he started again in the morning.

Robin, at the crawling stage, encased in layers of wool, rolled into the hole in front of the toilet and it took some effort to extract her. She was an almost spherical bundle, very roly-poly and without much to get a grip on.

Christan was a great help. Each morning he'd sit up in our bed on the floor and announce, 'Me want do some banging!'

Even at one year old he was good enough with a hammer that I was prepared to hold the nail for him while he got it started. Robert made him a board with pegs that could be hammered through to the other side, then turned over to do it again, but within weeks Christan was bored with it and hammered nails into it instead. At three, he was very handy with a hammer. Working with recycled timber, most of the nail holes had to be drilled anyway, and Christan was quite capable of following after Robert to hammer each nail into the prepared holes.

By the time Robert had finished closing in the extension to the back of the house, we had a completely rebuilt bathroom which was more than twice as big as the old one had been, with a handbasin, a wringer and a shower cubicle. Only the toilet was in its original place. After knocking out the wall between the bedroom and the new part, the house seemed enormous, and it took me a while to budget enough time in the day to sweep it all at once. Everything was double-wrapped in layers of insulation paper, so the house was a lot warmer, and as Robert had been building at the beginning of summer rather than the beginning of winter this time, we also had a lot more ventilation which was very important with the stove going to cook for four people and our bed being up high in the hottest place. Robert can be very one-track-minded so that when he was trying to make the house warmer he wouldn't do anything about cooling it, even if I thought about it for him.

I nearly had kittens when Robert told me he'd just come down the bluff carrying two-year-old Christan on his shoulders. I'd been up that way and it was pretty steep. Half the time you are climbing up trees to get up the steep rockface behind them. Even Robert thought that perhaps he wouldn't do it again.

Two hunters, the Kershaws, were up on the top of the hill the following day and found little gumboot prints.

'If you didn't know you'd think you were seeing things,' said Bruce Kershaw.

Another person who spotted little gumboot tracks in an improbable place was Robert's friend Johnny Rogers from Brisbane. He had tramped down the coast on the same day that we went up, and somehow we had passed him on Sandrock Bluff. We were on the track, but evidently he was not. When we stepped back onto the beach on the north side Robert saw a footprint, really no more than a depression in the shingle, and declared, 'That looks like Johnny.'

We knew that he was probably coming sometime, but had no idea when, so I was quite sceptical.

'How can you tell from that?'

'It just looks like him ... only it's a bit small.'

'Yeah, right!'

Robert comes out with the most outrageous things at times, but the fact remains that often he is right. Two days later at Barn Bay I found another set of footprints, and this time Johnny was still in the last of them. He was wearing cycling shoes, which explained why his footprints were smaller than if he had been wearing boots.

When Johnny saw little gumboot prints in the sand on the south side of the bluff he told himself that it was just me out for a walk with the kids. The fact that this was about 10 kilometres north of Gorge River was not about to convince him to turn around and go back again. He was looking forward to a hot shower and a meal, but was disappointed to find nothing but rice and split peas left in the food cupboard.

'That's why we are going out to the shop,' was my answer.

We were stuck at Barn Bay for several days of rain and Johnny had brought some sultanas, hoping that I'd make Anzac biscuits for his birthday. Sultanas were a good start, but we were sadly lacking most of the other ingredients. Still, I did come up with something edible. I cut pictures out of fishing magazines to make a card for Christan's birthday three days later, and made some uncooked oatmeal fudge, like most people would use biscuit crumbs, shaped it into a wee mouse for each of us with peanuts for ears and a fruit leather tail. We also had a cake that we thought was pretty yummy on the walk to the Cascade, but by that night out in Haast no one wanted another piece, thank you. Brian Wildbore, who had been here during the previous Roar, gave Christan and Robert a ride up to the shop from the Arawhata Bridge, where they bought all sorts of things to eat and collected the mail. With a packet of mini Mars bars from Brian and his very own pair of scissors from Granma, Christan was very satisfied with his fourth birthday.

Chapter 10
OTHER PEOPLE'S TIMETABLES

Robert's parents were talking of coming to Queenstown for Christmas 1995, but when they tried to book accommodation they found everything fully booked and the earliest they could get was 9 January 1996. They would meet us in Haast on the fifth with a hired van.

Back in May, Christmas shopping hadn't seemed very urgent, so now, in September, I bought a packet of gold-wrapped muesli bars at Ian Rendell's shop in Haast and asked Mum to send something urgently. Christan was old enough to be looking sideways at all the other kids when we came out so close to Christmas, and the fact that Nana and Grandad would bring him all sorts of things didn't really let Father Christmas off the hook when he was passing by with his reindeer. In November, a helicopter pilot collected our mail, but, when he developed engine trouble and a lot of other Robinson R22s were grounded due to a batch of uncertified tail rotors, he never got back to deliver it. I got increasingly exasperated as Robert kept finding things such as a packet of popsticks, and handing them to Christan, saying, 'I guess it would have been a good Christmas present.' He made Christan a wee herring net that would have blown his socks off if he'd found it on Christmas morning.

In December, Robert had to fly out to Haast to make a statement to the police after a nearby helicopter accident, and before he left he asked what we needed from the shop. I knew that there wouldn't be anything there in December that hadn't been in September, but I asked him to try to get something Father Christmassy. He came back with a marshmallow Santa, but had also collected the parcel from Mum which contained a Buzzy Bee for Robin and a pack of Winnie-the-Pooh playing cards for Christan — just in time to save Father Christmas from dying out before Robin was even ready for him.

> 'Twas the night before Christmas and all through
> the house
> Not a creature was stirring … except for a mouse.
> And a stoat!

The weather forecast dictated a Christmas Day departure, so at two in the morning, with travelling food cooked and some sort of Christmas organised, I was packed and ready to go. I was heading to bed when something started squeaking loudly outside and running up and down the side of the house. Next, there was a scuffling sound as a stoat came through the gap under the front door, through the workshop and into the main room where it sat up on its haunches and *squeaked* at me. I reached for a stick from the wood-box, whereupon it shot out again, under the door and away, but it occurred to me as I replaced the stick that it might have been Stoata Claus wishing me a jolly Christmas. I had failed to recognise him without his wee red hat.

It wasn't much of a Christmas. We had a hurried lunch, whatever it was, and the yummy jelly pudding I'd promised didn't come up to expectations. Then we bundled Robin into the pack and left by 2pm to camp in the tent at the Spoon River. The coming rain chased us up the beach, although we kept ahead of it most of the way. We only had to walk the last kilometre or so in it and set up the tent.

In the morning we woke to a pattering sound on the roof and thought 'Oh no!', but as when Christan was tiny, it turned out to be a perfectly fine morning and the pattering was all the sandflies that were sharing the tent with us. We carried on to Barn Bay, where the kids had a lovely time playing with all the toys while it rained for a couple of days and then while we waited a couple more for the Cascade to go down.

Sometime later, back at home, I heard Christan singing along with his guitar and strained to catch the words over the racket.

> *We got to Cascade and river not look very good*
> *So we found a wubber ducky*
> *And we went across in the wubber ducky.*

And that is what happened. We could have stopped at Maurice's hut to wait until the morning, hoping that the

TOP Retailing magnate Dick Smith and his wife, Pip, called in to visit in their JetRanger. Pip took this photo of the Cabbage Tree Helicopter's Beansprout Mark 1.

BOTTOM We were often full of ideas for art and craft projects, and it could be very frustrating to wait months for a trip to the shop to buy what was required; in this case pasta and gold paint supplemented by shells from the beach.

TOP Tea was cooked in instalments with a single hotplate on top of a 12-gallon oil drum, which also covered a wetback from the original coal range. The hot-water cupboard was to the right of the stove.

BOTTOM Birthday cakes were cooked in the camp oven on top of the stove. Most of the gifts were also home-made.

TOP My family visited for Christmas 1997. L–R: My mum, Rosamond; my grandmother, Marjory House; my niece, Madeleine; Robert; Robin; Christan; my brother, Andrew.

BOTTOM An 8-cake and a teddy bears' picnic in the bush.

TOP The kids were keen gardeners, and grew our first-ever pumpkin crop.

BOTTOM The gladioli flower in time for my birthday each year. The plants were growing here before Robert arrived.

TOP At six and even before, Christan was very handy with a hammer.

BOTTOM More recent technological advances include a greenhouse and two solar panels. Some vegetables are now grown in cages as the possums also advance, relentlessly.

TOP I enjoyed knitting as long as the patterns were colourful and interesting. I sold a few to friends and occasionally to a shop in Queenstown.

MIDDLE A Tasman storm delivers tonnes of fresh firewood on the beach, ready for gathering.

BOTTOM Rinsing nappies in the river on a sunny summer's day. Where else would you want to be?

Whatever Christan is into, he does with total enthusiasm,
whether it be playing cricket on the airstrip or building
goal posts and a whitebait stand from driftwood.

TOP Usually Christan copied Robert's oil paintings in acrylics on calico, but sometimes Robert would be inspired by Christan's less-inhibited technique.

BOTTOM Robert's painting of the view of the Cascade Valley to the sea from the point on the road where we were married. Robert supports us financially with his painting and craftwork.

river would go down a bit further, but there was more rain to come, probably before daylight. As if by magic, an inflatable boat lay out on the riverbed with some other gear, apparently left by a whitebaiter. We decided that Father Christmas must have made a sharp turn in his sleigh and dropped it there. Thinking that the whitebaiter hadn't come back we tied it up in the bush, but several months later when Maurice Nolan was wondering where his boat had got to, we gave it back.

'Lou Brown's canoe is away down the river,' he said. 'Some joker paddled it down there and couldn't get back up. I've been meaning to bring it some time when I'm down there in the jetboat.'

'What if I gave you $50?' Robert asked.

'Yeah, that would help,' said Maurice.

He brought it up and left it in the bush, but by the time we got back there it had gone again. And the following year, Father Christmas delivered a rubber ducky safely right to Gorge River.

We had a few days to spare at Neil's Beach, but the day that we had to pack up and hitchhike to the Haast pub to meet Bob and Ngaire was also the day that Christan needed to stay in bed. He'd come down with the sort of sudden illness he was prone to from the age of six months through to about 15 years, almost every time we came out to town. Whether it was a 'flu, a tummy bug or just the result of being too busy or stressed or having too many late nights, it would start with a fever, he'd be unable to keep food down and, skinny as he was, he'd go downhill fast. I'd been working on it for a couple of years, but this time Robert saw that I knew what I was talking about and wasn't just nagging for nothing whenever he arrived home late from a mate's place with Christan in tow, tired and unfed. 'I gave him some sultanas,' he'd say, and wonder why that cranked me up another notch.

Up at the pub everyone was happy to see everyone else, and Bob got to meet his second granddaughter for the first time. As soon as I politely could, I got Christan into bed while Nana and Grandad buried him in a pile of presents. When he keeled over amongst the Lego and puzzles, Robert and I took it in turns to stay with him while the others adjourned to the dining room.

As Christan seemed much better in the morning, it wasn't possible to leave him out of the proposed picnic at Jackson Bay when he wouldn't need to walk anywhere and he could sleep in the van if he wanted to. But he was sick again in the evening, and we were booked at a motel in Wanaka for the next night and Queenstown the one after, where we dragged him off to the doctor. A diagnosis of bronchitis, otitis media and conjunctivitis meant a prescription for antibiotics, and for the second time they made no difference. It seemed to me that, with him being a Libra, perhaps ear infections threw him off-balance more than they should, and for a long time afterwards. It was not an enjoyable week in our motel room in Queenstown with a screaming child and medicines dripping down the walls. We continued to take turns to stay with him until a different antibiotic finally fixed it, and, as I had lots of things to do in town after seven months, Robin spent most of her time in my pack until she came down with the 'flu, too.

Robert and I were hanging out to get home, and the plan was for Ngaire and Bob to drop us off at the hangar on Tuesday morning before they headed back to Christchurch. So with Robin sick on Sunday and the potential ear infection before us, it looked like we'd be unable to fly and certainly not up to walking home. The on-call doctor had gone out to an accident but arranged to meet us at the Frankton Medical Centre at two that afternoon. We waited in the van until five, by which time we decided that Robin would be far better off in bed and that we might as well get her started on Christan's antibiotics.

On Monday morning the doctor said she had no secondary infection but prescribed antibiotics anyway, and, having started, I knew that you should finish the course rather than breed up multiply-resistant strains of bacteria.

We said goodbye to Ngaire and Bob early on Tuesday, and were happy to rest in the sun on the airstrip while we waited for Roger to come at lunchtime. Then Robin threw up. With very little water, I changed her clothes and my own and bundled all the smelly stuff into my pack to deal with later at home where everything was so much easier. When she developed diarrhoea as well, I refused to go on giving her medicine that was killing her and that she didn't need anyway, and allowed her to begin to heal herself. We were so glad to get home.

I had spoken to Alison on the telephone the day before we flew home. She was planning to bring her husband and kids to Auckland and could we come to meet them? I said that, as much as we'd like to, we wouldn't be going anywhere for a while, but we would have to come out again sometime in May.

Her next letter arrived late in March announcing their expected arrival on 1 May. Instead of coming out in May as we'd planned, we'd have to be gone by the second week of April.

'Great!' said Robert. 'We won't have to go.'

Clearly he could see that leaving so early was simply not

possible, and I had to reconsider my own priorities. I had never said 'No' to anything Alison had asked, but travelling with two kids was a major effort and put a huge strain on us all. Robert was working hard to finish the new bathroom and extension to the back of the house. We had a large hole in the floor where our bed had been, and another to dig for DOC's new space-aged fibre-glass toilet next-door.

On the other hand this was my sister whom I hadn't seen since her first child was a month old and I was four weeks pregnant. We'd had three more babies between us in the interim, and it seemed impossible for me to not see her if she was in the same country. I went out to the garden to dig potatoes while I thought about it.

'OK, she's coming for three weeks,' I brought up the subject again later. 'What if we fly out and walk home, instead of the other way around as we usually do? And if we didn't get there until her last week, that would give us an extra four weeks here first.' And we agreed to that.

Having arranged with Roger to fly out on a certain date, we kept an eye on the forecast. 'Northerly and rain by the evening' it said, so we were all packed, tidy and ready to go the day before. But Roger hardly ever seemed to have the same forecast as we did. Flying over Big Bay on the original day after all, he commented on the fact that it was raining and it promised to be a horrible flight.

'It was a perfect day yesterday,' we told him.

After travelling to Christchurch by bus, Dinah met us at the airport with Ned, who flew with us to Auckland. As Dad had also come over from Australia, it became a full family reunion at my brother's place at Bethells Beach on the Waitakere Coast. With two sons-in-law and all seven grandchildren making a lot of noise, I looked up to find

Mum, Dad and us three kids sitting around a table for the first time since Andrew had left home to come to New Zealand more than 16 years before.

I made my first kids' book about this trip to Auckland, to give the cousins an idea of how we lived and what it had taken for us to get there. It was a bit of a cheat since we'd actually flown, but I used photos of the Christmas trip with the partly flooded river. Anyway, we had yet to walk home. Apart from the two births, this was the first time we had flown out, although we were getting used to flying home at the end of a trip, exhausted and often sick. It was therefore also the first time the kids had arrived in the 'Big Smoke' without already being worn out from the walk. The difference showed in their state of health, which made a nice change.

Coming home we spent the last night in the tent at the Spoon River and woke up to drizzle. It wasn't enough to stop us walking, but just enough to make it cold and miserable. So long as we kept moving I was able to keep Christan's spirits up, but he knew that we didn't walk in rain, for very good reasons. Robin, in the pack on my back, was dry and warm, and Robert went on ahead at his own pace as he would have to blow up the rubber boat to get across the river and bring the dinghy back for us. I 'got ahead of myself' as Robert would say, and went straight up the track to the place I expected him to collect us, imagining a warm fire already blazing in the stove as we walked into the hut. We called and called, growing colder, wetter and more miserable by the minute, but the way the echoes work in the valley meant that he couldn't hear us from his position a couple of hundred metres downstream, on our side, where he was trying to blow up the boat by mouth after a sandhopper had chewed tiny holes in it. Eventually he appeared out of the bush and we helped to put up the emergency piece of black plastic he always carried. The kids howled while we struggled to dry the boat enough to patch it in various places with sticking plaster and added a pair of artery clamps from the first aid kit for the biggest holes. When we couldn't blow it up any faster than it was going back down, Robert jumped in and rowed as fast as he could to get across the river while his bum sank lower and lower and his feet rose higher. Still, it was much better than swimming.

Chapter 11

EDUCATE THE CHILDREN

The professor of Inorganic Chemistry at the University of Western Australia in 1983 began his first lecture by writing on the blackboard what he considered to be the most important formula we would ever learn.

B x W = D

That is: *Brains x Work = Degree*,' he elaborated. 'Regardless of how big the first factor is, if the *work* factor is zero, the result with always be zero.'

Denise Black, the midwife at Christan's birth, first introduced us to home-schooling and told us about the requirements of the Department of Education. I read a few books ahead of time, including some about Rudolph Steiner's methods and *Teacher* by Sylvia Ashton-Warner. Consequently, it seemed silly to me to say 'Today you start school', when really it was a gradual and continuous process. Whether Christan was doing puzzles, at age two with me to help, painting or carving with Robert, gardening, fishing or collecting firewood, the idea that his education began at age five or six was a bit irrelevant considering that a child learns more in their first few years than at any other time in their life.

Like any other animal, children learn a lot by watching their parents. Christan rubbed greenstone on his own piece of sandstone at the end of Robert's bench, holding it up to the light to see through it, imitating Robert's mannerisms. Waking up each morning, he'd grab the potty and insist that Robert pee in it before he would, no matter how desperate he was. At one year old he sat on a whale vertebra with his feet in the hole that the spinal cord runs through, 'carving' it with a rasp. Later we'd read a book and he'd retell the story using words he wouldn't normally use: 'This one is an active volcano and this one is a stink volcano!'

I wrote a letter to Sandi Meha, a friend from Jackson Bay to whom I had sold some skincare products. With help from my brother and sister, I had been trying to run a small business in Nu Skin, a pyramid sales company like Amway. At four, Christan sat beside me writing too, lots of Hs and Os. He told me what it said, so I wrote the interpretation for Sandi.

'You got your skin fixed?' he asked her.

Next, he made an observation: 'Mum, a zebra's skin is really, really…' (each 'really' squeakier than the last) '… *really* close to its blood.'

'Mmmm,' I agreed, still writing. 'What about an elephant?'

He reached out a hand and patted my double chins.

'Like that.' *Rotter!*

He made up for it a few days later when I was talking skincare again and how I was trying to make myself beautiful. In a tone that showed he wondered why I should question something so completely obvious, Christan said, 'But . . . you're beautiful!' and of course, I forgave him for everything.

I have read several women's stories of supervising their children through the Correspondence School years, and they all tend to have in common a fear of inadequacy. Robert and I, on the other hand, were always confident that we could teach our children satisfactorily, even if we were a bit unorthodox. We are both well educated, and we had the bonus of having two highly intelligent children. I would have found it an awful lot harder if either of them had had problems, but, actually, home-schooling, Correspondence, or at least individualised teaching are very good options for children who do have a learning difficulty.

It seems to me that so long as they can read and write by the end of primary school, they can pick up any finer details that may have been missed later on. The rest of it is just how you keep them interested while they are doing it. I do believe that a solid grasp of mathematical concepts is absolutely essential at the primary level, and I can understand someone being nervous about the teaching of it, but most of us can manage primary school Maths well enough, and the Correspondence teachers are usually very good at supporting their supervisors. In upper secondary school some people who simply don't have a 'maths brain' may have to accept their limitations in this area and choose a path that suits them better, but in my opinion this should not be done any sooner. Every child should have as much as possible pounded into their brains in the blind hope that some of it may stick some time. A student's achievement should never be limited by any lack of trying on behalf of the teacher, but I believe that many people are very capable teachers regardless of official qualifications.

Aim high in all you try for, Catherine, wrote my teacher, Miss Rose, in my autograph book at the end of my first year at Goldsworthy Primary School.

Even if you fall slightly short of your goal, you can be sure that you couldn't have done any better. I had high expectations of my children, often too high, which led to many battles. It is important not to push them to the point of burning out or all-out rebellion, but if you expect nothing from them you shouldn't be surprised if that is what you get.

My dad wrote in the same autograph book: *Courage is fear that has said its prayers.*

Before Christan turned six we applied to the Ministry of Education for an exemption from enrolment. Robert filled out a long and complicated form explaining how we intended to do everything, but the only legal requirement was that we teach him 'as well and as regularly as a registered school'. Every six months we signed a statement in front of a Justice of the Peace to that effect, and in return we received $740 per year as a supervisor's allowance, which helped with stationery, postage, etc.

At first Liz Brown, who had supervised four of her children through their Correspondence schooling at Barn Bay for the previous eight years, was indignant that home schoolers received 90 per cent of the same allowance as Correspondence School pupils, as she and other parents had fought hard to get it. I pointed out that she also had everything provided — schoolwork, marking, library books, art supplies, postage — while we had to buy everything with that. The books that teachers photocopy from were always very expensive, although later home-schoolers were able to buy some of them without paying for the photocopy licence.

Whenever I mentioned to a school teacher how much we were given per year, their first reaction was to say, 'Wow! That's pretty good', but after thinking about it they decided that it was pretty much equivalent to what their students received as a stationery allowance. On top of that, each student enrolled at a school has a teacher, a building, grounds, equipment and all of their work provided.

As home-schoolers we had the right to use the National Library and some regional school resource centres, as well as local libraries and those set up by home-schooling associations, so there were plenty of options available to us. Postage was our main expense. We'd been home-schooling for 18 months before the first payment arrived, so at first we tried to save most of the allowance to cover later costs. I spent hours making activity sheets, like those a teacher would run off on a photocopier. I cut things out of magazines, drew diagrams, wrote out lists of sums or questions with blank spaces for the answers — then Christan would finish the sheet in five minutes flat! Spending more of the money made sense, but we still saved quite a bit of it, which helped to pay for their final year of school at Mt Aspiring College in Wanaka.

An important part of teaching is to remember what it was like when you were a child yourself. For example, I remember failing my Junior certificate five times while learning to swim. Commenting on my breaststroke, the instructor said, 'You're turning your foot in.'

'Huh?'

What does that mean when you're seven years old? Time after time they said it: 'You're turning your foot in.'

I failed my swimming badge at Brownies, too, which made six times.

Finally the light-bulb went on: 'Oh — I'm turning my foot in!' So on the seventh attempt I passed. Talk about 'If at first you don't succeed...' After that, I progressed quickly through the Intermediate and Senior certificates, followed by Elementary, Proficiency, Survival and Life Saving without any problems. But I still turn my foot in when swimming breaststroke because I can go faster.

I also remember the day when I figured out how to stop Mum whacking me. Just stop being a ratbag! There was that same sensation of the light-bulb flashing on. I had one relapse after that (and I was 13 by this time), swearing at my sister, unable to stop myself despite Mum's descent from a great height. Perhaps I was a slow learner, but I remembered it while watching Christan struggling to get on top of his more childish behaviours.

It was hard to teach our kids to swim. Many people of our generation who grew up on the West Coast still can't swim. The kids were in the water all the time, and I would have to say no in the middle of winter when they showed no sign of developing any sense themselves. But it was always too cold to stay immersed in the water long enough to learn to swim properly, and they didn't learn to swim until they were each four years old on holiday in Australia. They both refused to swim again after coming home, and didn't until after their second holiday over there, three years later.

From then on they were fine and very confident in the

cold water, although they could still benefit from swimming lengths of a pool. In December 2011 Christan swam 50 metres at −1.8°C in a polar plunge near the Amery ice-shelf in Antarctica.

The Teachers' Resource Centre in Alexandra was very helpful and generous, but by the time a large box full of books had been flown in and out of Gorge River, not to mention paying for it to be couriered to and fro, we felt obliged to read every word in them. We'd have books about trains, cameras, seashells, clocks, amphibians and Cyclone Giselle. The rest of the box would contain reading books at the appropriate level.

In the mornings one of us would light the fire while the other stayed in bed in order to keep the kids there until the house had warmed up a bit. In the winter when they were small it was a necessity, but so far as schoolwork went it became a compulsory start to the day. There was a lot of really interesting stuff in these books, and the better ones would lead on to school projects, story writing or experiments later in the day.

The Seven Wonders of the Natural World led to 'the seven wonders of New Zealand', which was one project Christan was really enthusiastic about. By the end of the second week he was unstoppable, working on the index, introduction and cover page to get it finished. He was so proud of it that he showed it to visitors who landed here in a helicopter.

Mind you, we'd had a particular boost towards schoolwork at the time. Our best friends, the Bellerby family, had been staying for a week. Their boys Cam and Lochie are either side of Christan's age, and Fern is six months younger than Robin. They were the first children we'd had here since the Browns had moved away from Barn Bay before Robin was born.

The Bellerbys have been here three times altogether, and we have often stayed with them on their farm near Te Anau or met them in Wanaka or Queenstown for a birthday or a day's skiing.

This first visit was in February 2001, when Cam, Lochie and Fern should have been at school, so for part of each day the DOC hut became the official school room. They had material that had been set by their teachers, and Christan and Robin were delighted to have someone to work alongside. I could hardly believe my eyes when Christan sat at their table, head down, mouth shut and not a complaint to be heard.

When he'd finished a 10-page story about the week he'd had with his friends, I commented, 'You know, the only problem with this is that now I know you can do it, I will expect it all the time.'

I typed up his story the next time we were in town, and made it into a book for him with photos Lucy had sent of their holiday. Some of his sentences were incomplete, and I nagged to have him work on them further, meeting the usual stubborn resistance.

'I want it to say it like that — under the photo.'

I was happy to negotiate once I realised that it was a proper idea, rather than deliberate obstruction.

Lochie also made a book that he was very proud of when he got back to school, with the help of his teacher.

Christan went on to write another very long story about camping five kilometres up the beach with Cam and Lochie, catching fish, crayfish and paua to cook over their fire, so the next time the Bellerbys came to stay we took photos to illustrate another book.

Rather than straight facts, we preferred books that told a story. We enjoyed the series on *The Abbotsford Slip*, *The Sinking of the Wahine*, and *The Tangiwai Rail Disaster*, and read the *My Story* series and other fictional accounts of children caught up in historical events.

While reading *Black Boots and Buttonhooks* by Phyllis Johnston about May Tarrent's childhood, the kids were inspired to learn the poem that May recited at school in the early 1900s. We recorded them on tape, reciting alternate verses of 'The Fighting Téméraire' by Henry John Newbolt. 'Oh! to see the linstock lighting, Téméraire! Téméraire! Oh! to hear the round shot biting, Téméraire! Téméraire!...'

Later they learned Banjo Paterson's 'The Man from Snowy River', but they had no concept whatsoever of saying it together. If one started reciting, the other would rapidly turn it into a horse race which worked quite well towards prompting and correcting each other. They loved shouting it in the bath with the doors shut.

I would have found it much harder if my kids had had any problems, but they are both very capable. The hardest part was dealing with Christan's attitude. By the time Robin started, she accepted that this was part of a normal day and she wanted to be doing it, too. For Christan it was all new and he didn't see why I should insist that he sit still and do things he didn't want to do. Robert didn't make it easier by walking in the door and saying 'Let's go fishing' or 'Let's go gold mining.' He always had a lot of ideas about how it could be different or how it shouldn't have to happen at all, that Christan had been learning perfectly well by following him around doing all the things that he did. In the old days a boy grew up to do whatever his father did and it was only the Industrial Revolution that took parents out of the home so that children had to go to school while they were away. Although I agreed with him, no amount of talking about it changed the fact that, today, this has to be done. We'd made a commitment to the Ministry of Education as to what we planned to do and we just had to get on with it.

Christan is quick and intelligent, and when Robert or I explained a new mathematical principle to him you could see the understanding in his eyes. 'Yep. Yep. Yep,' he'd say. But the moment always came when I handed it over to him to start figuring out, and his whole demeanour would change. He'd hunch down on his stool, hat pulled down over his eyes and say, 'So what do I have to do?' Sigh.

In holiday time Christan would ask good questions like 'How does a compass work?', knowing that it couldn't be turned into schoolwork like everything usually was. It seemed to me that schoolwork might as well be about something they were interested in, but inevitably it happened too often. He'd also ask questions late at night, which was a great ploy to avoid having to shower and go to bed.

Then, a week before we should be starting school again, I offered to put it off a bit longer on condition that they tidied up their desks, threw away all the old school books and got rid of a few tonnes of junk. Christan had trouble deciding whether he'd prefer to start schoolwork a week early or tidy his desk!

Robin, following along behind, was generally much easier to manage. It was more in her nature to please me than to bang heads, and anyway she wanted to do whatever Christan was doing. At four, she insisted on being provided with her own task sheet so that she could do Maths, too. She climbed up onto the high stool at Christan's desk to do her work, and when she couldn't reach the top of the page — which she couldn't read anyway — she turned it upside down and carried on filling in the boxes. No problem.

As she went, she kept up a continuous stream of questions: 'Sixty was it? Two sixes? Oh, six zero. I know how to write a hundred...'

As it turns out, we have a family history of home-schooling. My grandmother was taught by her father in China until she was 12, before she went away to school in England. He'd regularly say, 'Blast and damn you to everlasting Hell!' and clonk her on the head with the book. It was in the same semi-humorous frame of mind that I once did it to Christan — before the 'No Smacking' Bill was introduced into Parliament. But Christan was outraged by my appalling behaviour and moved straight in with the guilt trip. I was a bit chagrined but still laughed at him.

'You have no idea how lucky you are, boyo! I could tell you some stories.'

Like the one told by Twiggy, a whitebaiter at Big Bay. The master at the Catholic school he attended was in a rage because he couldn't track down the perpetrator of a particular crime, so he announced that he would belt the whole class. Twiggy and his friend made sure they were at the back of the line and watched him working his way along it, growing more and more red in the face, with sweat pouring off him. Finally, he reached Twiggy and friend, and, glaring, said, 'And you two can come back tomorrow!'

As the first child it was also Christan's job to break in his parents, and Robin got to breeze along in his wake. By the time three years had gone by, things that had seemed so important once often left me wondering what all the fuss had been about, or else perhaps I had just given in and chosen to drop the subject. Routines that I'd fought so hard for were either established by then or compromised on, and generally the battles were being fought on new things at whatever stage he was up to next.

No matter what I wanted, Christan would always argue with it, so rather than set a strict timetable it was better to set a few limits and allow him to work things out for himself within them. These limits changed regularly, as I was forced to compromise often and kept searching for something that would actually work, but for Christan any set limit was something to push against. If I said he could do it whenever he wanted to in the day so long as it was finished by tea time, he'd leave everything to the last possible moment when he was tired and grumpy, then try to get out of it. If that didn't work he'd grizzle that the work was too hard, which it was by that time of the day, whereas first thing in the morning with a fresh brain, it wouldn't have been. After a few days at Mararoa School, he decided that I made him do much more than other kids had to. Although I didn't agree, it was better to back off a bit and leave him feeling like he had some say in the matter.

If I went away for the day the kids would enjoy mucking around and creating havoc while doing their schoolwork without being nagged. At least, Christan said he'd enjoyed it. Robin said she couldn't hear herself think!

In the last year or two of home-schooling, they'd come to me in the morning to ask, 'What's my schoolwork today?' and I'd say, 'You tell me.' They knew what the choices were and how much was required of them, but I was thoroughly sick of telling them what to do just so they could argue about it and tell me they didn't want to.

Social contact was our potential stumbling-block with the Education Review Office (ERO) while we were home-schooling, but they agreed that as our alternative was the

Correspondence School, that wasn't going to solve the problem.

One weekend early in 2002 an aeroplane landed, bringing our mail. While anyone is here we drop everything to talk to them and usually have a cup of tea, so it isn't until after they have gone that we open our mail. Sometimes after a long gap, that may occupy most of the rest of the day. On this particular day we opened a letter from the ERO which informed us that someone would be coming to review us. They would be in Haast at 9.00am on Thursday and could we please tell them if there was anything else they needed to know.

We managed to get a letter out within two days, stamped FastPost, so that it probably arrived by the Tuesday afternoon, telling them it was all fine by us but that they might have to walk the last 45 kilometres from the road-end, or alternatively, they could fly by helicopter from Haast.

Three years passed before we heard any more from them. They didn't even send a note to say, 'Sorry we didn't make it.' In 2004 Russell Cannon reviewed the Haast Primary School and heard about us from the teachers, as we usually spent a week or two at the school twice a year when we were there. Russell arranged to fly in with Dave Saxton to review us on a Monday, in April 2005, but again it didn't happen, so he asked us to come and see him instead the next time we were in Dunedin. By then Christan had enrolled with the Correspondence School, and the following year so had Robin.

As the kids grew, not only did they eat more but their needs changed. While home-schooling we needed school books, books, paper and other stationery, paint, brushes, glue, etc. It didn't arrive in the post as it had for the couple of years while we were enrolled with the Correspondence School's Early Childhood Programme up to the age of five.

Some people are amazed at the amount of junk we have in our house, but it isn't a very big house and we need to have things on hand because we can't just go and get something.

Although we made a lot of our own games, books and puzzles, this has still required a supply of paper, cardboard, glue, contact plastic, and so on. The kids needed pencils, pens, paint and brushes, and, as they grew, these things were always on the shopping list when we got to town. We usually went out twice a year, but one trip would only be as far as Haast and Queenstown, neither of which had much of what we needed at a reasonable price at that time. So with only one proper shopping trip per year, the list was a long one.

Having started on brown paper from flour and potato bags, by the time Christan was three or four he wanted to paint on calico — 'Like Dad!' — with paint that came out of tubes. Up to the age of 10, when he suddenly lost interest and took up sport instead, paints and brushes were always on the shopping list and the Christmas list, and he bought finer and finer brushes as Robert did: a 0, a 00 and even a 000. He made himself some pocket money, too, selling his paintings and bone carvings to friends, and once we caught the post in the nick of time to send two of his paintings to an exhibition at the COCA gallery in Christchurch.

His first financial transaction is a family joke. While Robert talked to Ross Crump about the painting he wanted to order, Christan, aged six, showed his painting to Ross's friend. Robert thought he had seen something changing hands, but he didn't say anything until later when they were hitchhiking back to the bach we were staying in at Neil's Beach.

'Did she give you some money?'

'Yes.'

'How much?'

'It had a twenty on it.'

'Was it paper or a coin?'

'Paper.'

He bought some paint, a fancy paintbrush for fine work, and a birthday present for Robin and Robert. He also bought some stamps, as he had been enjoying writing letters at the time.

Holidays in Australia included Christmas a few times, so travelling home again with all the shopping we'd done there plus Christmas presents was a major effort. Neither Robert nor I weigh very much, and with two small children the airlines were usually quite generous towards us when it came to excess baggage, at least before tickets got cheaper and restrictions tighter. We even managed to bring home the *Encyclopædia Brittanica* over two trips. You might think it would have been easier to buy it here, but it would never have happened. These people wanted to sell it having bought the CD-Rom version, and Robert's father was keen to pay for it, so transport was the easiest part. We turned up to the check-in counter with it packed into suitcases, hand-luggage and duty-free bags, and went back a couple of years later for the rest of it. It was really handy to have it on the shelf to refer to for schoolwork or even general conversation, and for me it meant that I wasn't always wrong anymore and didn't have to wait three months to prove it.

One day while looking up 'Nickelodeon', I found Gorge River mentioned in the first few lines at the top of the page, as one of three places in the world, with British Columbia and the Urals, where nickel-iron occurs naturally. This must be the heavy silver-coloured metal that Robert finds in the gold pan, locally known as awaruite. Now, what is the chance of opening up the *Encyclopædia Brittanica* to the (presumably) one page where Gorge River is mentioned, I wondered? And I actually did it again after the Indian Ocean tsunami, looking for the Nicobar Islands.

Once we had the internet, of course, the kids scorned the encyclopædia, and I'd race them to see who could find the answer first. After a year or so, they generally beat me, but I still win on a cloudy day when there is no power to run the computer at the required time, unless it is something that wouldn't be in a 1987 encyclopædia.

Letter-writing was a popular school subject. The kids put their names into the Kiwi Conservation Club newsletter asking for penpals, and Robin received six interested answers. Her schoolwork for the next week was to write to them about her trip to town six times over. Whenever we had the chance to work on a computer she typed her letter and sent off six copies.

At nine, Christan made a bet with Robin (six) that he could read *The Wright Brothers* faster than she could read *The Littles*. He lost to cries of 'It's not fair!' on the second day, and took four more days to finish. He had no idea that Robin was reading quite so well, but mostly she would be right up there for any challenge.

Christan's handwriting lesson when he was 12 took the form of writing in a diary each day. Among all the reports of the cricket and rugby scores, how many possums, stoats and rats he'd caught and whether Chooky had laid that day, there is the occasional scathing report about his little sister spilling her porridge on the floor or climbing into Mum and Dad's bed during a thunderstorm. ('The chicken!') She could get her own back, though. On the front of the book where there is a space to write your name he had written *Christan Long* in black, and someone else has come along later with a blue pen and added *is dum*.

Most of my ideas were treated as boring on principle, but one success we had was the writing of newspaper reports. Christan produced the front page of 'The Gorge Weekender' for Sunday, 2 February 2002, price 80 cents, after Howard Paterson and his four friends tramped through here.

The main article stated: 'Howard Paterson is the richest man in the South Island. He owns many large sheep stations and 55% of the eggs in NZ are laid by his chickens.'

As well as other small articles his front page contained:

- sports results — 'Mum beat Christan and Robin at cricket on Saturday', followed by the scores
- advertisements containing prices he'd found on the labels of the meat the trampers had left behind — Bill the Butcher Specials:
Fillet steak	$19/kg
Loin chops	$18.50/doz
Venison leg steak	$18/kg
- an index and the editor's contact details including a fictional website — www.gorgeriver@sw.nz — the only websites we had at the time were at the end of the parry ducks' legs.

I taught them about the five Ws and an H to be used when writing a newspaper report: who, what, when, where, why and/or how. Robin's article (three years later) was entitled 'Egg Laid'.

Who? — the hen belonging to the Longs

What? — laid an egg

When? — the date, February 2005

Where? — in her box, the usual spot

How/Why? — because it was certainly about time she did!

There was also an advertisement for new-laid eggs: 'Be quick, cheep!'

This was a small article to fill up the front page. The main headline arrived in a couple of Long Ranger helicopters, on 4 February 2005. We'd been sitting in fog for five days but could often see blue sky just up through the gorge, and the helicopters flew in from there.

John Grove, a Lancastrian businessman from Hong Kong, owned the first one. His partner, Thea, was with him, resplendent in white shorts and diamonds. They introduced us to Monica in short tights and a short, frilly dress, and her very German mother, Esther.

'Is she your sister?' I asked Thea as John handed around the insect repellent. She looked enough like her to be, and Thea was also German.

'No!' she answered, quite definitely. Oops.

Jeff Sly appeared from the far side of the chopper. He'd taught John to fly on his twice-yearly trips to Millbrook, near Arrowtown, and still came along for safety's sake on flights through the mountains.

The second chopper landed, piloted by Mel Jones who owned the hangar in Auckland where John left his helicopter between visits to New Zealand. He had onboard Martina, an athletic-looking lady in Nike clothing, Stefan who was introduced as her coach, and a blonde curly-haired lady from Auckland who was the tour guide. We couldn't remember her name but she looked like our friend Cathy Mountier, so in Robin's newspaper report she is called 'Cathy Ringlets'.

We invited them in, and as I handed out cups of tea Martina commented that she'd never drunk so much tea in her life as she had since landing in New Zealand. Jeff asked Robert to show them his greenstone carvings, and he handed around dolphins and penguins in various stages of production. You don't often get to see a finished one around here, as generally as soon as they are finished they are sent or taken to whoever has asked for them. This time, however, he had a finished painting for John and was concentrating on him to finalise the payment, and so it was some time before Martina could get his attention. When she asked about the prices of the carvings Robert answered vaguely, not realising that she had taken it as a final quote.

'How can I contact you? Do you have an email address?'

Robert, sitting beside her, pointed out that she could just ask him.

Having made a definite order, she now had his full attention.

'What's your address?' he asked. 'To send it to.'

'Just send it to Mel,' she said, but Robert was reluctant. We didn't know Mel, but helicopter pilots in general can be unreliable. They have so many customers that they can hardly be expected to remember one from sometimes several months before.

'I'll remember,' Mel assured Robert.

By this time Jeff was just about busting to tell me who these people were who didn't want to give any names or addresses.

'Have a look on the front page of the newspaper,' he said in an aside to me as we walked back out to the choppers. Robert at the workbench inside the front door was still being convinced and writing down Mel's address in Auckland.

On the front page of the copy of *The Press* they'd brought us, Martina Navratilova and Monica Seles had played a charity match the previous day in Christchurch, against Andrew Mehrtens and Carlos Spencer.

When Christan enrolled with the Correspondence School for his secondary schooling, it was a relief for everyone. He really needed something coming from the outside world, and he loved communicating with his teachers, particularly his form teacher, Pam Henson. He was happy to do all sorts of projects that he would never have done for me, and was quite — well, at least moderately — enthusiastic. It was so different to working all week just to have your mum say, 'Oh yes, good work. Now do it again next week.'

Robin kept up the tradition of disinterest and argufying for another year, until she enrolled at intermediate level, as Christan should have, in hindsight. Her teacher was more worried, not for the standard of Robin's work but for her lack of social interaction. Speaking on the phone once or twice a year while we were in town, she found Robin to be a master of monosyllabic answers, which isn't unusual amongst children of that age but is definitely disconcerting at the other end of a phone-line. After Pam visited us, tramping through here during the summer holidays, she was able to reassure Robin's teacher that she enjoyed a rich and varied life.

Not that it was all perfectly wonderful, even on Correspondence, as evidenced by my letter to friend Lucy Bellerby in 2007: 'Schoolwork is driving me nuts. Christan is supposed to be doing exams as soon as they arrive with the mail but can't remember what he learnt yesterday. I've given up on him which seems to have made some difference.'

So unfortunately, although delighted, I was a bit scathing at first when Christan won not only the prize for the best student studying Science in Years 9, 10 and 11, but also the Rural Women's New Zealand Golden Jubilee Prize for excellence and attitude to schoolwork for any student living in a remote area.

'Excellence and attitude?!'

On reflection, I had to agree that they would hardly know about his attitude, and I wouldn't send anything away until it *was* excellent.

Two years later, Robin won the Award for excellence in Science in Years 7 to 10, then the Rural Women's Prize at the end of Year 11. Each of them was invited to Wellington to receive the latter prize.

Chapter 12

THE FAMINE OF 1999

We had asked Roger to call in sometime with a load of groceries while he was in the area during the Roar, but by mid-April 1999, it became apparent that he wasn't coming. We sent a letter out with the last hunting party to say that we would need him by the end of the month, and whenever a plane or helicopter flew by we'd stand outside to watch, trying to identify the pilot and speculating on their purpose. Still, there was no sign of Roger.

The last day of April came and went, but on 1 May we all trooped out at the sound of an approaching plane. We knew that it wasn't Roger, always recognisable by his approach, and indeed the plane was flying high above the hill behind us. We'd already turned to go back to work when it banked and began to lose height and, for the first time since I'd been here, a Cessna 206 landed on the strip. David Bunn, father of Roger's partner, Debbie, brought the news that Roger had put his tail wheel into a pot-hole on a rough airstrip and bent the frame of his plane. It was nothing too serious, but, with two other planes in the same condition waiting for the 'jig' in front of him, it looked like it would be a long time. Meanwhile, we had a nice visit from David and a large load of supplies to be going on with, including a 25-kilogram sack of milk powder which was to make all the difference in the months to come.

There was plenty in the garden, and the boys were always keen to catch fish or collect seafood. With stored dry goods we managed well enough until it was time to walk out to Haast in July. Roger's news was of further delays and hold-ups, but he thought he'd be in the air in three weeks and would come to us straight away. Morgan Saxton offered us a flight back home in his helicopter, but, knowing that he wouldn't take much money from us, we didn't like to load up too much with food. We took enough to get through three more weeks with what was left at home, and it was the best helicopter flight I'd ever had.

Three weeks passed, then a fourth. The flour was long-gone, and there was no more wheat to grind. Eggs, butter and rolled oats were distant memories. The kids were eating brown rice all day, with sugar, sultanas and milk. The beans had gone, but there were still lentils and split peas for days when it was too rough to fish off the rocks at the end of the airstrip. We rarely caught more than one yellow-eyed mullet in the net in the river mouth during the winter.

At the end of five weeks we took stock. Cooking oil was gone, sultanas and sugar finished, and there was enough rice for five days. It was time to do something about it for ourselves.

A fishing boat passed by and we asked Darren King-Turner to make a phone-call for us. Remembering that the last time we'd asked him for anything, he'd forgotten to stop to take us out to Milford Sound two weeks before Christan was born, we didn't count on him too much, but as he had two children of his own by this time it was worth a try.

Next morning Robert headed up the coast to round up all of the emergency caches of (can you guess?) rice, sugar and sultanas, which we store on both sides of the river. Enough for another week. While he was away Darren called back to say that Roger would be here in three more days. It turned into five days, but at last he came.

Four days after that he was back again. We flew to Big Bay, fished for whitebait for a couple of weeks with Graeme and Anne Mitchell, and returned home well fed. The kids always appreciated a good feed of meat after a lean winter, and we often seemed to eat half as much food afterwards as we had been before we went.

One day, Mitch was getting frazzled trying to co-ordinate the aeroplane landing with the weather as well as with driving a load of frozen bait across the river on the tractor while the tide was out. During a pause in the radio conversation he looked across at me and observed, 'You don't have to worry about things like this.'

'We've just waited for five weeks,' I pointed out.

Because our food reserves had been exhausted, we told Roger that we would need him again in two weeks. Even a huge load of food doesn't go far without our usual backstop, and during the whitebait season, when the plane always carried a full load, there was no room for anything extra.

Ten days later, Paddy Freaney and Rochelle Rafferty from

the Bealey pub near Arthur's Pass tramped by on their way to Big Bay and the Hollyford, and happened to mention to Roger that we were going out soon. This was the case, but we needed food to get out and he didn't come.

Again the weeks went by, but Christan and Robert were catching a wee bit of whitebait. In the fourth week we had four lots of visitors, all bearing loaves of bread, and we lived on bread and whitebait. One loaf was fresh from a bread-maker on a barge moored on Lake McKerrow! Peter Bowmar brought a pound of butter and some cheese with the bread. At the end of the week Rick Aubrey, from Dalrachnie Station near Omarama, landed in his Cessna 180 with his mate. After a cup of tea, they walked down to check out the airstrip, and while they were gone I looked for more wheat to set behind the stove to dry before I could grind it. I was stunned to find that this was the last of it! Having little else, we'd eaten nearly 15 kilograms of wheat in a month! We asked Rick to ring Roger again, please, and find out what was happening. Roger got the message but was mustering for the next few days on his high-country station, Mt Soho, and yet another week went by before we saw him.

Having given up on him, I packed up the last bit of ground millet and rice to make porridge, the last of the hand-ground wheat flour, and various other last little bits and carried it 12 kilometres up the beach to the other side of Sandrock Bluff. The kids, aged eight and five, ate more than they could carry and we were also well-loaded with raincoats, lifejackets, a large piece of black plastic that we could camp under in case of emergency, foam mats, sleeping bags, etc. We counted on having a day or two off at Barn Bay, as it was a long way for them to walk without a break. We had run out of time for Robert to take a full load of food to Barn Bay, as we wanted to be in Haast before the end of the whitebait season. Robert had paintings to deliver to people who would be heading back over the hill as soon as the season finished. If I carried the food over Sandrock Bluff, he could ferry the extra load for the last stretch while the kids and I walked more slowly to Barn Bay. I also left a small amount of food to replace our emergency caches on either side of the Spoon River.

I arrived home to find that Roger had been, and we had bacon and eggs and fish and chips for tea! There was cheese and butter and all sorts of things. Three days later, although we weren't hungry anymore, Robert noticed that actually he'd felt better before! The good thing about going through a tough time or doing things the hard way is the feeling of accomplishment you are left with at the end of it. He felt razor-sharp and enjoyed being totally focused on putting food on the table to feed his family. We often look back at that time with a shared sense of achievement and occasionally even with nostalgia, when the cupboard is bulging and the eggs are going off faster than we can eat them or we arrive at the shop without having actually run out of anything for ages.

Still we have not quite reached the end of the story. At Christmas, Roger arrived with a small box of new potatoes and asked, 'Don't you have any in the garden?'

'Well, no,' I replied. 'We ate them and had nothing left to plant.'

A hundred and fifty years ago in the pioneering settlements at Jackson Bay and Martins Bay you would go hungry rather than eat your seed potatoes. Even when things get tough around here, it isn't really that far to the supermarket.

Chapter 13

FAMILY DYNAMICS

F irst deserve, then desire.

At the beginning of the transcendental meditation Sidhi course I took in 1989, we were promised: 'For a sidha, everything you desire will come. If it doesn't come, go and get it. If you can't find it, make it.'

It is human nature to hanker for something different. The grass is always greener on the other side of the fence.

'Which do you prefer, Master?' asked the chela. 'Uphill or down?'

And the master replied, 'Down when I am going up, and up when I am going down.'

W alking over boulders, I look forward to the sandy stretch five kilometres ahead, temporarily forgetting that carrying a heavy pack on sand is a real killer. Sweating up the beach to Barn Bay on a hot, windless, bug-filled day in the summer, I can't wait for the cool, shady bush track out to the Cascade the next day, which is also muddy and boggy and may involve climbing around windfalls.

For a long time I wanted a stainless-steel sink, thinking it would solve so many problems. We had scrubbed the yellow Formica bench-top so many times that it was mainly white, and in places even the white had given way to the dark wood underneath. Through a crack in the join between the sink and the bench, it also dripped into the food cupboard below if you were not careful, and so was hardly hygienic. I complained to Robert that the bench didn't drain back into the sink properly and that water pooled in the back corner.

'It will probably take me all day to fix it,' he said.

'That's about how long I've spent already, wiping it down,' I insisted, so he had a look. By inserting a small stone underneath the corner, the water ran off beautifully. Shortly afterwards the whole sink was moved to a different place in the rebuild of the hut, and, although the drainage wasn't bad enough to complain about, it wasn't as good as it had been.

So I thought all my dreams were coming true when we found a stainless-steel sink bench in a wrecker's yard in Dunedin, and some months later it arrived home in an aeroplane. It was a huge improvement and I love having it, but I also learned a valuable life lesson from it: no matter what you have, there will always be bad points as well as good points.

The bench came with a 15-centimetre-high back on it to protect the wall, which was great but meant that we had to raise the shelf behind the sink by 15 centimetres. As we didn't want to raise the next shelf as well, it is now very pokey to get into, particularly when there are cups hanging on hooks in front of it. Then, as the sun gradually dropped lower in the sky in the autumn, we needed a curtain on the window until mid-afternoon to stop the glare of the reflection off the stainless steel. Although it was so much easier to clean, I'd forgotten how much it would show all the water marks, particularly when our water comes off a limestone face. And yes, you guessed it — it doesn't drain!

We bought a second-hand toilet cistern from the same place. Although beautifully clean and white, it took a lot of work to stop it leaking…

Happiness is in wanting what you have.

Neither of our families has really understood how hard we work, and how we each have to play our part. For example, when my grandmother died in January 2007 and I flew out to spend a couple of nights in Dunedin with my sister and talk on the phone to Mum and my brother, I left a gap that the others couldn't easily fill. While I was away, Robert, Christan and Robin had flown to Big Bay with our 30 possum traps. They had also made a drop-net which they planned to throw over any unfortunate possum whose path they crossed, to slow it down a bit until Christan could hit it. While they waited for night to fall, they had cooked paua and thistlenuts over a fire on the beach six kilometres away from the hut. Armed with torches, the drop-net and a big stick, they had caught five possums on the way back, before boiling a few sausages on the wee gas cooker at about midnight. After the meal they cleared and reset the nearby traps, many of which would catch two possums in a night. With 30 traps they caught 87 possums in three nights.

They hadn't been in the hut long enough to collect wood or light the fire, though, and there wasn't enough gas to waste on heating water to wash the dishes. So on walking through the door, my first job was to light the fire and wash all the greasy plastic bowls. That done, I started to cook the enormous amount of food that had to be dealt to if we didn't want to carry it all home with us in two days' time, ahead of the next front. If I cooked it, they'd eat it; but they were working too hard to have any energy left over to bother about food or dirty dishes. Whenever we arrive back at the hut after we've been working together, three of us flop down exhausted, but the fourth — me — has to cook a meal before getting to stop. I'm an important part of the team, and without me they can work on only three cylinders.

'Half a cylinder,' Robin says.

The following year Christan had a better spotlight — mounted on a piece of elastic around his head, and its battery carried in a canvas belt he'd made. While I stumbled behind in the dark, he could run up the bouldery creek bed and through patches of gorse chasing after possums with a club. They don't run very fast, and if they didn't climb too far up a tree he could often catch them. Big Bay was crawling with possums, and again we went home with a good load of fur.

When Christan pulls the skin off the head and front legs of a possum, it makes me think of him as a toddler yelling 'I don't want to have a bath!'

I don't want to kill, pluck or skin a possum or even set a trap if I can get out of it, but I'm happy to carry loads, bury carcasses in the garden, and wash all the stinky clothes at the end of it. These days Christan might get home for only a week or 10 days, and sometimes when he leaves, having worked up to the last moment, there'll be piles of traps and smelly clothes, skins on boards, off boards, and waiting to be tacked out — possums everywhere in various states of undress — and an almighty mess of fur and unidentifiable disgusting bits in the workshop. We wave goodbye and spend the next three days finishing the job, but we might have 80 skins to be dressed at the end of it and a big bag of plucked fur worth $120 per kilogram. This has provided Christan with a respectable amount of money to pay off his student loan and to buy all the expensive toys he seems to need. Another time after a long spell of growing soft in town, Christan had blistered hands by the end of the first night, but he carried on plucking and skinning for three more days after the blisters had burst. We are proud to see the work ethic that he has learnt from us. Robert gashes his finger on a sharp rock, binds it up with orange route-marking tape, and plucks the next three possums with his left hand before he goes back for a Band-aid.

It is not unusual for Robert to paint until one in the morning in order to finish a section before it starts to dry, and on average he works 10 or 12 hours a day, seven days a week. In Mooloolaba someone is always telling me that I work too hard, whereas there I'm just having a holiday. Even the neighbours lean over the fence to tell us that you can't work after 10 in the morning because it is too hot!

We do more work in the first three days back at home than in a month over there. The house takes several days to make habitable again, having first slashed a path to the front door through the weeds in the garden. Rats and spiders have to be evicted, although luckily spiders don't bear a grudge. Inevitably, they are invited back the next day to deal to the sandfly problem, particularly when I get too enthusiastic about cleaning years' worth of spiders' webs out of cracks around windows. It is a bonus to fly home on a no-sandfly day, so we can have all the doors and windows open to air out the smell of mould tinged with mouse. After Robert finished rebuilding the floor and we'd shovelled out the compost heap that had been supporting it, the smell was more the other way around as the mould problem was so much improved, but the West Coast is always a damp place.

One day we received a message from a TVNZ producer in Auckland that she was coming to see us within two weeks, so we began cleaning. Apart from spiders' webs and all the daily stuff, I aired bedding and towels, cleaned out dirty corners, found various rotten potatoes in the middle of full bags that had been around for a while, cleaned out the food cupboard, washed my hair about 50 times, baked cakes, changed, washed and mended clothes, even washed the windows behind Robert's workbench. On a Sunday, imagining that we were fairly safe, we cleaned out the shed only to get a fright when a helicopter landed, albeit not with the expected TV crew. We then spent two days hauling seaweed off the beach, carted firewood back to the shed, tidied up outside the hut a hundred times and just about wore out the broom, before we decided that she must have changed her mind — while expecting her to arrive with a moment's notice, just when we were in the normal state of chaos.

Robert has called me a workaholic, and certainly in a rough spot I will stomp out and dig something or haul loads rather than resort to the whisky, if we had any. That attitude certainly comes in handy around here.

Within a week of arriving home one summer, a huge load of seaweed settled on the beach about a hundred metres beyond the end of the airstrip, whereupon we all downed tools and gathered as much as we could for the next two days. We carried sacks of it and dumped it onto a pile at the nearest point on the strip where it would be safe from reclamation by the sea. In fine, hot weather it begins to compost quickly, and gives off so much heat that the kids put a billy full of water into it to see how hot it would get. Generally it rains before long, which halts the process, and we cart it back to the garden over the next few months by the trolley load.

This seaweed pile washed away during the second night — 'Too bad,' we said, 'but we've got enough for now' — but was back again two days later, another hundred metres further down the beach.

'Oh great!' we groaned — and went back to work for 10 more days.

Robin says it is one of her favourite smells of childhood, from the time when they were babies and had to accompany us. They played in it or collected samples to stick into their book for the Early Childhood teacher at the Correspondence School. As they grew they had their own small bag to collect it, but even at 50 cents a bag they required a lot of cajoling to do much. I'd nag and harangue and set minimum limits of 10 bags each, then grumpily make my point by collecting 40 or 50 bags myself. It would be more like 20 or 30 for the next couple of days, then 10, sometimes day after day, until I'd be praying that the sea would just take it back, please.

This day seemed like a good one to employ Robin's emerging stubborn streak. She had spotted a possum-skin kiwi in a shop in Queenstown just before we came home and she *wanted* it. But it cost $18, and there was *no way* she was having it.

'I'll buy it with my own money!' she cried, and still it was 'No!'

'If you get 36 bags today, I'll buy you the possum-skin kiwi. At 50 cents a bag that's $18.'

And she was into it! We got nine bags before the tide came in too far and made us stop for a break. In the afternoon we got another nine bags and stopped for a swim. Before we finished the next nine bags, Robert and Christan, who had carried 25 bags, walked up the beach to go diving, and I had to be home by 6.40 to hear the weather forecast on the radio. So we carried straight on. Robin finished her last three bags alone after I'd gone home with a trolley load to put on the garden, and later that night I wrote a letter to our friend Debbie McColl in Arrowtown, explaining the situation and asking her to spend the enclosed money on Seaweed, the possum-skin kiwi at the Kiwi Gift Shop.

Sometimes, a pile of seaweed stays only for a single tide and we dodge between incoming waves to grab a bit more as they take it away. One morning after a big flood, I found myself lifted bodily and carried 10 metres up the beach in a surprisingly large wave, in a solid soup of leaves and seaweed. I stood up spitting and laughing, with beech leaves in my hair, down my shirt and in my ears, still clutching a sodden, heavy bag half full of the stuff.

'That's enough!' I called, exhausted but exhilarated, and headed home for a hot shower and breakfast.

Chapter 14

FATHER CHRISTMAS LANDS ON THE AIRSTRIP

It was very special to me to have my family here for Christmas when the kids were little. The only time my grandmother saw my kids, she was 83 and had recently been diagnosed with Parkinson's disease. As I helped her out of the aeroplane and supported her, she clutched me saying, 'I'm not standing yet.'

I was sad at seeing how old she'd become and how she was withdrawing into herself; sorry that my kids would never know her as I had. Christan, who was six, remembers her fairly well, but Robin was only three and hardly does. A steady source of energy and strength, she was the driving force in our family for as long as I could remember. Still, she was their great-grandmother, not grandmother, and they would have to remember her differently while having a great time with their cousin, Madeleine.

'I don't know how you ever get anything done,' my grandmother said to Robert. 'I had a holiday in Italy many years ago, beside the sea. We were going to write letters and do all sorts of things, but we spent the whole time sleeping. The sea is very soporific.'

'Yes, I love lying in bed,' Robert answered, 'and the rain on the roof...'

On Christmas Eve in Mooloolaba when Christan was five, an aeroplane flew over silently with landing lights flashing, on approach to the airport at Coolum.

'Look, Christan, there goes Father Christmas in his sleigh!'

The next time we were there, the kids were seven and four and they each had a gift for everyone — mostly things they had made, like pictures and bookmarks. It was lovely to see them get as much pleasure out of giving as receiving gifts, and it diffused the frenzy of unwrapping one present after another.

While we were there we went to see Father Christmas at the shopping mall, a middle-aged man with his own grey beard and a broad Australian accent. His jokes were truly dreadful, but he was quite funny when he laughed and jiggled the pillow up his coat with both hands. Christan was definitely unimpressed and so, rather than have him disillusioned, I told him (as I had always been told) that this was just somebody dressed up. The real Father Christmas only came on Christmas Eve and was far too busy to be visiting shopping malls around the world.

Christan wanted a fishing rod, which was easy, but Robin wanted a dolls' house. It wasn't possible to buy anything I wanted to give her for a reasonable amount of money, and there was also the issue of getting it home. But she was delighted with a small plastic fold-up case with dolls in it. We also found some dolls' furniture on flat sheets of craft wood that pushed out and fitted together. It wasn't any great favourite and quickly disappeared into the toy box with lots of other junk, but it solved the problem adequately at the time.

A couple of years later we made a proper dolls' house at home from stones and plaster on a wonky wooden frame. I lined the inside with cardboard and decorated it secretly for Christmas, making some of the furniture to add to a few things I'd bought. I was very proud of my velvet lounge suite, bookshelves, sink bench and stove, bath and toilet, and the cross-stitched cushions on the kitchen chairs. Robin had a Maori doll and a baby, but it was five or six months before we were able to buy a matching father doll. We explained his absence with a story that he was Tuku Morgan, a NZ First MP who at the time often featured on the Radio New Zealand news. He had to be away a lot in Wellington for the sitting of Parliament. Later we set the dolls' house up outside with a landscaped garden, took photos of everything and turned it into a book. Tuku Morgan, in a blue suit and tie, flies home from The Beehive, courtesy of Buzzy Bee, and we also see him in the bathroom in his infamous red satin underpants!

I called Christmas a good one when the kids played for at

least the first 24 hours with whatever they were given. Christan was eight or nine when I bought him an antique set of Meccano from a dealer in the North Island, and, although it didn't seem like very much at first, we decided that if it had come in a box with each different-shaped piece stacked in a slot in a plastic tray, it would have looked like much more. The man had also included a clockwork Magic Motor, and Christan built a crane and raised increasingly large loads of blocks to see how many it could lift.

'It can lift 20 blocks!'

'It can lift 40!'

'It can lift 100!'

Sadly, it couldn't manage 132 and that was the end of that. It was a valuable lesson in the consequences of pushing the limits, and one we often reminded him of over the years.

Robert built the new shower cubicle with a wall 80 centimetres high at the front to help keep the wooden floor dry. 'I didn't build it that high for you to see if you can splash right over it!' he told the kids the first time they bathed inside it in the fish-case.

In Mooloolaba for another family Christmas, now aged 10 and seven, the kids wanted an electronic piano with a lot of urging from Robert. Dick Smith Electronics had four in their range, two of which were not what we had in mind. We checked out the other two in terms of how we could run them at home, as I didn't want to be keeping up a constant supply of batteries (eight size Ds at a time), and even the cost of rechargeable batteries and a charger was far more than I was prepared to spend. The top one in the range appeared to be capable of running on 12 volts if I could get an appropriate adaptor for it, but by the time I'd sorted that out they were out of stock.

I asked the assistant to ring around to see what other stores had one on hand, as there was not enough time to order more in before Christmas, then I attempted to negotiate with Grandad about it.

'Why not buy the next one up or down?' he said.

'The next one down won't run on 12 volts, and the next one up would have to be from a proper music shop and would be much too expensive.'

So I persuaded Ngaire to detour on our way to visit the cousins in Brisbane — and, after all that, there was new stock in the local shop with days to spare before Christmas.

After the kids and grandparents were in bed, I baked brioche and muffins for breakfast, as Christmas Day was also Ngaire's birthday and there were 15 people in the house. When at last I came to bed, Robin woke up before I'd had a chance to put the batteries in the electric piano, and so I had to wait until she went back to sleep, without nodding off myself.

Getting Christmas presents on time became quite nerve-wracking after we were caught up in the Queenstown flood in November 1999. I had wanted to buy two boogie boards for Christmas, but the shop was out of stock. They would get them for me when the flooding subsided and the courier van could get through the Kawarau Gorge, and then post them out to us care of Roger. We flew home over Wanaka, still flooded to the shop fronts, and waited for Roger to come before Christmas with groceries and mail.

On Christmas Eve I looked at the clock and said, 'He's got about 15 minutes to get here if he wants to be home before it's too dark.'

He was on the ground in five minutes.

'I've got to get back,' he said, 'or Santa won't come.' He was a busy man.

Yet another year, I had a mask and snorkel put away for Robin and something else for Christan when his flipper split down the back. So now I was in a fix! It was going to look pretty strange if Father Christmas didn't bring him new flippers when he so badly needed them. In the end, I asked a tramper for a big favour: could she please buy a pair and post them to us.

Finally, though, I got careless, and Robin was dreadfully disappointed to discover an empty packet that I hadn't thrown away properly.

To make schoolwork a bit more exciting at the end of 1999, the kids had written letters to themselves and put them into stamped, self-addressed envelopes inside another envelope addressed to the NZ Post Stamps Centre to be postmarked on 1 January 2000 in Gisborne, the first city in the world to see the sun rise that day. They also entered a poster competition for a convention to be held at Massey University early in the new millennium to discuss renewable energy. The topic was: 'How would you capture the first rays of sunshine of the new millennium?'

Christan painted a sunrise up the Gorge River valley, with himself sitting in the workshop, solar panel on the roof, working with the 12-volt grinder on a greenstone dolphin — a symbol of peace for the new millennium — with dolphins swimming past the front door in the sea.

Robin would be turning five before the end of the year, so we also entered her poster. She painted a sunrise with a glittery gold sun shining down onto our solar torch, which shone into the green, metallic reinforcement-ring eyes of a possum in a trap. Below that, she made a pot of 'Millennium stew' with orange paper carrot rings and peas punched out of green paper. Our thinking was that if all the world's computers did succumb to the widely predicted Y2K bug, and the financial world ground to a halt, we would survive on possums and Jerusalem artichokes.

On 28 December 1999 Morgan Saxton flew in a middle-aged couple with their deckchairs, chillybins, a gun and a fishing rod to watch the sun set on the twentieth century. They had a satellite cellphone which we were keen to have a look at, but we left them alone at first thinking that there was plenty of time for them to come and see us when they wanted to. Just then a tramper arrived to be rowed across the river, and later we saw him sitting shirtless in the sun in one of the deckchairs talking to the other man. About three hours later we were swimming in the river when Morgan returned. The chillybins and deckchairs were reloaded, and I caught a glimpse of the lady's long blonde hair under her pretty hat as they climbed back in and flew away. I hadn't even said hello to her! The tramper told us that the sandflies had been bothering her, and inside the hut all the holes in the screens had been taped over. Perhaps she found the bathroom facilities a bit primitive, too, but I wondered where she thought she had been coming to.

We had seen the oystercatchers making a big fuss on the other side of the river and had spotted two chicks, so we set up a couple of stoat traps nearby to hopefully improve their chances of survival. In the late afternoon of New Year's Eve we saw them again but on our side of the river, and were surprised that they could swim so well when they obviously couldn't yet fly. But the most noticeable thing about them was that, although they were only 12 centimetres long, they were completely black and looked exactly like the adults in miniature. A couple of days later the adults were bathing in a relaxed manner in the river, obviously unencumbered by chicks.

It rained all day on the thirty-first and we weren't very hopeful about seeing the last sunset of the old millennium. According to the tide tables, the sun had set in Hokitika and Greymouth by 9.15pm, but at 9.20 a ray of light burst through the clouds in the sou'west.

'Quick!' we cried, and dashed out to see what we could of the sunset.

But where was Robin? Although she was only five, this was an historic, never-to-be-repeated occasion. Whether she remembered it or not, it was important that she should see it, so I went back to find her. At that time of the evening in the summertime you can't go out without grabbing a hat and some extra clothing for protection from the sandflies, and Robin, who was very keen on nice clothes, had never mastered the quick grab-and-run technique the rest of us had. Sure enough, I found her crying into her clothes box because she couldn't find a pair of pants that she wanted to wear.

We listened on the radio to New Millennium celebrations an hour apart around the world. Fireworks by radio are quite unimpressive.

'Ooooh! The red ... and the green ... and the bluuue!'

On the first of January, I asked Robin what she thought of the new millennium as she climbed out of bed.

'Not much,' came the reply. 'Didn't see any fireworks, no balloons...'

Chapter 15

FISHY TALES

Robert had speared an eel through the net, and was trying to grab hold of it without lifting the spear which had no barb. We were hungry and there was no way he was going to let the eel go, but meanwhile up on the bank two-year-old Christan had got his pants down to pee. Since he couldn't get them up again without help, he was yelling his head off with about half a million sandflies biting his backside.

At two, Christan was already a keen fisherman and whitebaiter. When we had hitchhiked to Christchurch to meet Robert's mother at the airport and driven back down with her to fly home, every time we crossed a river or a creek Christan asked, 'Whitebait? Eel?'

In Mooloolaba, as we walked past the pet shop and saw fish in tanks, he'd ask, 'Tea?'

He was six before we let him have a fish-hook to wave around and catch in someone's ear. Even when he found a fancy lure in his Christmas stocking, his overly careful, living-on-faith-but-God-helps-those-who-help-themselves parents had removed the sharp bit. He was perfectly happy even with a rock tied to the end of his line.

By the age of four he could tell 'big fish that got away' stories like no one over seven would even try. While this tendency to tell tall tales didn't start when three possum hunters camped in the DOC hut for three weeks in 1995, their visit certainly encouraged it. It was the best year we had ever had for rata flowering, and the last two trees on the river bank stood in scarlet magnificence until the end of March. We had been surprised to see the possum trappers at all, since we'd barely seen a possum at that stage, but it seemed that they were monitoring the whole of South Westland. Mike Bygate said they would see how they got on, as he sprinkled a bit of flour here and there, and if they caught three possums he'd have to get a bit more organised. But first, they were going fishing.

That night's fishing was literally the making of a legend, at least for the family of a four-year-old boy. Mike, Richard and Guy fished all night from the end of the airstrip, and, having lost the hook twice, they caught a *huge* shark — a one-metre grey boy — with three hooks in its mouth! Christan spent the next year or two trying to catch the fish that had taken so many of his 'hooks', while the fish itself grew bigger and bigger.

We scored the remains of a large bag of flour and a few other things when the boys flew back out, including a fishing reel with a hook and sinker. We didn't realise that Christan had taken it to the river by himself and set it in the best place to catch an eel, as we had assumed that all his talking about it was just that — talk. So imagine my surprise when he and Robert came back and he held up an eel almost as big as he was — his first true catch and a great photo for the book Gorge River Press was making for him: *Gone Fishing*. The kids loved these books, which were mainly about themselves and the things they were doing. It was a way of recording a bit of family history and a good thing to do with photos, and they could 'read' them before anything else.

This favourite was about Christan's fishing exploits throughout the changing seasons, and it was a delightful mixture of fact, fiction and fantasy. For example, having got an inflatable boat for Christmas, there had been endless discussion about rowing out to sea to set a craypot and how big the captured crayfish would be. Of course, Christan was never allowed in the boat alone, except perhaps in the river on the end of a rope, but in the book we have him apparently rowing out to sea in his rubber ducky. In the next picture, dressed in his fishy shirt, he poses beside our hand-woven, supplejack craypot, triumphantly holding up the crayfish (which was actually caught by Paul Cooper, a pilot from Makarora who'd been diving out at the island).

It was almost 10 years before we could hope to catch a crayfish at the end of the airstrip, by which time the fish were recovering well as a result of the Quota Management System. Still, a bit of fiction made a lovely story. When he snag-hooked a kahawai that was already stuck in the net, we took a photo of Christan standing beside the river with the fish lying on the sand beside him at the end of his line; he couldn't have lifted it. In the whitebait season he had a little net set in front of the big net, and, if Robert had the chance, he slipped a handful of bait into the little net before Christan got there. As for fantasy, on the last page of the book Father Christmas brings Christan a fishing lure to catch that great big fish that keeps taking all his 'hooks'.

Checking the net was usually the first adventure of the day, and Robert would come back in with the news: 'Two kahawai and five herrings' — and 'Two kaiwai, five ewwwing' came the echo.

When Robin was big enough to tag along, too, there would be two echoes. One day, when she was aged about three, and developing an extraordinarily direct way of seeing to the heart of the matter, she arrived home alone. I waited for a moment, as it wasn't often that she got to tell me the news first.

'So what's the report?' I asked as the silence continued. But instead of 'Three herrings, no kahawai', she replied, in a confiding fashion: 'Well, the *silly* part was Dad was carrying the whitebait and the fish-case and he dropped the bucket and all the whitebait landed in the sand and he picked them up and I helped pick out the rocks...'

At first Robert filleted all the fish, but sometime after Robin was born he taught me to do it. Christan would stand up at the sink for lessons in fish dissection, and Robin would get into the bucket to play with their eyes. Christan had a wooden knife at first, which he could use to scale fish, and he carried it around in a sheath 'like Dad do'.

At two years old, Robin showed a good grasp of anatomy by picking up one of Robert's carved dolphins and pointing to each end in turn. 'There head, there bum.' Luckily when Nana's friend gave Robin a doll a few weeks later, she didn't notice Robin's equally succinct assessment.

The first time Christan truly had a kahawai on his line, he played it, letting the line out and out as he'd been taught — until suddenly it *all* ran out and the fish took the lot! The line hadn't been tied on to the reel. He was disgusted, but it was a lesson well learned; to always tie your own gear and never trust anything made in China. The next time he hooked one, he was so determined that he hauled it straight in, never giving an inch.

The eel population has also recovered lately, and often in summer if we catch a few fish the eels get to them first, leaving a great tangle of net and just a few scraps. The time comes when Robert has to catch an eel to (a) have something to eat and (b) give them the message. Eels are highly intelligent, and it only takes one or two to be caught before the others back off from pinching fish for a while. They never get caught in the net, though. Once, Christan set an eel line using a piece of the previous eel for bait. As he watched, an eel came in to check it out, but suddenly veered away as though it had hit a barrier when it recognised the smell. It never came back.

Robert doesn't fuss about getting rid of the slime on an eel. We don't eat the skin anyway, so he splits it down the backbone and smokes it or grills it over a fire on the beach. I can't bear to watch as it twists and writhes in his hands. He stops after each cut, to change to a better grip. Even after it has been cut up into bits on a plate it still twitches, and if you sprinkle salt on it, it wiggles like it's ticklish and jumps off the rack!

It always reminds me of the great big mud-crab Dad caught when I was six. Its one big nipper was about 10 centimetres long, and Dad had tipped it out of the bag into the laundry sink. Whenever he tried to pick it up, it slashed at him. Finally he poked it with the hose from the washing machine, and, when it latched on to the hose, he grabbed it behind the nippers and dropped it into the big pot boiling on the stove. We heaved a sigh of relief as he put the lid on, but half a minute later we looked back to see the crab climbing out of the pot!

Fishing stories filled many of Christan's letters to his friends. 'We caught a kahawai with a trout in its tummy and the tail was sticking out of its mouth.' 'We caught a fish in the net and its tongue was sticking out and there was an eye in the middle of the tongue' — actually a whitebait in the fish's mouth.

My letters also often referred to the state of the fishing, but with the focus more on what there was to eat. 'We haven't been catching any fish lately. It would help if the net had more holes in it; that is, lots of small holes rather than just a few great big ones.' 'We expect Roger any time with a load of food — at least, we hope so. He gets a bit distracted once the whitebait season starts. We caught seven whitebait yesterday which is seven more than the first day last year so it could be a good season.'

There isn't much whitebait in this river — if there was, there would be half a dozen huts here — but given that the whitebait season is also spring and three of us have birthdays coming up, it is an exciting time of year when the grey warblers sing their whitebait song.

Often I would look at the quarter-cup of bait they brought me and wonder whether to waste an egg in it. On the other hand, if I added an egg at least there would be something to eat. Robert reckoned that being creative was about making something out of nothing.

'Oh, aye?' I replied. 'I'll take it down to nothing, but once we are out of everything it will be over to you.'

If you asked my Uncle Neill what flavour chips he wanted, he'd ask for 'fish and custard'. So imagine my glee when Robert, who is not very good at checking on the contents of a jar before pouring it into the bowl, grabbed the custard powder while making a batter for fish! (Mind you, I once poured cold porridge onto the top of a pie instead of the mashed potato and egg mixture in the other bowl.)

In his teens Christan was very keen to catch whatever whitebait he could. First, he built a stand across the river with driftwood and bits of rope, made screens and a net with sticks, supplejack and shade-cloth, and added buoys to keep the net floating when the tide came in. The next year, he bought himself several metres of whitebait netting and made a perfectly respectable sock-net on my sewing machine. With a screen on a long pole and a pair of waders for his birthday present, he spent so much time in the river that schoolwork could hardly be squeezed in sideways. He certainly didn't have time to fill the wood-box or tidy up his mess.

Our windmill produced 24 volts on windy days (and zero otherwise) to power the freezer, so he could keep his bait for a few days. The rest of us helped to sort it while keeping them alive, as often we'd pick half a kilogram out of three or four of dark, gutty bait, and we always let the others swim away. Overall, I guessed that we let 95 per cent of it go and considered ourselves good farmers of the resource. The possibility of having to eat it all in the case of a power failure also limited the amount we were prepared to keep unless we were expecting someone to arrive. But picking 1500 tiny, wriggling fish one at a time out of several kilograms? Do me a favour!

In October 2008, Roger and his co-pilot, Teresa Wilkins, flew us home from Big Bay in a gap between storms. Out at sea I could see a wind shear in the clouds, and the mist and spray of water spouts below it. I tapped Roger on the shoulder and pointed them out to him.

'I remember the first time I flew in a Cessna 180,' he told

us, unfazed. 'It was a day just like this and we flew all the way up the South Island. We had the shit kicked out of us!'

A five-minute flight to Gorge River was not too much to put up with, and Christan was staying safely behind at Big Bay to keep on fishing, but Willy Todd needed to be flown to Arrowtown that day with venison and whitebait. Now Roger knows his way through the mountains almost like the back of his hand — the way the wind flows over the tops and where the down-draughts are likely to be. But that day he couldn't fly quite where he would have liked to be, and they hit a big bump. When he had a chance to look back, Willy was sitting there with his headphones skew-whiff and the deer in his lap. One bucket of whitebait had fallen back down on its corner, whereupon the poorly fitted lid flew off, spilling bait everywhere. Roger's log book had flown out of the seat-pocket in a great flutter, before snapping shut with whitebait between each page. An email arrived later from Warrick Mitchell at Big Bay. The photo showed the aeroplane safely on the ground near Arrowtown, with whitebait dripping out the door: 'We're having such a good year, we're pouring it straight into the plane!'

Chapter 16

FEED THEM, CLOTHE THEM

Having done a Diploma in Naturopathy, Robert wanted to feed Christan a gluten- and dairy-free diet for the first year. At six months we started him on potato and yams, and gradually introduced other vegetables, and brown rice, millet and buckwheat. In hindsight, it should have been at least a couple of weeks sooner, as he could have done with something extra and I was pretty skinny and finding the walk out to the Cascade hard work.

My brother stayed with us at Neil's Beach for a few days before our wedding, and Mum and Dad were in another bach further down the road. One morning I looked everywhere without finding the food I had prepared the previous night for Christan's breakfast.

'Have you seen a cup with a bit of porridge in it?' I asked Andrew.

'Yes, I threw it out. I considered it my duty to rescue my nephew from cold porridge.'

Exasperated, I eyeballed him.

'We *fight* over leftover porridge. And what am I supposed to give him now?' I didn't want to light the fire just to cook half a cup of porridge when we were trying to be sparing with someone else's wood supply.

Once Christan was feeding himself, I made him little chapattis from leftover porridge or mashed vegetables, with enough buckwheat flour to hold it together, floured them and cooked them on the top of the stove. We also made balls with oat flour, and I could put all sorts of things into them like mashed swede without Christan objecting. Being skinny enough to appreciate any food meant that he was not a fussy eater, and he would eat most things we gave him, so long as it looked like he was eating whatever we were having. Robin, a child of easier times, was fussier.

We almost never had sugar, and we kept Christan off lollies until he was nearly three. At two-and-a-half he asked me for salt to sprinkle onto his orange, as he'd watched other kids putting sugar on theirs. Often someone arrived with a packet of lollies for him, but he didn't mind if we ate them. Fishermen Swag and Elmo radioed especially to tell Robert to row out to *Chinook* and collect some Easter eggs 'for the wee feller'.

'He hasn't got any teeth yet,' Robert objected.

'He won't need teeth,' Swag assured him.

Rowing out to a boat is not a simple process, and it was a couple of hours later, as Robert climbed off the boat into the dinghy, that Elmo said, 'Now don't you go eating them.'

We put them into a jar for Christan to roll around on the floor, and he enjoyed the shiny foil wrapping. We were very restrained and didn't eat them for about three weeks, by which time they were going downhill and had to be cleaned up.

Dave Saxton, the well-known helicopter pilot from Haast, always brought lollies amongst many other things, and one day stepping out of the chopper he opened a packet with a great flourish and presented Christan with his very first lolly. Christan took a bite, was unimpressed and dropped it, but this only lasted until our next visit to Neil's Beach. There, someone offered him a lollipop, and again he gave it a try before offering it to Robert, who accepted it with such obvious enthusiasm that Christan reconsidered his decision and took the lollipop back.

Sometime after that, with an air of having made a great discovery he said, 'Sugar's really nice!'

We stood on the beach one day, watching Robert row back in to shore after visiting Swag on *Sharcaree*.

'Last time Dad rowed in he had a piece of bread with jam, and he was bringing it in for us. It was sitting on the seat safely all the way in over the bar until he stood up, but when we grabbed the rope to pull the boat up the beach, the bread fell into the water in the bottom.'

Silence ensued as Robert negotiated a wave, waiting for a lull before the last dash into the beach. Then, 'Ooo-hooo . . . jam on!' Christan wailed.

But most of our food has to be prepared from scratch, and it doesn't always turn out as planned (or why you really don't want to know this recipe.):

*Separate 6 or 8 eggs. (This depends on how fast
they are going off, and how long it is before we
are due to walk out.) Add a pair of beaters, then
wander off to do something else, such as get the
fire going. In the meantime the bowl tips and
all the egg whites disappear down the plughole.
Start again.*

*Shake the sugar container to loosen the sugar.
Check that the lid is secure first. Alternatively,
clean up sugar from the bench, shelves and floor,
and wash the rest down the sink.*

*Now the flour. Hmmm… perhaps I should
just add it to the sink. (By this time, Christan is
laughing so hard he can barely stand up.)*

*Add a healthy shake of baking powder. Oops.
Now scoop some dry bits back out.*

*To bake: Place in a camp oven. Put plenty
of wood in the fire and cook until someone asks,
'What's burning?'*

*Alternative method: Get the fire going under
the camp oven, go gardening for several hours
and return to uncooked, soggy mess. Start again.*

In 1993 we were helping out at Barn Bay while Liz was
away. I was flabbergasted when Jennifer asked, 'How
come you are such a good cook?'

I'd never considered the possibility. Nor am I a good cook.
But Jennifer was nine at the time, and having anyone come
into your house for a week and cook something slightly
different would be a wonderful change. The food was nothing
flash, but it was perfectly presentable to three hungry
children and two fishermen who'd been out all day. The

ingredients were all provided, and the wood-burning stove worked wonderfully. It seems to me that virtually anything cooked by someone else is a good meal.

At three, Christan was keen to bake 'cakes'. He'd mix up hand-ground flour, water, sea water, lots of sedge grass seed, and maybe a bit of cinnamon. We didn't have sugar. When he was ready to begin the baking, I would come along and tactfully suggest adding a couple of things to make sure it would end up approximately edible.

By the time Robin was at the same stage, the food cupboard was in a much healthier state. Although Robert and Christan still ate leftover porridge cold, she wouldn't even finish it if it went cold in her bowl. When I made a loaf of bread she had her share of dough to shape into a loaf. Other kids would have got to pop their loaf into the oven in their own tin. However, as I didn't want to cook it separately after I'd cooked my own loaf, I convinced her to let me put it on top of mine or plait it and lay it on the top, so it could all be cooked at the same time. While she was fussier about food, she was otherwise easy to please.

Disastrous birthday cakes are almost a tradition. I made a particularly fancy one for Robert's birthday and put it into the camp oven while attempting to settle Robin to sleep at that point where she'd pretty much decided she didn't need an afternoon nap. The cake had been smelling suspicious for some time before I got back to it — to find I had all but cremated it.

I often made a soft cheese by draining yoghurt through a cheese cloth, but, although it tasted like cream cheese, it didn't behave like it. Still, I took some time to be convinced that it wouldn't work for cream-cheese icing, especially as I'd only try it once or twice a year for a birthday. There would be a grand plan of a yummy cake, but when we added icing sugar to the cheese it just went runny. For Christan's eighth birthday I made two round cakes with the middles cut out to form a figure '8', but the icing continuously ran off. It was a great laugh and a memorable occasion, and we took it into the bush with various bears for a teddy bears' picnic.

A few days later an 8-shaped birthday card arrived from Anne Mitchell at Big Bay saying, 'Hope Mum made a cake and you *ate* it.' We wrote back saying:

> *Mum made a cake*
> *Shaped like an 8.*
> *It looked a real mess*
> *But it tasted great!*

For Christan's tenth birthday, I made the worst-but-yummiest cake ever: a blackcurrant-jam-marbled sponge cake with too much butter. It rose beautifully . . . then overflowed the pan, before burning on the bottom of the camp oven. Smelling the burning, I opened the oven, whereupon what was left in the pan sank and finally came out distinctly concave. Robert declared I had hit the lowest point in my cake-making career.

Plenty of other cake disasters take their place in our family history. Once, when I'd left the bowl of beaten eggs and sugar sitting in the sink where it couldn't tip over while I collected a full jar of flour from under the bed, Christan came in and, without noticing anything, ran his hands under the tap. 'You've just washed your hands in the *cake*!' I yelled as he took off out the door again.

Making a buckwheat cake when Peter Bowmar was here, I'd skipped the baking powder on purpose, as the buckwheat never seemed to rise much anyway. He was unimpressed.

'Surely there is something we could do about this?' he commented, politely.

Another time, back in the days when the cupboard was mostly bare of ingredients, I served one of my oatmeal concoctions to Sax, warning him that it was crumbly. He must have thought that this was something of an understatement when it virtually exploded into a shower of crumbs at his feet.

'Isn't there something you could put in it?' he asked.

'Well, an egg would be a good start,' I replied dryly. It was a long time since we'd seen an egg. Or butter, sugar or fine flour. We were down to rolled oats, cooking oil and hand-ground wheat.

I think that was the same day he saw me wearing two left gumboots.

'How did you do that?' he asked, scratching his head and looking at me as though I was missing something up top.

'Both the right ones have holes in them!'

Max and Lisa always seem to turn up in their Piper Super Cub when I've forgotten the baking powder. Grant and Linda drop in with their Robinson R22 helicopter just in time to share the last piece between them. Geoff Robson always times it right and arrives by R44 when there is something to eat. After all, it's only food.

But if you really want a recipe, here's the Chocolate Potato Cake. My grandmother once told me that when she was a child in China, her cook made a wonderfully rich, moist chocolate cake which had potato in it, and she regretted never getting the recipe. Even though I had nothing to compare it with, I gave it a try. The potato must be without lumps, so you might want to put it through a sieve. I mostly use instant mashed potato left behind by hunters during the

Roar, as packets of it tend to accumulate at the bottom of the cupboard.

> *Start with 2 or more cups of mashed potato and*
> *add enough water to make it fairly wet. Melt 200*
> *grams of butter into it while it is still hot. Add at*
> *least 2½ cups of sugar, probably more, as I never*
> *seem to use enough. If the mixture is not too hot*
> *now, add 3 or 4 eggs. I generally use plenty as*
> *I figure they are just as good for you in a cake*
> *as they are sunny-side up on a plate, and often*
> *we have too many of them needing to be eaten.*
> *I have made it without eggs, but reduced the*
> *potato quite a bit and used very little water.*
>   *Add 2 cups of flour, 4 teaspoons of baking*
> *powder, and ¾–1 cup of cocoa. Mix it and cook.*
> *You could add milk powder or use milk with the*
> *potato instead of water, but I never do.*

When I recommended this recipe to my sister, she was unimpressed and thought it sounded like bangers and mash with chocolate sauce. I said that I didn't see why it should be like bangers and mash any more than a chocolate cake with flour and water in it was like glue. She replied (by the next mail):

> *If flour and water makes glue, how come flour*
> *and water, butter and sugar makes a cake? —*
> *Well, what do you think makes all that butter*
> *and sugar stick to your hips?!*

Although she was well-travelled, Chooky always preferred to be at home, and preferably inside the house for a cuddle.

TOP Young wax-eyes gorged themselves on sandflies
on the window screens, to the point where we held them,
unconcerned, between mouthfuls.

BOTTOM Christan with an organic chemistry
assignment from the Correspondence School.

I spy a paintbrush, a whitebait net,
A ruler-rotor and some wood to get,

A boot, a bear, four pumpkin seeds,
A puzzle piece and a clean pair of tweeds.

TOP A page from one of our homemade I Spy books, showing a cardboard model of the hut and an aerial view of Gorge River on a sandy, mossy spot on the side of the airstrip.

LEFT Paddling up through the gorge in the rubber ducky.

TOP Robin and I spent two weeks on Codfish Island
volunteering for the Kakapo Recovery Programme. This
wee feller is ready to leave the nest.

BOTTOM Christan doing the 'Polar Plunge' and a 50-metre swim
at −1.8°C at the Amery Iceshelf, Antarctica, December 2011.

Growing up.

A view from
Gorge River: the
Tasman Sea in all
its beauty.

Many of our
visitors come
by aeroplane or
helicopter, and
otherwise on
foot or by boat.
These photos
show our house
from two different
approaches.

TOP Christan graduated with a diploma in Outdoors Leadership and Management in just one year with a scholarship from Mt Aspiring College to help towards his fees.

MIDDLE A recent photo taken by Neroli Nolan at the Haast School reunion.

BOTTOM It looks like they'll be landing soon. I'll get the fire going under the kettle and have a quick tidy-up.

After an urgent call for some bigger clothes for Christan, Mum sent us three fleece all-in-one suits, and the very first time I washed one it disappeared into the depths of the river while I wasn't looking. A week later I found it 500 metres away down at the end of the beach, wedged under a rock that was far too big to be moved by anything less powerful than the sea. It was quite a macabre sight and left you wondering what had happened to the baby!

I put Christan down to crawl while I was busy one day in spring, and when I looked again he was completely covered in bidibids. Picking them out of any sort of knitted fabric became the bane of my life for the next few years, until the kids were old enough to take responsibility for it themselves. As everything was knitted and he had nothing to wear that wouldn't collect the bidibids, I spent the afternoon hand-sewing long sleeves onto a woven-cotton Peter Rabbit shirt, to keep out the sandflies, and making a pair of odd-legged cotton pants from scraps.

Before Robin was born, my friend Robyn Kennerly gave me a sewing machine that just needed servicing. It was some time before we could get it home, but, while in Auckland when Robin was 18 months old, we visited the Singer shop in Manukau looking for a hand-winder.

'You can only put it on certain models,' the shop assistant insisted. 'It screws on where the external motor goes.'

'You don't want to worry about that,' Robert assured us. 'I'll make it fit.' And he did, simply by drilling holes in the casing of the machine wherever they were necessary. He did a perfectly adequate job of it, and 16 years later it is still working beautifully.

Dear Mum,

*I lost those woolly pants you made in a flood
and they are sorely missed. I have got others
but they were particularly good. I could have
grabbed them with a stick if I'd had one. I had
plenty of time, but I wasn't going to jump in after
them on the winter solstice.*

L iving as we do, it is never a good idea to underestimate the power and unpredictability of natural forces. Once, I ventured down to the river at high tide after a big flood, with an enormous sea pounding in, and unwisely I didn't turn around to go straight back home. I thought I would have more chance of getting the washing rinsed safely further up the river at the bluff, and so I put the buckets down well above the waterline. Normally I would put all of the washing into the river, weighted down with rocks, but this time I put in just a few things at a time so that I could grab them if necessary. Sure enough, when the Big One arrived I had three pairs of Christan's pants and one of his shirts in all at once; in fact, almost everything he had apart from what he was wearing that day. The wave washed a fish-case full of gravel tailings from Robert's gold-mining activities — which was at least 1.5m above the level of the river — right off the concrete block it had been sitting on for two years or more. Luckily that broke the force of the wave, so I didn't lose my buckets as well, which were still full of clothes. I only had time to run for it, and more than half of Christan's clothes were lost in one great whoosh, although I rescued one pair of pants several minutes later as they came back down the river.

He'd had a run of leaving things too close to the river that week, and was overdue for something more respectable, so I spent the rest of the day on the sewing machine.

I usually had a stash of second-hand clothing that people had given us, so all I had to do was cut them down to size when the kids were ready for them. At other times I cleared out some of Robert's old clothes by asking if I could make them into something for Christan, who was delighted to move into a pair of pants already covered in Dad's paint. I often tried to get the kids to throw away old ragged things from their clothes boxes, but they'd refuse to part with old favourites even if they barely came down past their bellybuttons. And I had been reluctant to make anything just so that Christan could yet again smash the world record for how quickly you could rip the knees out of a pair of pants while diving after cricket balls.

When Christan started to climb out of bed each morning with as many feathers on him as Chooky had, I found a 30-centimetre tear in his feather quilt. His duvet cover had contained a lot of down, but it was time to extract the feathers from it and make a new duvet with the down-proof cotton fabric I'd brought home from our previous visit to the city. After making one for each of us over the years, I also made him a new sleeping bag, as he had grown out of the small one I'd made to save us from carrying full-sized ones when they were younger. By the time I'd finished transferring all the feathers, the garden looked like someone had been plucking chickens and I'd be blowing them out of my nose for a week.

I sewed Christan a new down jacket when he was 15, copying the old one, and decided that I was in fact quite mad. It had zip-on sleeves, press studs on a front flap outside the zip that went right up to the top of the collar, internal waistband, pockets, etc. He and I were both pleased with the result, but it would have been difficult enough if I had had a pattern and set of instructions to follow. I wondered why I had ever volunteered in the first place, vowed never to again, and immediately had to make Robert a down vest, albeit a much simpler task.

Robert's mother, Ngaire, had given me a lovely pair of pale pink pants that she'd finished with, and while she was here I asked her to help me take them in. I was delighted with the result and wanted very much to get them out to Haast for our next trip. As it was not possible to carry anything extra, we had tried storing spare clothes at various sites on the way out, but without much success. Often the clothes would have got damp and mouldy and someone would have cleaned them out, or the shed we had left them in would be locked when we came back. We were always the worst-dressed guests at any party.

While Ngaire made all sorts of suggestions to solve my problem, this left me more and more exasperated as she simply didn't understand the complications. She lived in a world where almost anything is possible by paying for it. Things can also be much more difficult when you need people to go out of their way for you, particularly when you know that they will refuse to take any payment offered. We had asked Dave Saxton to take out six of Robert's paintings that we really didn't want to carry, as well as getting him to buy postage stamps for a load of school library books when he was already extremely busy during the Roar. After he'd arrived with a second load of groceries, apologising for having missed something on our list because his daughter Lisa was pregnant and exhausted from driving down from Christchurch when he'd asked her to shop for us, I was not going to request yet another favour. I could try posting a parcel of clothes out with someone else, but there was a good chance that Sax would collect our mail in Haast and deliver the parcel back to us.

I'd been trying to change the subject for some time when Ngaire left me flabbergasted by concluding that I'd just have to buy a pair when I got out. But that would mean the next time I'd have two pairs of pants I couldn't get out, and I wouldn't get to wear these ones at all, just store them. And apart from that: me? Buy a pair of pants? Where? Wanaka or Queenstown before the last day of our trip out, and at what price? While it is possible to buy reasonably priced clothing there today, back then retail shopping was not an option.

Robert's paintings got larger and more numerous, his greenstone carvings heavier, and the kids' spare clothes bigger, until eventually we had to ask Roger to fly in a week before we left to take it all out for us. We were also having trouble fitting enough food into the aeroplane on the flight home with two growing kids squeezing into the back seat with me, so it made sense to have him bring in a load of non-perishables to store and some fresh stuff for a good feed before we left.

As for the pink pants, I wore them for the next few years until my sister looked at me sideways and asked, 'Are they supposed to be that colour or did you wash them with something red?'

Other than sheepskin slippers, shoes couldn't very well be made at home, although Robert often mended or altered them. Apart from the fact that the kids didn't stay in the same size for long, the rough terrain our shoes were subjected to made it a constant job to keep up the supply. I visited every second-hand shop I could while in town and bought anything suitable.

Shortly after Christan's birth, I had a really good pair of second-hand sandshoes that fitted perfectly — a rare event over the next 20 years. Even the occasional new pair that seemed to fit in the shop would let me know by the time I was halfway to Barn Bay that tramping for the next year or two was not going to be an enjoyable experience for the 'feets', but they generally didn't last long. Robert once pointed out that just because he walks in bare feet it doesn't necessarily mean they don't hurt, and I added that the same applies for wearing shoes.

If the kids had a bad pair of shoes on the walk out, I'd try to get them something else for the next trip, or Robert might have to operate on the bad ones. Once I had to send an emergency letter out to Lucy Bellerby to ask for the next size for Christan. I knew she was a keen collector of second-hand things, and — with a boy either side of Christan's age and a girl a bit younger than Robin — she was often worth asking.

Unfortunately, the mail didn't get to us in time for the walk and Christan had to make do, but we collected it at the post office in Haast. Lucy wrote that when she started sorting through her stash of shoes, she'd felt like Imelda Marcos! The parcel contained one or more pairs of each size, and this kept us going for the next three or four years.

Robin didn't believe me when I said that you can't make shoes, at least not a pair that will work properly. Having made herself a blue silk dress with the 2012 Mt Aspiring College formal in mind, beginning by designing her own pattern, she was determined to make a pair of high-heeled shoes to match. She took a piece of hard black plastic from a washed-up bait basket, and, by softening it in the fire, shaped it to what she wanted. Next, she carved two wooden heels and screwed the plastic to them. The tops were of blue silk beautifully decorated with sequins and ribbons, stitched to an inner sole of multi-coloured craft foam. This was painted black along with the heels, before being stitched and glued to the base, and a piece of black rubber from the inner tube of a tyre was glued onto the ball of the foot and the heel. Test trials showed them to be too high and inadequately secured to her feet, so after a rethink she lopped off two centimetres and added parts of a blue nylon dressing-gown cord to the ankle. They worked perfectly and the whole outfit, including a hand-made and matching blue silk mask, cost her $20. She and her dancing partner, Eugene, won the prize for the best dancers at the masquerade ball, which led on to a part in the school musical.

Chapter 17
FUN AND GAMES

R obert asked Christan, age three, if he'd ever seen
fairies.

'Yeah,' came the matter-of-fact reply.

'Where were they?'

'Down at the bluff.'

'What were they doing?'

'Jus' flying around...and san'fies.'

Robin had read that if you balance grains of wheat on a four-leafed clover you will see a fairy. Although I didn't disbelieve her, it was a different matter for me to go along with her to see for myself. After sitting for a while I suggested that I was probably scaring them away, so I'd go and maybe they would come just for her, which worked.

However walking up the track through the bush in the poor light, I saw a butterfly out of the corner of my eye. Yet when I turned to look there was nothing there — and at 5.30pm at the end of July there were no butterflies in the dark bush!

On her sixth birthday, Robin was poncing about in her pink fairy dress. It seemed a bit silly really, but hey! What's the point of having a little girl if you can't make her a fairy dress? I was very pleased with it as I'd had no pattern and insufficient fabric, having to add panels of lace to make it bigger, along with a few fancy bits saved off something that was being thrown out. She had a lace (cobweb) frill around her neck, ribbon flowers and a bit of gold glitter. The reconditioned, gold, glittery butterfly wings were not such a success. As they got in the way anyway, she mostly left them hanging on a nail until her next flight. They never show fairies in books struggling to get through a doorway! And how do they get their clothes on and off?

I made her a fairy game based on Cluedo. The board had six different types of flowers, cut from wrapping paper, with a paved pathway made from paint sample charts. You had to guess which of six fairies had lost what in which flowers. We had a set of fairy stickers, most of them from Cicely Mary Barker's beautiful paintings, which I used to make the cards, and I attempted to make the fairies out of modelling clay. They were fairly ugly but recognisable, and we were all quite pleased with them.

'Lilypad Leapfrog' was another game we made, this one based on Chinese Checkers, only rectangular. Freddo Frogs come in many different types in Australia, so having eaten 10 each of the milk chocolate, white chocolate, strawberry and caramel flavours, we brought the clean wrappers home with us to make blue, white, red and yellow tokens. The kids were not keen on peppermint, so we skipped the green frogs. Freddo Frog ice-cream wrappers made a lovely title picture on the outside of the folded board. We used a sponge to make blue watery patterns, then cut and glued 10 waterlilies of each colour and 68 green lily pads in regular lines.

The best game of all was 'Holiday — we walk out and fly back'. Based on the commercial game which we had enjoyed playing with our neighbours Missie and Hobo during a wet spell at Barn Bay, the second part of the title came from a song Christan sang while banging away on his guitar, aged four. I am fascinated by the different ways you can record family history other than the most obvious one of books, so this game contains many memorable events in our lives and was improved on and added to through the years. We 'walk' out to Haast, stopping to camp at river crossings, with various pitfalls along the way ('step on a kina — miss a turn'). You can pick up a 'helicopter' card with opportunities for a quick trip ('Sax stops and offers you a ride'), or be delayed by threatening weather forecasts ('Rain, flood — miss a turn at the next river'). Once the road is reached, these change to hitchhiker cards with opportunities to make or spend money ('You meet Dale. He gives you a bag of walnuts and $50 and promises to pay you the rest sometime'). We collect mail at the post office and pay bills, bus fares and accommodation. Ultimately, you have to accumulate $200 to buy groceries in Queenstown before flying home.

Another game we tried to make never worked, and we learned about the intricacies of such things. From it, the kids learned to make up their own card games or change the rules for existing games, but sometimes when fights erupted I'd point out that often the rules were there for a reason.

The idea of alternative methods of recording history came up in conversation when my cousin Margaret and her husband, Fred, visited us while on holiday in New Zealand. She looks exactly like her mum, my Aunty Marj, and I felt a lovely sense of continuity seeing Margaret and Fred stepping into the vacancy left in the family by the recent deaths of her parents.

Fred is a carpenter with a holiday shack on the coast north of Perth, before you get as far as Geraldton, and I was delighted when he spoke of the stories the shack could tell. The roofing iron had come from Aunty Marj's place in Collie when he'd rebuilt their roof. It had been on two other houses before that, and is almost 100 years old! The framing timber had arrived by mistake on a building site somewhere, and the interior walls were of oregon — 10-metre-long finger-jointed lengths that had been the packing case on a shipment. We responded with some of the tales of our hut; the reason the roof sags in the middle, and how we took the corrugated iron off the walls to replace the roof, then covered the walls with what had been taken off the walls of the DOC hut next-door when it had been re-clad. Although the nail holes had completely rusted out, Robert had 'thatched' the walls with the shorter bits that were still adequate in between. Mind you, it's only 30 years old now and won't last another 70 in this climate!

I'd always wanted to make my own 'I Spy' book, and when a digital camera arrived in the mail from our neighbour Anne Mitchell, it became possible. I made the book with the Mitchells and a few other people particularly in mind, so I included things that they would spot in the pictures. On 12 double pages I recorded as many of our activities and special treasures as I could squeeze in, beginning with an aerial view of Robin's toy aeroplane in front of a cardboard model of our hut, and then passing through the house, showing the kids' desks, quilting projects, carvings on Robert's shelf, games on the floor, baking and favourite cups on the sink, and the view out of the window with a real aeroplane sitting there.

Finally, there is quilting. I started making Robin a quilt when she was 10, with scraps of fabrics from favourite clothes or other quilts that we have made for friends and family along the way. In a 'crazy quilt' design it records memories of people and events, most of the birds we see, seals, whales, dolphins, fish, insects, shells and plants. Christan sewed a whitebait net on it using a scrap from his real net. My sister embroidered the robin that came to us before Robin was born. Most of my family has done something on it, as well as several friends and Robert's sisters when they were here for Christmas. His mother sent an embroidered patch in the last parcel we had from her, and Robin helped Grandad make a twist of gold thread to sew onto it in the days after her funeral.

The kids had a lot of fun with Robert's whiskers, and Robin even kept some of his trimmings in a matchbox. While eating alfalfa sprouts they'd put a large handful halfway into their mouths and mumble through it 'I got some whiskers!' And with bubble-bath in the fish-case bath, they'd make beards with bubbles all over their faces.

> *Oh they're always in the way,*
> *The cows eat them for hay,*
> *They hide the dirt on Daddy's shirt,*
> *They're always in the way!*

The first spring when Robert shaved his beard off, I *hated* it! I had to hold a book over his lower face to make sure I was talking to the same person. I didn't like it the second time either, but I'd learned to bite my tongue more by then. The third time wasn't so bad and, by the fifth time he shaved, I decided that the benefits of not having whiskers up my nose definitely outweighed any problems of appearance.

Anyway, by that time his beard was mostly grey. He worried that he might look like a townie, clean-shaven, though, so for a couple more years he would let it grow when we went out. Finally I told him that he looked 10 years younger without it, as his hair is still dark, and that did the trick.

While staying at Hawea Motorcamp as guests of our friends, the Cotters, Michelle sent her youngest kids off to their rooms to bring a gift each for our kids, aged three and six. Tim gave Christan a truck and Teresa arrived back with a beautiful china doll. Half an hour later, Teresa confided to me in an agonised whisper, 'She's going to call her *Whiskers!*'

By the next day I was able to reassure her that the doll was Treasure Zoe Whiskers. Zoe for Zoe Steck, whom she loved playing with at Okuru; and Treasure for a girl at my high school who had yellow hair one week, pink the next and blue the week after that — a story that had obviously impressed Robin. Treasure Zoe lived with us for many years.

For another of Robin's small dolls I made dresses from scraps of fabric, one of tartan and one with leftovers from Robin's pants which featured seahorses and fish on merry-go-rounds. I also made her a Lycra swimming suit, mask, snorkel and flippers, and Robin called her Pretty Tartan Dress Seahorse Dress Mask and Snorkel, which I shortened to Pretty Tart.

Robin was three and Christan six before the last section of the floor was finished, as it had to wait until the 12-gallon-drum stove needed replacing. The floor sloped down towards the fire, and Christan spent many hours rolling down it on his plastic motorbike before crashing into the concrete block that supported the stove; a pleasure Robin was deprived of once the floor was rebuilt level.

By that time, however, we had two bathroom doors and the children pushed each other around the table, through one door and out the other, alternately yelling 'Faster, faster!' and 'Stop! Stop!! I said *Stop!*''

It was a sad day when the final crash deprived the motorbike of a handlebar that was never successfully repaired.

Four is the age at which children seem to learn to put their shoes on the right feet, so I smiled to see Robin's last relapse.

'Your boots are on the wrong feet,' I pointed out mildly, but she dug her toes in.

'They're right,' she insisted.

I continued to humour her.

'The left one is right, but the right one is wrong.'

'Well they must both be lefters,' she concluded and, turning her back on me, stomped out.

When Robin wanted to know who made God, I read her AA Milne's poem about Elizabeth Anne who wanted to know how God began.

'Goodness gracious, it's time for tea!' her nan said.

'What put *that* in your quaint little head?' asked the Lord High Doodlum after she'd run around the world to knock on his door.

So she ran back home and asked her doll, who replied 'in her usual way, by squeaking':

'What did she say? Well, to be quite candid,
I don't know but Elizabeth Anne did!'

I suggested that Robin asked her Squeaky Bear, and the next day I heard her up on the bed saying, 'Who made God?' *'Squeak squeak squeak.'* 'Who made God?' *'Squeak squeak.'*

After that, playing card games — for example 'Fish' — she'd say, 'Dad, in your usual way of speaking, have you got a six?'

We'd been reading a lot of Enid Blyton's books, including descriptions of hoopla stalls, and Robin wanted one to celebrate the winter solstice. A box of goodies arrived from Mum just at the right moment, so we guessed how many jelly snakes there were in the jar, and made a chocolate wheel from the spinning wheel, with second-hand books, clothes and stamps for prizes. The coconut shy was an empty coconut shell standing on top of a cricket wicket, and we ate a spoonful of desiccated coconut every time we knocked it off with a ball.

Sometimes the competition could get heated, such as the time I took Christan, Robin and my sister's kids up to the Pine Hill school oval in Dunedin one winter's afternoon to run around the 200-metre track. At first we did 75-metre sprints and time trials over 200 metres. They had been around four times each, timing their laps, when Robin failed to stop, carrying on for a second lap, then a third, and a fourth. By the time she was on the tenth lap, I was telling the others about the annual fund-raising Jog-a-thon that had been held each year at Riverton Primary School when I was there. We used to ask people to sponsor us for a maximum of 10 laps, and if you walked most of it that was still OK. I agreed to pay them 50 cents per lap with a limit of 20 laps each, but I wasn't paying for walking, since Robin, sailing by on her eleventh lap, had not stopped once.

'That's five weeks' allowance,' said Kevin, heading for the track.

Christan, as usual whenever we were in town, had a cold, so he piked out after six laps and I wouldn't pay him full price to start again. He got more and more grumpy, as he hadn't expected the others to go on so long. When they absolutely had to have a drink I allowed them to jog over to the fountains and back, so long as they also continued to jog on the spot while they drank.

Robin was smaller and not as fast as the others, but she made up for that with determination. As they finished 20 laps each, she was almost at 30 and still refused to stop. At 33 laps, as it was getting dark and cold, I told her that we would have to go and she could jog home with us.

After years of entertainment from cardboard boxes, whether sitting in them, sleeping in them, stacking them on top of each other or row, row, rowing the boat, their last round of amusement came in the form of a pinhole camera. We stretched a jersey over the whole thing to make it completely dark, and they put their heads through the neck hole into the box. A white piece of paper made a screen on the side opposite the pinhole. The low winter sun on the continuously moving ocean made the best video picture, with flax or cabbage trees as black shadows on the screen, and the kids spent most of the day walking around with the box on their heads.

Christan was mad on cricket. He received a miniature set of bat, ball and wickets from the Haast Social Club's Christmas party, and later he moved onto full-sized gear, mostly from the Wanaka

Wastebusters recycling centre. A red six-stitcher, slightly soft cricket ball made another Christmas wonderful, but mostly he used tennis balls — and lost them in the flaxes by the dozen.

Hunters or passing trampers were pressed into a game whenever possible. Robert and I tried to get out to play with him most days. Robin improved in time if you bowled nice, slow, bouncy ones. She'd bowl high, underarm lollipops to me, but I kept whacking high balls into the bush.

If he couldn't get anyone to play, Christan practised bowling at the wickets or listened to the Black Caps playing the Proteas or the Aussies on the radio. One of his most treasured possessions was a Black Caps T-shirt given to him by my brother and his partner at the time, Lee Cooper. His conversation was full of Chris Cairns and Sachin Tendulkar, 'one-dayers' and Nathan Astle's double century. On holiday in Australia, there were serious disputes with the rest of his cousins over test matches. When the Black Caps won in an extremely close one-day match late one night they almost lynched him, but in the morning the newspaper claimed an Australia victory! Perhaps the reporter had taken himself off to bed confident of the result. Christan gave his cousins heaps.

His passion was tempered by a measure of reason, though. When asked: 'You know, you'll never get to play for the Black Caps playing with your mum on the airstrip. Do you want to do something about this?', he replied, 'Oh that's OK. I'll probably want something else by then anyway.'

Chapter 18
QUICKER THAN WALKING

Loading the aeroplane at Arrowtown in fair weather didn't necessarily mean you could count on good flying weather on the other side of the mountains. But you wouldn't be in the air for long before you started to suspect that all was not well at higher levels, particularly in the long valleys on the eastern approach to the passes. In the back seat of a light aircraft with two small children, you are completely isolated in a world of potential chaos, and the occasional 'How're you going?' from the front seats offers only a brief distraction. You're watching both kids to judge which one will throw up first, while suspecting that it may actually be you.

Flying up Lake Wakatipu one day with a green frog in an ice-cream container, we hit the biggest bump ever. Apples and oranges rained down on us, and boxes of supplies packed behind the seat leapt forward into the back of my neck. Two slightly less dreadful bumps followed as Roger turned away from the lake, searching for a calmer patch of air.

Then came the long haul up the Beans Burn, where the prevailing wind from whatever is happening on the coast tumbles and swirls through the pass and down the valley into your face. Clutching Robin in one arm and the vomit cup in the other hand (I forget what had happened to the frog by that time), I heard her singing to herself, over and over, 'Kangaroo! Kangaroo!'

'Not far now, Mum,' Christan called and, bracing myself against the window frame, green to the gills, I realised that our roles had reversed and that *he* was reassuring *me!*

At last, we shot out over the saddle.

'Down, down,' I begged silently. Lake Wilmot, the Upper Pyke, Waiuna Lagoon, Big Bay, then out over the sea, a much smaller hiccup over Awarua Point and the Gorge Islands came into view.

'Down, down.' I wanted my feet on the ground. More firma, less terra.

Zoom! The low pass to check that the airstrip was clear of driftwood and anything else, and I shut my eyes and tucked my head down for the 3G turn. The Steeples, the river, the flaxes and at last we were down. Roger braked and turned at the far end of the strip, then stopped and opened the door with the propeller still going.

'You want to get out?' he asked, grinning over his shoulder.

'That's OK, thanks. We'll make it from here.'

But on a good day it is hard to beat a flight in a small aeroplane through the Southern Alps. New Zealand is such a small place, and I've never tired of the thrill of looking down on it all laid out for me as on a map. Mountains, valleys, forest, glaciers, fiords, it's all here within reach. Fly up the Skipper's and watch the narrow road snaking its way along below you. Turn over Lochnagar and take a close look at the Bonar Glacier on Mt Aspiring at 2500 metres. Look down the Arawhata to Mt Maclean and Jackson Bay before turning left over the Red Hills. The airstrip on the Gorge Plateau looks much the same as it did when the bulldozer first cut it out over 40 years ago, and you can't see the washouts from up here. Only five minutes to Gorge River International Airport.

Returning from a Christmas visit to Robert's family on the Sunshine Coast of Queensland, the direct flight from Brisbane crossed the Cascade coast of South Westland before descending into Dunedin, with Lake Wakatipu on the right hand and Lakes Wanaka and Hawea on the left. To the north we could spot Barn Bay, Cascade Point, Jackson Bay and Mosquito Hill at Haast. Looking south, there was Big Bay, Martins Bay, the Kaipo, Milford Sound. Even Poison Bay was visible just before Fiordland faded into the mist of distance. But we couldn't see Gorge River, as it was right between our feet.

A year or two later we watched Freedom Air's Boeing 737 fly overhead bringing Nana and Grandad to Dunedin on their way to visit us in February 2000. Two days later, when they landed on the strip, Christan told Grandad, 'I saw you fly over in the plane!'

'Yes, love, we flew over.'

'No! On Thursday. In the big plane.'

We had asked Bob to bring us a new broom, but he was a bit nervous about it. 'You have to be careful about buying your daughter-in-law a broom,' he said. I reassured him that it was perfect for sweeping the carpet. Up until then I had used a banister brush on hands and knees.

It rained for two or three days while they were here, and Bob commented on how well-behaved our kids were; his other grandsons would have been climbing up the walls. Even so, when Christan was 13 or 14 with a teenager's excess of energy, he could be hard to put up with in a small hut. He was a great tease, and at least two of us were always ready to rise to his bait. I had to speak to him about taking responsibility for his own energy levels and doing something about it, rather than sitting in here bouncing ping-pong balls off the back of his mother's head. He was growing up by then, and I was highly impressed, and relieved, when I only had to ask him once.

We had been visiting my family in Auckland for a couple of weeks, and, at four and seven, the children were not babies anymore. It was time for an adventure, so rather than return home by flying to Christchurch, we took the overnight train from Auckland to Wellington and transferred to the morning ferry.

It was the worst trip either Robert or I have ever had across Cook Strait. The Lynx had already been cancelled, and changing our minds to fly to Blenheim would have been worse still.

We had the kids' lifejackets with us so took them on board, and they came in handy later when they fell asleep on them. Before the boat met the first big swells I made a quick dash inside to grab a few paper bags, knowing that I wouldn't want to go back in there. Robert, on the other hand, was getting cold and thought we should all go inside.

'No way! I'm staying out here. And you will have to be ready for them to throw up.'

He was back within minutes, as it was so horrible in the lounge and there was no room to sit anyway. We were all sick except Robert, who wished he had been. No one else on board was saying a word, apart from a blond, loud-mouthed guy who looked like a yachtie: 'The best thing for seasickness is to shove as many meat pies down your throat as you can. Pies and beer. It's the only way.' Everyone else groaned and wished he'd go away or shut up. Thankfully, he announced, 'I'm off to the cafeteria for another meat pie.'

Christan woke up as we entered Tory Channel and the boat came back to life around us, but Robin slept on. I was reluctant to wake her, but if I hadn't she would have missed the only good part of the whole trip. In Picton we hired a car for the first time. Even with a one-way trip and drop-off in Queenstown, it was cheaper than paying for four people on at least two bus trips, plus we could load the car up with all our gear and stop along the way to visit people for a change. First, we were going to Nelson to see one of the pioneering Cascade River whitebaiters, Ted Buchanan. He wanted to show Robert his collection of the greenstone artifacts he'd found during his 50 years of whitebaiting at the Cascade River mouth.

Usually it was my job to keep up with car-sick kids, but as Robert didn't have a current driver's licence I did all the driving. I was trying to tell Robert to get ready for it, but he was busy watching the road and still recovering from the boat trip himself. Robin was sick four more times before we reached Nelson, by which time we were thoroughly over our great adventure — and I bought 'Sea Legs' before we carried on the next day.

Chapter 19

LIVING ON FAITH

A favourite question people ask us is: 'What do you do if you have an accident?' The answer? 'Well, mostly we don't.' Clearly, though, when such situations do occur being able to get help is crucial, particularly after the children were born. But at various times, changes in our circumstances have prompted us to be a bit more prepared 'just in case' and communication with the outside world is an issue we have addressed several times over the years.

For example, we borrowed a single-sideband radio for a few months before Christan was born. The nearest we came to needing to make a call, though, was with a threatened poisoning sometime after we had returned the radio, when Christan, crawling, swallowed a potato sprout. While we scratched our heads wondering quite what to do about it in the absence of a phone number to call for advice, he threw up and solved the problem. As he became mobile and inquisitive, though, we anticipated potential problems and hazards, clearing several plastic containers of noxious substances that had been left behind in the old freezer shed from Eoin Wylie's time here.

During our second pregnancy we scored a hand-held VHF radio. There is still a gap today in VHF reception between Cascade and Awarua Points, unless you are far enough out to sea to pick up a repeater on Jackson Head, Mt Watney or Mt Pembroke, but we could get a message to a passing fishing boat in line of sight. Robin was almost a year old before we had an emergency locator beacon.

At first I had been unsure how serious a problem would have to be before we could justify activating the beacon, although I felt that we wouldn't wait as long with the children as we might if either of us were sick or injured. However, Robin Manera, the policeman at Haast, didn't even hesitate before he said, 'Just press the button', which was very reassuring. Fortunately, the kids have grown up safely without us ever having had to call for help.

The most nerve-wracking time came after we had made the decision to buy a locator beacon, but then returned home without it. As it happened, two of the bad moments we did have were in those few months before the beacon eventually got here.

At this time, Robin loved playing in a bouncer which hung from the roof beam. She sat in a harness made from a pair of jeans, with long straps that hooked onto a bungee cord around a carved piece of wood. Robert had first made it for Christan and we hung him from it in his baby pack, but he was so small that he couldn't see over the edge of the pack and, with his little skinny legs sticking out of the holes, he looked like a spider on the end of a web. With a few alterations and the denim harness it worked beautifully, until the day when he was suddenly too heavy for it and the bungee cord gave up the ghost.

At three-and-a-half, Christan could now swing from the piece of wood, spinning around on the rope. Of course the day came when I forgot to take the bungee cord away and he got the hook up his nose. There was blood everywhere, and it was several minutes before we could see that it wasn't too serious. I knew that an eggcup-ful of blood can go a long way and that noses could be particularly messy, but I kept one eye on the fishing boat out at sea to be sure it didn't go out of VHF range before the bleeding had stopped.

Often in the summertime, when Robert caught a lot of yellow-eyed mullet in the net all at once, without refrigeration it would be a race to eat them before they had to be thrown away. He didn't like to fillet anything because it wasted such a lot, so whenever there were too many fish in the net he split them down the backbone and smoked them in a drum that sat on the roof over the chimney.

From about 18 months, Christan had been very good about bones, and if he did come across anything in a mouthful he would simply spit out the whole lot. We talked about the husks in our hand-ground porridge as 'bones', and even any missed bits of cores in stewed apples. At two-and-a-half he was mostly able to pick through a fish for himself, but inevitably the next big drama ensued when he got a fishbone stuck in his throat.

He was gagging, throwing up and bleeding a wee bit, and it was quite awful to watch. I tried sticking my finger down his throat a few times, but of course he'd gag. There wasn't much we could do. We gave him paracetamol and Bach Flowers Rescue Remedy, and he — very wisely but most uncharacteristically — fell asleep. We didn't have any bread, but after he woke up we fed him about two weeks' rations of lollies, Milo and dried fruit leather (an annual and much-treasured gift from our friend June Hayward), hoping that something would shift it. He cried a lot, but with plenty of cuddles and a chocolate cake with custard for tea we got through the day. By the next morning he'd all but forgotten about it, only commenting several times that yesterday had been a long day.

After that, all fish was filleted carefully. We realised that there really wasn't that much wasted on a mullet, and quite often we'd end up throwing away the last couple of fish anyway if we couldn't get through it all. We ate fish and chips up to six nights a week throughout the summer, and it was only during the winter when we might catch only one or two that we'd cook the whole fish to not waste anything.

Anyway, the smoker drum was causing the chimney and the roof to rust quickly. Having trodden the corrugations out of a piece of corrugated iron to make a new chimney, Robert decided to build a new smoker down at the river. This was a great improvement, as I couldn't cook anything or even boil the kettle for six or eight hours while the fish was smoking. Robert and Christan would bring back delicious smoked eel, mullet or kahawai, ready to eat. Although I haven't eaten eel for years, in the first seven years when I was pregnant, nursing or both, I was skinny enough to really enjoy it.

It was Christan's miniature cricket bat, however, that brought us within a whisker's width of our first serious accident. Robin, one and toddling, appeared to collect it square in the mouth and sat down on her backside. Robert barely had time to gasp, but couldn't believe his eyes when she didn't even cry! She must have been at the absolute extreme limit of his swing and it never touched her. We live on faith.

Several different types of splinters have caused problems over the years. Towards the end of February 1996, Robert and Christan were working hard on the floor when a spark flew off a rusty nail, landing in Robert's eye. It was 'down tools' for that day, as his eye watered continuously and he could barely see. Still the fragment didn't wash out. I looked several times but couldn't see anything. Early the next morning, Phil Wright, a helicopter shooter, stopped in for a cup of tea to lessen the load while pilot Stewie Fever flew a load of deer out in his R22 chopper. Robert would have been still in bed otherwise, struggling with his eye. Phil had Xylocaine in his emergency kit and gave Robert a squirt, which helped enormously. His boy Jason had once had a piece of metal in his eye, and Phil hadn't been able to find anything until the next day when it went rusty!

'Yeah, I figure it will rust away eventually,' said Robert.

'I don't know about that,' Phil replied, dubiously.

Although it still bothered him, it was much more bearable by the time the Xylocaine wore off, and it wasn't until later that day, looking at Robert side-on, that I could see something embedded in his eye. Looking straight at him as I had been up to then, I couldn't see it against the black of the pupil. I tried licking it out of his eye, gently at first but quite roughly when it still refused to budge, but by this time the cornea had healed over it, so it wasn't as scratchy as it had been.

We were expecting Roger any day, hopefully by the end of the month, but being a leap year made February longer. I said that if this was my eye I'd want it seen to and I wouldn't be prepared to just sit and wait for Roger to come. Only later did I remember my First Aid training that said for any injury of the eye, *both* eyes should be covered. Robert kept peering through the blur, testing it to see if his eye would still work and ultimately straining it badly.

Early on the seventh day, as Robert sat in his seat with a cup of mint tea, his eye started watering furiously and the metal splinter washed out. And a couple of days after that, Roger arrived.

Robin also had an unpleasant incident involving one of her eyes. Something was in it, but as I couldn't see anything and there wasn't much more I could do, I said, 'Just keep your eye shut and it will come out eventually.' For half the afternoon and all evening she kept it shut without any improvement, but still I thought that it would come out overnight. On looking again in the morning we found that the splintery side of a tiny chip of hardboard had caught against the ridge inside the edge of her eyelid, and no amount of eye-watering was going to shift it. It had sat there for over 18 hours by then. Poor kid! Robert suggested getting it out with a match, but I wasn't game. Having rounded and smoothed the end of a match into a tiny spoon, Robert was able to get it out deftly and easily.

Robin collected a splinter of glass in her foot one day, aged about three. I could have grabbed it between my thumb and fingernail if I'd been quick enough, but while I looked around for tweezers to do it properly, she walked on it and pushed it in further. It turned into a huge drama as I attempted to dig the splinter out with a needle and she screamed until I had to give it up and let her go. She stormed out to the workshop, and was so wound-up that she fell asleep on her stomach with her foot stuck straight up in the air. Later when she was in a deep sleep I tried again, before handing the job over to Robert who is more patient. It took three-quarters of an hour for him to carefully work around the wickedly long splinter with a needle and extract it without waking her. On my own, I would have had to take her to a doctor. From this experience, I learned to be more patient.

It was certainly patience I needed in the aftermath of Christan stepping on the underside of a deer skull which had been carefully left by a hunter in the flaxes with the antlers pointing into the ground. His foot was lacerated and full of dirt, and had it been an option I would have taken him straight to Accident and Emergency. Again, it took most of an hour to get the wound clean, but by then I could see that, although deeply cut, the sole of his foot was thick enough that only one or two of the cuts had drawn blood. He kept a sock on it for a few days and it was fine.

Up the beach on a spring tide, checking out marine life in the big rock pool, Robin once again collected something in her foot — this time a kina spine. This was the first time I'd had to deal with one, but Robert had often regaled us with the harrowing tale of jumping off the bow of Dale's boat at Big Bay to wade ashore, landing directly onto a kina. Lou Brown had been with him and had found an unopened bottle of Dettol on the beach right there. Then he pulled a piece of stainless-steel wire off a craypot and dug about a dozen spines out of Robert's foot before they could walk around to the Mitchells'. Robert took off running, and Lou could hardly keep up. He was picking spines out for a month, by which time he'd been all the way to Greymouth and back.

This spine (singular) was in Robin's big toe. If it had been under the toenail it would have been nasty, but it was actually completely embedded in the meat underneath it and was impossible to get at.

'It will be really sore if we wait too long. Better to get it straight away.'

Back at home we worked on it for quite some time before Robin had had enough and — shall we say — put her foot down.

'OK, I guess it will come out more easily when it gets a bit infected.'

We tried again over the next couple of days, but it wasn't hurting her at all, there was no infection, and digging at it was by far the worst bit. So we forgot about it.

Four weeks later we were back at the rock pools on the next new moon when Robin called out, 'That kina spine just popped out!' It could hardly have been simpler.

We also have a gory photo of Christan wearing sandshoes, cutting a spine out of his big toe with his pocket knife. Both his shoe and sock had matching holes big enough for his toe to stick straight through.

Somehow, it is the close calls that really freak you out as you think about what might have happened. In late April 2004 we climbed up Mt Malcolm, the highest point around here at 800 metres. It is relatively easy to find the way up a mountain, as the ridges all converge on each other. Coming back down, Robert led the way, concentrating on finding the correct ridge to follow rather than end up in steep, gnarly country further up the river. Stepping into a deep hole in a rotten log, he rocked over forwards but stopped in time without damaging his knee. It was then that we realised just how easily we could have had a serious situation. I was unsure whether I could even find my way home, let alone get back again to find him. It was getting late and cold, so would I have taken both children with me or left one behind to help him?

After this incident and with Christan going out into the bush alone more and more, trapping possums, we bought a smaller, hand-held beacon for him to carry, rather like giving your child a cellphone. I explained that there might be times when he'd have to wait for us to come and find him before making a decision as to whether or not to call for help, but I told him that if his leg bone was sticking out the side of his leg, he might as well press the button and get the process started.

It was funny how, once we had this locator beacon, we found we couldn't go anywhere without it. The kids worry about us as much as we worry about them, and they insist that we also carry it while doing many of the things we've been doing for years.

Chapter 20

EARTH-QUAKE, STORM AND TEMPEST

'Doesn't it rain all the time on the West Coast?'
Sometimes it does seem that way. On average,
we have the same number of sunny days in a year
as Auckland has, but when it does rain, we get a lot more all
at once. Our average rainfall at sea level is 5000 millimetres
per year. Inland, at the head of Milford Sound, the annual
average is twice as much, and in Te Anau, on the other side
of the mountains of Fiordland, it is only 10 per cent of that.

Greetings from the West Coast, under thirty-five thousand feet of grey cloud. We did have

256

some good weather for a week or so in the
last month but it is getting hard to remember.
Gales, thunderstorms, huge — if not actually
monstrous — seas interspersed with various
forms of precipitation such as rain, hail, drizzle,
downpours, showers, squalls…

B ut as soon as you wake up in the morning to a sunny blue sky, you forget all about it.
My second favourite sort of weather, after fine and sunny, is sou'west squalls. I like the way the sea changes colour, and the smell of the wind as the next band of rain and black cloud bears down.

In March 1998 after a night of heavy rain, I headed up the hill in the morning to get the water-pipe going again. Partway down the airstrip through a gap in the flaxes, I saw the beach buried under two metres of logs, branches and, at the far end, leaves and sawdust. I went back to the house to get the others to come and see. It was all bright red, fresh wood that had been living trees only the day before, and we found and ate a crayfish that had drowned in the fresh water. The net — and the log it was tied to, well above normal flood levels — had been washed away, but we salvaged some of it from the tangled ball amongst the jumble. Seagulls gorged themselves on giant earthworms 30 centimetres long. There was not a stick of driftwood left on the riverbed, which was layered with thick mud. It seemed that somewhere up the valley a slip had occurred large enough to completely block the river until it blew out in a big wave. Luckily, it had happened in the middle of the night and we were far enough away from it not to be in harm's way. The river ran muddy for a month as the slip continued to wash down, until a spent cyclone came down the coast and a huge sea piled up all the driftwood again, a metre deep, right to the edge of the bush. Over the next year tonnes of moving gravel reduced the depth of the river to one-and-a-half to two metres in places where it was usually four to six metres. As the gravel moved further out, we had spectacular river bars across the mouth. Another big flood washed it away and dumped it onto the beach where it stayed for the next five years. In 2009 a huge flood left wood only 30 centimetres deep all down the beach, beginning a similar cycle, and it was hard to quite comprehend that 11 years earlier, it had been six times more than that.

So far we have always been together during earthquakes. Sometime in my first two or three years here, Robert and I were sitting at Dee Creek, halfway between Barn Bay and the end of the road in the Cascade Valley, watching all the trees swaying during what seemed like a smallish quake. At the Martyr homestead the water had been sloshing out of the tank, and back at home a week later several books had fallen off the shelves. I came to realise that the experience of an earthquake depends very much on where you are sitting at the time.

In 2006 we were whitebaiting at Big Bay, staying in the Mitchells' hut on the north side of the Awarua River. Safely tucked into bed in the sleepout, the quake was a good one but not at all worrying. Robin slept through it as usual, and Christan was right beside us in the next bunk. At breakfast the conversation was lively and excited, especially while the quake was discussed over the DOC channel on the single-sideband radio. While the woman in Te Anau chatted away about the earlier shock, we sat there rocking around with the next one. When the other person finally got a word in, he said, 'Actually, we're just having another!'

Sitting inside this time in daylight, seeing the large glass windows bowing in and out and pongas swaying around outside, the aftershock seemed a lot worse than the first quake had. Being surrounded by nervous people also made a difference, and with several small aftershocks throughout the day I was jumpy as I'd never been before. Every time someone bumped the table I thought it was another one. I really feel for the people of Christchurch doing that for months on end.

Our worst one by far came in the middle of the night in 2003. Centred in Doubtful Sound, of magnitude 7.4, it had the corners of the house shrieking. It also had me sitting up in bed wondering at which point I should do something, such as start putting some clothes on. While Robin had slept through it, Christan was jumpy for weeks.

In July 2009, Christan was at home for school holidays when a 7.8 magnitude quake occurred in Doubtful Sound. We sat at the table looking at each other while everything shook for about a minute. There was plenty of time to wonder if this was the Big One, as it gradually increased in intensity then decreased again just as gradually. There were a few aftershocks over the next couple of days, but nothing fell off the shelves and it certainly wasn't the worst we'd had.

It was interesting to hear on the news that in fact this was a big one if not *the* Big One. It sounded much more exciting in the newspaper accounts, and it was the biggest earthquake recorded in the world for that year until Samoa had a really big quake complete with tsunami. Of course, Doubtful Sound is 200 kilometres from here, and it was bad enough for the few people who were on the spot. We heard one story in which all the seals jumped up onto the rocks except one which jumped onto a fishing boat instead. When the water drained out and the boat rocked over on its keel, the seal slid across the deck into the toilet!

After Christan had gone back to school it rained for four weeks. We had a bit of a break for a week or so, then it poured for four days. As neighbour Warrick Mitchell commented, at least it had only rained twice.

On the fourth night Robert said, 'Did you hear that noise?'

'Well, yes, now that you mention it.'

At first he thought it was the sliding door of the bathroom. Robin was in the bathroom at the time and so could hear the noise better, and she thought it was the sound of an earthquake coming, only it never arrived. Meanwhile, the rain was thundering on the roof, the river was in full flood, and the sea was rough. The noise sounded to me like a retreating wave rolling stones back down the beach, but it kept going on and on. I started to think about waves and opened the front window to see if a tsunami was coming, but nothing more happened.

It wasn't until the afternoon of the following day that the rain stopped and I went out to have a look at the beach. Looking up, I saw a new slip on the hill behind us and my jaw dropped, quite literally. I scooted back to fetch the others, and as Robin stepped onto the airstrip I said, 'Turn around.' It was very funny to watch her jaw drop, too.

Although this slip looks impressive in photos, it was actually quite reassuring to have that much of the hill fall off behind us without it being a problem. It is 200 metres away from us and didn't go as far as the bottom of the hill. I'm now used to looking at it from here, but I still find it quite an ugly scar in my favourite view from a kilometre up the beach.

While Christchurch residents struggled through the

aftermath of the 22 February 2011 earthquake, Robert replaced our stove. The new one had been custom-made by Mr Wobbles and Geoff Robson in their Neil's Beach engineering workshop. When they had arrived here with it on 2 November 2010, I had tears in my eyes.

'Yesterday was our wedding anniversary,' I said. 'I've never had a proper stove.'

I suppose it would have been handy to have had this stove years ago when I was feeding hungry teenagers, but then I wouldn't be appreciating it so much now.

With ash and concrete dust thick on every surface and our eyes, throats and noses full of it, we thought how lucky we were that we could at least have a cold shower at the end of it or swim in a river that was unpolluted by raw sewage. Although we'd lost our chimney, the hole in the roof wasn't leaking or threatening to drop anything on us. The toilet still flushed, and we could cook on the stove in the DOC hut or heat enough water to wash with.

Chapter 21

THE GOLDEN HEN THAT LAID EGGS

Up until 2003 we had not had much success with pets. Often there would be a mouse rescued from a trap, which would be bleeding from the nose but otherwise apparently OK.

'Is there an antidote to rat poison?' Christan would ask, in tears.

The mouse would then spend half a day trying to jump out of a 20-litre bucket while the kids made its house nicer, hoping it would choose to stay. One mouse actually jumped right out, but mostly they'd be released at the end of the airstrip in the afternoon.

Creamy and Chocolate were two mallard ducklings who flew home with us from Arrowtown one summer. They were relatively undemanding, in that they would sit (and shit) on the back doorstep and wait for you to come back out, at least until they got too hungry to wait any longer and would lodge a loud protest. If we scratched amongst the leaf litter in the bush they would eat anything that moved, but if a brown moth stayed perfectly still they couldn't see it.

At first they swam in a fish-case and ate sandflies, but as they grew we carried them to the river to swim. Without a mother duck they weren't very waterproof and they looked very funny grooming their wet spikes. Their belly feathers grew in first, which made an interesting zoological lesson, because by contrast chickens grow in their wing feathers first to keep warm.

That summer a lot of greenstone boulders flew out under a Sikorsky helicopter. While the Pounamu Vesting Act had come into force in 1997, Darrell Munro, Harvey Hutton and Ian Boustridge held a claim at Awarua Point up to 2001, and as they were using the biggest helicopter we'd ever seen, it was the cause of much excitement. The ducklings also kept an eye on the 'big bird' while it flew to and fro directly over us. Literally *one* eye: they'd watch with their heads on one side, then, as the helicopter passed over, turn their heads and watch with the other eye.

Until we had them as pets, I never realised that ducks smelled so bad! As they got bigger, we herded them to the river each day for a good wash rather than just for a jolly swim. By this time the local paradise ducks were keeping an eye on them, too, and we wondered what would happen when they were big enough to be left alone down at the river. We hoped they would eventually fly away and be independent, but come back to visit and be fed occasionally. As it turned out we were to discover just how small a hole a stoat can get through, when I found them both dead in their cage one morning. They are buried under the oak tree.

Next we brought home a green frog, but had a problem working out how to keep it contained without keeping potential frog food out. It had a swimming pond in half a jerry-can, and mossy rocks to sit on, and we half-squashed sandflies into the pond so they'd still be moving. But when it apparently hadn't eaten anything in a week we let it go rather than watch it die in captivity, and told each other hopefully how happy it would be sitting out by the little creek.

In May 2003 one of the Toddies' chooks had abandoned her newly hatched chicken in a frost, and it was living in their house in a box. As it was a bad time of year to be a chicken in Central Otago it came home with us, despite all my misgivings about what we'd do with it when it was grown.

For four days we were alternately entertained and frustrated by this little fluff-ball that always had to be under your feet. Every time you moved, it would come running to see if you'd scratched something for it to eat, and it wouldn't let you out of its sight unless it was tucked into bed. Bed was a cardboard box with a hot-water bottle, a blanket and a wee nest made of sheepskin. You could tuck it into bed and put the sheepskin lid on, and it would stay quiet for ever-diminishing periods before climbing out of it and peeping loudly to be let out of the box.

In the wee hours of the fifth night I woke to hear the chicken calling out, obviously struggling with something. As I opened the box a rat jumped out, and the chicken was crying with an injured beak and foot. I held it, crying myself, sure that this tiny ball of feathers, bleeding at both ends, would soon be another on our list of dead pets. There wasn't much I could do except make it comfortable in its wee nest, and put the nest into one of the rat-proof boxes we keep our spare clothes and blankets in. It cried all night.

'How does a chicken cry?' my sister asked when I told her about it.

I have read about the discordant notes young animals have in their cries that their mothers find impossible to ignore. The sound goes right through your brain and breaks your heart, and no amount of helpful advice from your husband — 'You have to be tough or they will walk all over you' — makes it any easier, whether it is a baby, a duckling or a fledgling bird relying on you to feed it and keep it safe. Robin was seven the first time I held a crying baby and laughed to find myself immune to his theatrics, but the rat-attacked chicken and the hungry starling chick were still to come. Even now I can't bear the noise Robert makes carving greenstone with his Dremel. It sounds to me like a small child who doesn't want to have his hair washed, screaming 'Nah, nah, nah!'

Despite the tragic circumstances, it was quite a relief to have the chicken immobilised for a week while its beak healed and three of its toes turned black and fell off. Christan and Robert covered a beer crate with rat-proof mesh, which made a safe travelling-box for Chooky for the rest of her life, and she could live in it on trips out to Arrowtown or at Big Bay during the whitebait season.

First thing every morning when we took her out of her box, we'd carry her straight to the bathroom sink to wash her feet. Then she could fly down to the floor nicely. Next she learned to scratch. We gave her food in the lid of a small jar, and we'd hear 'Peck, peck, peck, scratch — *PING!*' as the lid flew out across the floor behind her. But the funniest thing was when she tried to scratch porridge.

She still didn't let us out of her sight for several weeks, which led to one very stressful day when we were all helping Robert to fix the roof before it started raining again. We'd be calling down the chimney to a distressed chicken looking for its mum, and Robin would dash down to see her whenever she could be spared.

I learned to speak 'Chicken' in the same way as I usually knew why my babies were crying. It had a three- to four-note song that sounded like '*hap-pee-chook, hap-pee-chook*', or at the scrawny stage when her crop was as big as a golf ball with hardly any feathers to cover it, it was more like '*crop's-gonna-pop, crop's-gonna-pop*'. When she was getting hungry there was a two-note call that said '*feed-me, feed-me*'. I could hear her asking one morning while I sat in bed.

'She's got food,' Christan assured me, but the call became increasingly urgent until it became the single note '*Mum! Mum! Mum!*', and I got up to find her full food bowl upside down so that she couldn't get to it.

Bringing her with us had been a spur-of-the-moment decision as we headed to Roger Monk's airstrip. At that time we had no way of asking him to bring anything extra that we'd forgotten, unless we could get a letter out to him with a tramper or another aeroplane or helicopter, so she was about a month old by the time he flew in with a load of groceries and mail. Another month went by before he came again, this time with some stoat-proof chicken wire, and by then she was spending the day outside, only coming in to sleep in her box at night. When allowed in each evening, she'd patter, patter, patter quickly through the workshop then stand still in the doorway and say, '*Here I am! Everyone's favourite chook. Now, I'll just have a quick peck, then who would like to cuddle me first?'*

She was so proud of herself sitting in her new cage out in the garden, saying, *'I'm a chook!'* And on the day her voice was breaking, I spotted her hiding behind the wood-pile practising her new *'brrrrkkk'*.

For the rest of her life, she came inside every evening for a cuddle and a few peanuts before we shut her into the cage for the night. Also on wet days we'd invariably feel sorry for her and she'd straggle in looking like a feather duster that had been mistakenly used as a toilet brush.

We were so lucky that she turned out to be (a) a hen and (b) a very pretty little hen who could ride in a backpack. It would have been so different having a big ugly rooster. When Robin was due for a full-sized pack for her thirteenth birthday, we had to search Queenstown to find one with a 'chook pocket' on the top: a zip-up pocket big enough for Chooky to sit in with her head sticking out, without being too squashed.

Apart from when we flew to Australia, she usually came with us on buses and later in the car. We'd shut her in a box to get her onto a bus, but the driver invariably knew she was there by the end of the trip.

'Is that a cat in there?'

'Ummm, a chook actually.'

'It only said four passengers on the ticket.'

We couldn't find a decent box at Gunn's Camp, so she rode to Te Anau in an empty six-pack with her head out one end, tail out the other, and a convenient handle to carry her by.

'Is it a kiwi?' an overseas visitor asked.

'The only family I know who'd bring a chook to Milford,'

said Wanaka Flightseeing pilot Andy Woods as we posed for photos in front of Mitre Peak.

It had taken us eight days to walk all the way to the end of the Hollyford Road, but Chooky didn't walk far. She wouldn't follow you like a dog does. Whenever we put her down her main focus was on what wanted to eat her next, so she'd generally head for the nearest cover. The only time she went in the right direction was on the bridge over Little Homer Creek when she only had a choice of forwards and backwards. The DOC huts had boot-scraper door-mats which were perfect for her to sit on, as her poops fell straight through to the ground below.

She laid her first egg halfway up the beach to Barn Bay on a trip out to Haast. She'd been making a fuss all day, but it was a new noise and we didn't yet know what she meant. Christan was carrying her in a sou'wester hat tied to the straps of his pack. When she squawked and jumped out, he found an egg in the hat! Of course we had to write a book about that, and, as we didn't have a camera with us, the kids drew a lot of the pictures for it. Later we took her and a camera up the beach for a walk to get a few photos, plus other people sent us some of her out in Haast and Arrowtown. Actually, *she* wrote that book — '*Tales of a Well-Travelled Chook*' by Hermione Cluck (affectionately known as Chooky) — and Gorge River Press published it for her. Then we had to get her to write another book with all the jokes we hadn't used yet. In *Chooky Checks Out Modes of Transport*, she travels by boat, pram, surfboard, backpack and shopping trolley, and finds a car with her name on the licence plate.

Over the next four years she laid a few eggs in strange places, one at Dee Creek and one at the Jerry River after we'd carried her up into the upper Gorge River gorge and back.

One day we opened her box in the back of the car to find her looking most embarrassed, as if she'd been sick. She'd laid a soft-shelled egg then sat on it, and was covered in egg yolk.

She travelled on the Cook Strait ferry, almost got to Cape Reinga, and pooped on the doorstep of The Beehive as a protest against the farming of battery hens.

On visits to the Toddies near Arrowtown she had to face up to other chooks, whom she considered very bossy and ill-mannered. She was definitely at the very bottom of any pecking order, and mostly sat on the doorstep waiting for us to come back. If the door was open, she'd come inside to look for us. The first time we had to leave her there for a few weeks when we couldn't take her on an aeroplane, she just sat at the door and moulted.

'If she pulls any more feathers out you'll have to knit her a woolly jersey!' said Toddie.

The Toddies' farm is something of a mixed menagerie. The first time we took Chooky back to the place where she'd hatched, Toddie was sitting at the table filling out a stocktake for the Ministry of Agriculture. Apart from red deer, he had a few fallow deer, half a dozen cows, pigs, goats, chooks, ducks, a couple of turkeys and a battered pheasant who liked to hassle the chooks.

'You're lucky you don't have to fill out these stupid forms,' he said.

'Now that Chooky is laying eggs, maybe we should expect one in the post,' I suggested, receiving a snort in reply.

Toddie had raised eight orphaned Canada goslings, which lived on his pond with various geese, mallards, grey teal, paradise shelducks, Australasian shovellers . . . the list goes on. Some of the ganders had grown up a bit demented, in the way that hand-reared birds often do. One defended his territory around a piece of water-pipe, as if it was his mate. Another hung around the dog kennels and hissed and charged at anyone who walked by. Toddie threw him back over the deer fence whenever he could catch him, but he always got out again. We wrote a poem for him.

'Goosey Goosey Gander,
Wither will you wander?'
'Upstairs and downstairs
And in my lady's chamber.

There I met Toddie,
Looking most intense.
He grabbed me by the left leg
And threw me over the fence!'

On one occasion on the farm in springtime Chooky was evidently 'on heat'. She dropped her wings down in a submissive gesture that says 'I'm ready for a rooster', but apparently without understanding the consequences of her behaviour. Next thing I saw her flash past the front door, followed two seconds later by the rooster. She took a sharp left turn and vanished into a tangled mass of vegetation as the rooster sailed on by.

A minute passed.

'OK, Chooky, you can come out now ... Chooky?'

I peered in to find her completely hemmed in by the short sticks of the wee hedge. She couldn't reverse out without help, and definitely couldn't go forwards.

She was a lot more wary after that episode.

One trip driving from Haast to Greymouth and Dunedin was complicated by the addition of six tiny, fluff-ball chickens to the poultry department. We had rescued them from certain death and were transporting them to the growing population at my sister's place in Dunedin, but this involved having them for three nights and a whole day in motel rooms along the way.

At Whataroa we arrived late and left early, so they just stayed in their box, but in Greymouth we stayed at Charles Court motel with friends, Helen and Ian Rasmussen, who were well used to us. Chooky usually had her own room there — the canopy of a small truck on the grass out the back of the motel where she was warm and dry and safe from dogs, cats and other potential predators. This time, however, the canopy was on the truck. Ian turned the truck around so that the rainwater would drain out of it, and of course the last thing I did when we left was to hose it out. The chickens mostly stayed in their box, but several times during the day they would come out to eat, drink, scratch, poop and generally make a mess on the newspaper. By the fourth day they were well-trained, and we had them perching all over the car in sunny spots or snuggling in our pockets between feeds.

Out of respect to Chooky, we'd try to be a bit tactful when eating a roast chicken, speaking of 'Uncle Harry' in whispers, until the day when Nana, carving the Christmas roast, dropped a piece onto the floor and Chooky scoffed it! Grandad called her 'Half a pot of soup', and certainly if you took the feathers off her there wouldn't have been much to eat.

For several years I've made Christmas cards starring Chooky. Robin had a trick of making her lie on her back without quite realising where she was, so we laid her in the baking dish surrounded by potatoes and onions in the middle of a decorated table. I took at least a dozen photos of her, and when she noticed the parsley on her breast she took a wee peck at it, completely unconcerned. Then suddenly she leapt up in a great flap, scattering potatoes and onions in all directions.

Apart from stoats, rats, dogs, cats and roosters, her main enemy was the falcons that would sit up at the top of the hill watching her. She was only six months old the first time they had a go at her, down by the river where she was eating sandhoppers. The falcon actually had her in the air, but the kids were there and were able to save her. She had puncture marks on each shoulder, and spent the rest of the day inside the house *under* the seat.

She got away with it for the next few years, but at times when the falcons were extra-hungry with fledglings she often wouldn't dare to come out of her cage. She could reach the front door in three great flapping leaps right over the silverbeet to come inside for a while each evening. I once saw a falcon fly straight through the 12-centimetre trawl mesh on the front gate, simply tucking its wings in before carrying on. It would sit in the cabbage tree right above her cage waiting for a chance. I had her out with me while gardening one day when there was an almighty '*Squawk!*' I turned and, through a great cloud of feathers, saw the falcon on Chooky's back repeatedly stabbing downwards with its cruel beak as she ducked her head to the right, left, right again. Although I was less than three metres away, there was nothing I could do before she wriggled out from under and dashed into the prickly gooseberry bushes.

In her last summer, Chooky seemed different. She was more than six-and-a-half years old, hadn't laid an egg in two years, and maybe she was getting a bit senile. She was much less cautious and would even wander out onto the airstrip flashing her tail feathers at anyone who might be watching from above. But she died on her perch in peace after an illness of only one day, and so far we haven't wanted another pet.

Chapter 22
MOTHER NATURE'S MULTITUDES

Nearly everyone asks, 'How do you deal with the sandflies?'

A rich lady steps out of a Squirrel helicopter to have a champagne lunch on our table. 'Oh, I could live here forever!' Then a sandfly lands on her and the pilot scurries back to the chopper for the insect repellent.

'You are about to discover why you don't want to live here forever.'

Most people will stop reacting to the sandflies after a couple of weeks if they stay long enough, but the sandflies still hurt when they bite. When the kids were small I never dressed them in shorts or T-shirts, which also meant that we didn't have to use sunscreen. As they got older they tended not to be as bothered by the sandflies as much as we are and could choose what to wear for themselves. Wearing a hat not only keeps them out of your hair, but mostly out of your face as well.

But Gorge River must be the only place on the coast without mosquitoes. There is virtually no swamp in this valley, which also means we don't get much whitebait. I can deal with sandflies because they mostly stop at night, but I am grateful that we have so few mozzies.

I remember the first year I was here, 'Spacie', a fisherman, had been into Barn Bay to Lou Brown's birthday party and couldn't understand how Lou could live with so many sandflies in the house at night.

'They have been particularly bad this year,' we said.

Various strategies have been employed for keeping them out of the house. We used to have plastic fly streamers over the front door which opened into the workshop first. With the inside door shut, this acted as a kind of sandfly trap. Once inside they tend to go to the windows, and I used to spend a lot of time squashing them there, as we almost never used fly-spray. Visitors often left half-used cans of fly-spray next-door when they left, and these accumulated for years.

We use repellent when necessary, and whenever I arrived during my first year Robert smelled of citronella. For a couple of years we added peppermint and eucalyptus oil as well, but this got expensive by the time there were three of us using it. A bottle of Dettol went a lot further, mixed with oil of some sort. Later, Robert always smelled of linseed oil.

We do get years with a boom of other things, too.

There was the Year of the Cicada when, lying in bed as the first ray of sunshine hit the garden in the morning, you'd hear a single *chirp* and the whole lot would join in on the second note and continue until the sun went down. A 'cicadian rhythm'. We walked out through the Hollyford Valley that year. At Big Bay the kids were collecting them, walking around with them on their hats. As we walked from Hidden Falls to the road-end there were stretches of the track where the sound of cicadas was absolutely deafening.

Then there was the Year of the Bumblebee. When Dick and Pip Smith landed here in their bright blue Jet Ranger helicopter, we suggested that they should shut the doors and it wasn't just for the sandflies. Half an hour later there must have been 20 or 30 bumblebees buzzing around their helicopter, as blue is the bumblebee's favourite colour.

The kids were stung several times a day, which hurts but is no big deal. We don't have any honey bees here. Once I stepped right into the middle of a bumblebees' tea party and was stung simultaneously on both sides of the foot. Ouch! And sometimes, after a narrow miss, I have looked down to see a pissed-off bee lying on its back, squirting venom furiously into the air.

But 2007 was the Year of the Sandfly in the South Westland calendar. By this time we had a screen-door and several windows screened with curtain netting, as they go through normal fly screen when they get determined — which is every morning and evening in the summertime. You can deal with them all day, but when they don't stop at night it gets to be a bit much.

From first light we lay with a shirt over our heads — the only summer we've had to resort to such measures. At night they flew up to the light then dropped onto the table, and Robin had to wear a hat to keep them out of her tea! We became used to using fly-spray, even in the main room, until all those half-used tins were finished for the first time ever. Mostly, we only spray in the workshop and shut the door until the stink clears and they are all dead, and sometimes Robert burns a mosquito coil out there.

That year was the year I went out to Dunedin at the beginning of February when my grandmother died. I left clutching my hat, knowing that I'd need it as soon as I got back. I bought fly-spray for the first time, and we continued to buy it for the next couple of years while the sandflies were still at the upper end of their cycle. I also bought fly-papers, which were brilliant! We hung them up by the light, and an awful lot that would have ended up buzzing upside-down on the table never got to.

The cycle ended with a cold, horrible summer, but I wasn't complaining. Not only were we relatively sandfly-free, but Christan had come home for Christmas and was unable to leave until two weeks into January — a double bonus.

Robert uses repellent a lot, as he tends to do outside, standing-still jobs. For example, it takes him two full days down by the river to strip the ropes off an old net with their lines of floats and sinkers and use them to make a new net. He comes back with red spots all over his feet despite all the repellent he uses.

Whereas Robert loves summer, I can't bear that hot muggy, buggy, overcast weather. By the beginning of February, however, we usually notice that the number of sandflies has begun to decline.

I prefer not to use repellent much, and these days I usually don't do any gardening on the worst days. It isn't all bad, though. On fine, no-sandfly days you can't bear to be stuck inside, and sometimes you can be looking forward to a wet day to get inside jobs done.

It is no accident that Otago Girls High School was the first girls' high school in New Zealand; an indication of the reverence the Scots held not only for their women but for education, too. They understood that if you educate the women, you educate the children. I am not a qualified teacher, but never thought that formal qualifications mattered very much. I am well educated and I have taught my kids how to look at the world around them, to ask questions and understand the way things work, the laws of cause and effect.

In spring we often watch muttonbirds flying south to the islands off Stewart Island to breed. On strong sou'westerly days they fly closer to the coast, looking for a reduction in the headwind. One day the wind was so strong that they were flying almost over the beach. When it is northerly, they fly so far out at sea that you can't see them. Through the binoculars we watch them going by, one after another, day after day, in a seemingly endless stream.

'There's tens of thousands of them!' Robert said.

'No, there's twenties of hundreds,' Robin insisted, in a higher pitch, and wrote it in her Nature Diary: *20es of 100es*. Robert read it aloud as 'zoes of looies' and the phrase stuck.

When all the flaxes flower, with six or seven stalks each, tui arrive from wherever they spend the rest of their time. Bright orange heads top iridescent blue, green and brown bodies. In the biggest mast year we'd had for a long time, they stayed long enough to nest. The bellbirds also raised at least one young one, distinguishable by its behaviour rather than appearance. The young tui, lacking a white throat feather, called pathetically to be fed between dodging irate parents who had evidently had enough of that business. A few days later it was furtively fending for itself, trying not to present the bossy elders with any opportunity to harass it. In the bush one day, I saw it duck into the top of a rata tree above me, hiding in the canopy like a blackbird in a cabbage tree when the falcon passes by. With a whirr of flight feathers the adult zoomed overhead, calling aggressively, but Junior stayed hidden for 15 minutes, digesting nectar and waiting for things to cool down a bit before venturing out carefully to the nearby flax flowers at the edge of the bush on the riverbank.

Across the river the beach is sandy for most of the next eight kilometres, and little blue penguins come up at night to nest in old rabbit burrows. A pair used to live on the side of the airstrip when Christan was little, but they disappeared for a while. Three or four years later perhaps the next generation nested there a couple of times, but we haven't seen them for many years. While counting little blue penguins' footprints on an early-morning tide-washed beach a couple of years ago for the West Coast Penguin Trust, we found two sets of bigger Fiordland crested penguin tracks on a short stretch that is normally rocky but where a bit of sand had settled temporarily. We counted this as two nests, and early the following year we saw four sets of tracks returning to the same place to moult.

Newly fledged fantails can often be seen outside Robin's window at the back of the house, being fed on a beakful of sandflies. The parent, probably the male, is usually the scruffiest-looking bird, quite worn-out after raising the brood. His mate may already be sitting on the next lot of eggs.

We had a tinted window in the bathroom, and Mrs Thomasina Tit often sat there talking to her reflection. There seem to be many more tomtits over the past few years, and visitors often comment on them, asking if they are robins. It seems that most people don't get to see them much anymore. The same is true for red admiral butterflies which lay their eggs on *Urtica ferox*, the ferocious tree nettle, which unsurprisingly is now scarce in most areas of the country.

Arriving here one summer we climbed out of the aeroplane to find a dead paradise duckling on the ground. The adults still had three more offspring, but within a day or two that had been reduced to two. I was hauling trolley loads of firewood on the airstrip when Robin, age four, came to me with a suspicious bulge up her shirt.

'Mum,' she began, as if she was about to divulge a great secret, 'next time there's a Pet Day near here, I want to go.'

'Why? What have you got?'

I had to persuade her to let the duckling go back to its mummy, but a few days later we were left wondering whether we should have kept it for the sake of its life.

After reading the book *Takahe — lost and found* about Geoffrey Orbell, who rediscovered the takahe bird thought to be extinct for years, we came across an unusual footprint on the beach. Robin bent down to measure it in a most scientific fashion.

'Do you think it is an extinct bird?'

'No, I fink it is a ecktink duck!'

In fact, it turned out to be a spur-winged plover — the first time we'd seen one here. The next day we saw it about an hour before the falcons lined it up. One of them dive-bombed and forced it into the river, then sat on a log to wait as it floated, unable to fly and drifting with the current. Just before it met the first wave at the river mouth, the other falcon flew down and plucked it from the water before they both flew away with it up the river.

Christan was in floods of tears, but Robin calmly

announced, 'He's taking him home for lunch.'

Two or three weeks later, walking across the Cascade flats with plovers screeching at us from all directions, Christan was over it: 'I'm sick of plovers now!'

I n the first few years I was here you could watch seven or eight kaka every night, flying from one hill to the other across the Gorge. Today there is hardly ever more than one or two at a time, as stoats continue to take their toll.

In 1996 a tramper, Pete Shaw, arrived having spent three or four days walking down the river. A possum hunter had reported hearing a kokako up above the Jerry River junction, so bird expert Rhys Buckingham had asked Pete to come down for a few days to play sound recordings although he had heard no answer.

'I'm making a pizza, but I've made enough dough for two,' I said.

'I've got the cheese and salami,' he replied.

'Great! We were having potato and seaweed.'

He told us that the last definite sighting of a breeding pair of South Island kokako had been in southern Stewart Island 10 years before, but the fishermen who knew about them kept it secret rather than have them interfered with. Pete, who had been working with North Island kokako in the Ureweras for several years, said that if they had known in 1986 what they knew at this time they could have saved them. Several people say that kokako are still out there, but at one of Robert's book talks in Nelson Rhys told us that although he has heard them and seen various signs of them, he has been unable to spot one and that he considers them to be functionally extinct.

Often as I walk down the airstrip with the trolley to cart

wood, a fernbird calls to me. If I stop and call back it keeps answering, gradually coming closer until it is more visible amongst the flax leaves. They are not particularly shy, despite their habit of keeping inside scrubby bush, but rather curious. Robin once had one come down onto the ground in front of her as she scratched up the dirt.

During the Roar one year, Dave Crichton spotted a bird he didn't recognise just before the helicopter arrived to fly him out for another year. Back in his office at Chamber and Nicholls' accountancy firm a couple of days later, there was the bird, a fernbird, on the front cover of the *Forest & Bird* magazine. We didn't hear that for some time, so later in the day I went into the bush looking for anything noticeably different and saw a bird I have never seen before or since. It was quite like a blackbird but significantly larger and chocolatey brown. I asked Gerry McSweeney of *Forest & Bird* about it sometime later, and rather than scoffing at the idea as I had expected, he said, 'That will be an Australian bird. They occasionally get caught in a big westerly storm and this would be the first place they reach.'

Whatever the bird was I never found out, but on 26 April 2008 Robert spotted an Australian castaway. From our holidays in Queensland, we knew the magpie lark that was sitting on the airstrip and on the roof of the DOC hut and, as Gerry had said, it was just after a strong westerly spell. Brian Glubb and Larry, from Haast, also saw something strange that sounded similar in the Cascade Valley a day or two later. Robin reported it to the Ornithological Society and it was the first official sighting since 1905.

Another bird that caught our eye by looking unusual turned out to be a young long-tailed cuckoo, as yet without a tail, squawking to be fed by its harassed foster parents. In the first year I lived here I saw an adult fly into the window, not hard enough to stop it for more than a moment, and it was some time before I saw one again, although we often hear them calling in the spring and summertime.

While boogie-boarding out at the island, Robin and I have seen black-backed gulls nesting, and the young ones, still fluffy but walking around, high up on the main rock. Up at Cutter Rocks, five kilometres north of here, we have seen one sitting on eggs on a rock cut off by the high tide. Later, once they have fledged, the young birds swim in the river while the parents watch from the high rock on the far side, until an argument erupts as to when the next meal should be. At a certain age, the parents chase them off, but twice we had a juvenile hanging around for several months taking food from us. Silky waited by the net each morning until Robert came down to the river to check it. He followed the boys down to the rocks at the end of the airstrip where they fished for wrasse and had to be watched carefully. After being fed on the fish frames he grew bolder and pinched the catch while their backs were turned, or took limpets from the pile of bait. We were astonished at how big a fish he could swallow, even to the point that he could barely fly. He'd wobble out to sea and sit there to digest it a bit before coming ashore to spit up and pick the good bits from around the bones. One day he took the bait as it landed in the sea, and Christan had a seagull flying around like a kite on the end of his fishing line.

Silky disappeared after a few months and we thought perhaps he'd gone to hang out at the Haast dump, but later Silky II returned regularly every month or two for a couple of years or more, even after he'd grown into adult colours. At first, while he was still flying with his parents, one of them flew over the airstrip and dropped an empty paua shell as if it knew that we fed Chooky from paua shells and it was asking us to feed the young one. We put meat or fish out for him when we had it, or even rice if there was nothing else, but he didn't think much of that. Christan fed him whole possum legs with the claws and fur on. He'd swallow one and still come back for more, but if he put his head down to take another piece the leg would fall out of his throat.

Seagulls eat a lot of cat's eye snails, and in good weather the rocks around Gorge Island are covered in regurgitated front doors. Silky II paid for his keep once by spitting up a pile of them just outside the fence where we usually put his food, including the biggest cat's eye we have ever seen around here. But generally he couldn't stay much longer than a week, as Bossy would chase him off while never brave enough himself to land on the airstrip to take food.

A pair of paradise ducks eat the grass on the airstrip and warn us of approaching trampers. They are the fourth pair that has lived here in the past 20 years. We watched the previous pair growing old together, particularly after they raised three and later one duckling to fledging. The male made increasingly heavy weather of the post-nesting moult.

'That's the funniest duck we've ever seen,' commented hunters Paul and Brent during the Roar.

He'd lost so many feathers that he could barely float, and if pushed to swim quickly the water flowed over his shoulders. The following year he couldn't fly at all for a few weeks. When I inadvertently frightened him off the edge of the airstrip, he had to run down the beach into the sea then swim all the way back to the river mouth.

Another time we frightened a young one into the river during a small flood, and, feeling dreadful, watched as he washed out to sea, not expecting to see him again. However, he made it ashore across the river, and in fact survived to fledge, so we christened him 'Lucky'. Sometime later we saw him on the riverbank with the parents and a fourth duck. Uncle Blue Duck had called in for a visit.

A pair of oystercatchers are also our near neighbours. The new pair came to live here in 1999. They have hatched chicks a few times, which is great fun to watch, but only twice have they raised one or two to fledging. We watch them from the bush, where they seem unaware of us although they are instantly alert should we step onto the riverbed. We saw three chicks hatch on Christmas Eve in 2004. Two were dry and fluffy, camouflaged amongst the rocks away from the nest while the adults continued to take turns to sit on the last egg until it hatched. They have a time limit, though, and will leave a squeaking, half-hatched egg when they have to for the sake of the others. On Christmas Day Christan had a telescope, so we watched them toddling around and being fed. The adults worked in shifts to search for limpets and other shellfish, and called to the others as they flew around the corner into the river. While the tide was high they searched for grubs under logs on the riverbed. After a couple of days, the whole family trooped out to the beach in the mornings and we watched them returning at night, a major trip for the two tiny fluff-balls over boulders and logs.

Their survival is generally decided by the weather in their first week of life; a day of heavy rain or a big sea will probably be the end of them. Often the adults nest too close to the river, and a flood or rough sea sweeps the nest away, but they don't seem to learn before the next time.

One year two chicks survived to fledge, after which the adults became much more relaxed, although the youngsters still had to be fed. We cut up possum meat into small pieces and fed them at high tide. Their beaks open at a hinge rather than disconnecting like a seagull's does, so they can take only small bits. One adult is usually off-duty and ignores them all, while the other comes close to take the meat. It carries it down the beach while the two fledglings follow behind begging for it. Sometimes one nags long enough, sometimes the other, and every now and then they both miss out as the adult swallows it himself. It is lovely to watch. We never fed them a lot and only when the tide was in, so that they would continue to do their own thing the rest of the time. A couple of years later when the next chick fledged we tried to do it again, but the adults had forgotten how and only one of them took a few bits and swallowed them.

One day while I was getting wood on the front beach, I kept feeling an urge to watch out for a whale, but resisted because I had to get the job done. But sure enough, along comes Robin calling, 'There's orca!'

Three females and a male were swimming by, outside the island. I watched until they were too far away to see any longer, but as I turned away I thought, 'There could be more coming yet', and watched a bit longer. Another pair surfaced about a kilometre offshore, and two more came along behind.

It can be hard to tell how big they are. They look just like dolphins, and it can be hard to judge the distance. Then the male surfaces and you have no doubt. As each of the males reached the level of the island, they stopped, lay on the surface somehow, and made huge flaps of their tails without going anywhere in a way that lifted them right up out of the water. Then we could really see how big they were.

It is amazing how deer seem to know whether or not someone wants to shoot them. The four weeks of the Roar in March and April every year is a busy season we look forward to, when the Gorge River DOC hut is usually full of hunters.

If the weather has been warmer than usual, the stags may not start roaring properly until right at the end or even the following week. One year we heard a stag roaring as we lay in bed the morning after the last party had helicoptered out.

Murray Bowes landed in his Cessna 185 with his son Marc and two friends to stay overnight. While the two younger men headed up the river in the boat with their rifles, Murray and his mate shared a conversation and a bottle of wine with us. Returning to the hut to cook a meal for the tired and disappointed hunters, they met two deer grazing on the doorstep.

We watch helicopters flying by, carrying people into blocks further south. This year, the young pilot Alex called in and pointed out a hind and fawn calmly grazing on the big slip behind us. After he'd flown away to collect his next load at the Cascade we watched the deer through the telescope for three-quarters of an hour, but when a party of hunters landed shortly afterwards there was no sign of the deer. Four weeks later, early on the first morning that the hut was empty, I could hear one of the deer moving around outside, breaking sticks three metres away from my side of the bed.

Today we are watching the wave of possums arriving. Thirty years ago, Robert could walk out the back of Dale's hut at Big Bay and collect fuchsia and broadleaf branches to feed deer in the holding pen before they were flown out. There are no fuchsias anymore, not even dead ones; only a few fallen logs rotting away. Tutu and even cabbage trees are stripped of their leaves, and grey skeletons of rata stand where once they flowered brightly red. This haze of dead rata is creeping up the coast towards us, and the number of possums Robert catches in his traps doubles and triples each year. The Gorge River serves as a barrier to them and is the 'end of the road'. The steep limestone face above us was bright with flowering rata only last year. Rata, kamahi, broadleaf, fuchsia; a gourmet delight for *Possumus munchii*.

———

Brown rats, black rats, gray rats, tawny rats …
Cocking tails and pricking whisker …

The Pied Piper of Hamelin by Robert Browning

When you live right beside the bush, rats are not only a fact of life but they can also be a source of much amusement — alongside the frustration and disgusting messes awaiting discovery.

In the first year I spent at Gorge River you could set your watch by 'the clockwork rat' who emerged from his yet-to-be-discovered lair, walked across the top of the bookshelf, climbed down the edge of the bathroom door, and ran across the floor to an exit behind the wood-box, off to work for the night. The lair turned out to be Robert's short wetsuit on a coat-hanger. The separate hood had fallen down inside and lodged in one leg, making a stable platform for a family of rats. As it was hanging in a dark corner, it was some time before I noticed something moving inside. Slowly pulling down the zip, I found a pair of beady eyes watching me. I zipped it back up and whacked the wetsuit while four rats came flying out of the other leg hole.

When there were small babies in the house I became more nervous about rats, so Robert patched up a few holes and for a year or so we were relatively rat-free inside the main room, at least during the winter with the doors closed.

After closing in the front verandah with a lot of windows, Robert covered the gaps above the top plate with phosphate bags to keep the sandflies out until he could get the ceiling in, and it stayed that way while we walked out to town in the autumn. By the time he got to it, several rats were living happily behind the sacks in the warm draught.

'It sounds like a case of zoological insulation,' Lou Brown commented.

Just last year, newly arrived home, I was in the hot-water cupboard and I could see a piece of string hanging down out of the ceiling. I grabbed it and pulled. 'Oh, surely not.'

Now, I've got nothing against rats so long as they stay in their upstairs flat and don't make loud gnawing noises at night or roll stolen walnuts around in the ceiling. Nor can a rat help where its tail ends up when it is dead, but still, this was definitely a job for Robert. There is often a drip above the hot-water cupboard, but when it drips onto a dead rat directly above the clean washing, we really are talking gross! You can only laugh. When I told my niece Elena about it when she was staying with us a few weeks later, she shuddered and declared that the words 'dead rat' and 'ooze' should never be used in the same sentence.

The food cupboard is mouse-proof and dry goods are stored in bottles, kerosene tins, jars, large plastic buckets and the like, although every now and then we have a rash of plastic-chewing while buckets and jars lose their lids. We came home once to find they'd chewed through a couple of two-litre bottles of canola oil and there was oil all over the floor. Next, they'd chewed the lids off two jars and added enough flour to make a roux. Two large buckets had the lids chewed most of the way around, with a bigger rat-sized hole on one side and two bags of rolled oats at the bottom of one of them, both chewed. Either this rat could count or he was on his honeymoon! It had even dragged pumpkin seeds and soggy tea bags from the garden into the bucket and was able to jump back out through the very small hole in the lid.

When we go away all our clothes and blankets have to be packed away into rat-proof boxes. Arriving home in the middle of one cold winter we found that the bed had a definite 'lived in' feel to it and smelled suspiciously of rat. We took off the mattress cover to wash it, and Robert wiped the mattress a bit — not too wet or it would never dry at that time of the year. We unpacked, had a meal, got a bit organised and piled into bed to start warming up. Ten minutes later it was, 'Oh, phew! Everybody out!'

There was no way we could sleep on that. The two mattresses had to be completely washed and they took three weeks to dry properly, including the last several days jammed into the hot water cupboard with the door roped shut.

Once in the whitebait season when Roger arrived and said 'Let's go', the lid wasn't put onto the peanut jar properly. Two weeks later we arrived home to a trail of chewed and digested peanuts leading along the shelf, across the sink and the floor, and up onto our bed. What a mess!

When I first arrived at Gorge River, Robert had various tin cans and margarine pottles hanging in strategic places, but it was funny how a drip would stop after a while or move to a new place.

One drip in particular, dubbed 'the travelling salesman' due to its erratic nature, has a place in family legend. We'd all lie in our three-metre-wide bed — plenty of room for all and no doubt, in today's speak, for family bonding time — and watch the drip form on a join in the hardboard ceiling. Then it would start its run, and there would be much hilarity as we watched to see who it would fall on this time. It wasn't quite so funny waking up in the morning to the full effect, and two or three trips up onto the roof were required to track down the source of the leak.

For a long time it was never quite bad enough to do something about it. You can't fix the roof while it's raining, and when it isn't raining it doesn't leak. Eventually, when we had to stand a bucket under one major leak and get up in the night to empty it, we acknowledged it had gone far enough.

Lifting off the old tin roofing-iron, we were amazed that it had kept anything out at all. Some of it was hardly more than a pile of rust flakes. With the tin off, all the details of Rat City were exposed to view and it was quite a lesson in zoology. There was the nursery nearest to the chimney, well-packed with dry leaves, several mummified remains of previous generations, and even the pink shower curtain that had gone missing about five years earlier.

This was one of those few times when there was no stopping for a cup of tea with a couple of arriving trampers. Robert rowed them across the river but apologised and said that we'd see them after dark, by which time it was raining again.

Chapter 23

MAYBE IT WILL WASH UP ON THE BEACH

During the early 1990s fishermen had to learn not to throw all their rubbish overboard. Trampers often complained about the amount of rubbish on the beach — cardboard bait-boxes and the plastic tape that secures them, stacks of plastic strips left after the plastic bags have been ripped off, buoys, ropes and even pots after a big blow. It was important to keep the deck tidy, so it all went over the side. Still, we'd reassure the trampers that the rubbish stayed at a constant level, rather than getting worse and worse, as apart from a few yellow oil containers which lasted forever, the plastic degraded in the sun and apparently disappeared. These days the total amount is much less but is still constant, and we see a lot more plastic bottles with Japanese writing on them.

Whenever we've needed something Robert would say, 'Maybe it will wash up on the beach.' And all sorts of things *have* washed up at times.

He uses logs for building posts, fence posts, poles for the wind-sock and radio aerial. He pulls all the nails out of washed-up timber and keeps them to use when he runs out of good ones. Steel from broken pots has been used to make digging tools for gold mining or axles for the firewood trolley, which is a washed-up fish-case on pram wheels. Other fish-cases are used for a wood-box, a bath, a worm farm, a reservoir where the water tank overflows in which we keep whitebait alive or milk and beer cool. Ropes are useful for many things, and even very short lengths can be used to tie possum traps to a tree or make a door handle.

Robert has found a sleeping bag on the beach and wet-weather gear, a door-mat, and a dinghy which we enjoyed for a short time before returning it to Bluff crayfisherman Elmo on *Mijay*. A glass fishing buoy and an unbroken light bulb were more surprising, and, once, Robert found a message in a whisky bottle: *Greetings from the officers and crew of the Australian vessel 'Australian Trader', thrown overboard* ... The latitude and longitude were recorded next, a point about halfway between here and Australia. It was dated 18 months prior to the day he found it, and the bottle still smelled of whisky.

These days, whitebait stands are more likely to be welded together than nailed, and the amount of timber washed up has noticeably decreased. When rebuilding the house, maybe half of the timber Robert used had been salvaged from the beach, carried for up to five kilometres or even more if it was particularly worthwhile. He also recycled whatever he could from what he was pulling out, but floorboards tended to get shorter as their rotten ends were sawn off and a few extras would always be necessary.

Robert uses buoys on nets and as track markers, and ropes are always in demand. When a huge tangle of trawl mesh washed up, Robert dragged it five kilometres to get it home. The deer numbers were building up as the helicopters were not hunting around here for several years, so he put the mesh up around half of the garden and we could tie it off when we were away. After a 1080 residue scare in feral venison in 2001, we hardly saw a helicopter for six years or more, and Robert brought a bundle of netting down from an old deer pen up the river to fence the rest of the garden. At night we hung the trawl mesh up across the pathways, as the deer didn't wait for us to go away anymore before checking out the gourmet cuisine in the garden.

One night shortly before Christmas we forgot to close the paths, and stepping outside in the morning Christan met Flopsy, the long-eared deer, on the back doorstep. On closer examination it became apparent that she'd walked in through the front entrance and taken a bite off every potato plant on the way to the back exit. Robert told the kids that their Christmas present for that year would be two gates to keep the deer out, and so long as the garden was secure he wouldn't have to hassle their friendly deer.

Using logs and long, straight sticks from the beach and the remainder of the trawl net, he worked all day while Flopsy ran in large circles around the house. He looked up to see her hiding in the bush and watching him through the fence, obviously wondering how she was going to get back in for some more of that good tucker if he carried on in this fashion. Several times, she'd dash across behind him, out onto the airstrip, then disappear back into the bush and around behind the house again.

With a couple of pulleys and more rope, the gates close themselves under the weight of driftwood burls.

R obert came in one day with a big grin on his face.
'What do you want next time you get to the shop?'
'Huh?'
'What do you *really* want?'
I rattled off half a dozen things.
'No, not that. What about at a hardware store? You said you wanted one a few weeks ago.' It turned out that he'd found a scrubbing brush washed up on the beach: 'Just what you were asking for!'

W alking home from Barn Bay, for no obvious reason I started recalling my visit to the last whaling station in Albany, Western Australia, in 1974, a year before it closed permanently. At that point we left the beach to climb over Sandrock Bluff. Back on the beach on the south side, we came across the backbone of a southern right whale, a length of about eight vertebrae, approximately six metres long, still joined together and smelly but clean of any meat. A kilometre further on was another length of backbone, then a lot of broken pieces of jawbone washed up amongst the driftwood. We never saw the rib section, but Peter Bowmar later told us that he'd seen it from the air, north of Sandrock Bluff, and I think it must have been the smell of it which triggered my memory of the whaling station.

'Out with the old and in with the… not quite so old,' declared Robert the morning after the beach clean-up of February 2012. Greenstone Helicopters pilot and former fisherman Geoff Robson of Neil's Beach, donated two helicopters and more than 20 hours of flying time to the project. In conjunction with DOC, seven people volunteered their time to pick up rubbish on the beach from Awarua Point to the Cascade River mouth, and subsequent trampers have commented favourably on the state of the beach.

We had 15 fadges of rubbish sitting in front of the hut waiting to be flown out to the road-end. There was a lot of stuff that we definitely did not need. In fact, we added a lot of rubbish that we had collected over the years from the beach to keep it tidy, at least within a reasonable distance of home. I often pick up plastic bottles while filling bags with firewood, and they fly out every couple of months or so with our own plastic rubbish, but buoys with broken eyes tend to accumulate and are not easy for us to get rid of. Christan used to tie a lot of them together to 'hang' under the driftwood helicopter to be his load of deer. When I sang:

> The green grass grew all around my boys,
> The green grass grew all around…

Robin heard it as:

> The green grass grew all around my buoys,
> And the green grass grew all around.

The trawl mesh that had kept the deer out of the garden for several years was deteriorating in the sun, and more and more holes were patched together with odd bits of string. So when we picked up at least two trawl nets on Awarua Point where most of the fishing junk settles, Robert decided to replace the fence and put the old netting into the fadge instead. The worms moved into a new home as three fish-cases were in good condition. We would have liked a new wood-box, but none of the fish-cases fitted into the usual space under the hot-water cupboard and it seemed a bit drastic to rebuild the house for the sake of a new wood-box.

Chapter 24
TECH-NOLOGY CHANGES THINGS

W̶e listened to a story on Radio New Zealand about a family who chose to disconnect all their space-age gadgets. For six months they went without cellphones, internet, iPods, TV and DVD players, hair-straighteners . . . They even turned off the hot-water system for the first two weeks and went swimming instead. Their purpose was to reconnect as a family, and each of them made permanent changes in their lives as a result of what they had learned during that time.

Robin thought that it would be much harder to stop having things that you were used to, whereas for our kids everything they got was new. They didn't miss what they'd never had, and if they did want something enough they would eventually have it.

Before 1987 Robert lived here alone without so much as a transistor radio, and once went for a month without seeing another person, boat or aircraft, not even a jet-stream in the sky. Since I came to live here we have never been so long without seeing man-made machines of some sort, but we have been without speaking to any outside person for six or even seven weeks at a time.

We entered the Age of the Wheel after Christan was born, when Arrowtown friend Janice Hamilton gave us a pram. He slept in the top of it in the garden and, with the addition of a plywood tray, Robert made him a 'high chair' to eat in. And with a fish-case tied to the wheels we had a trolley for hauling firewood and loads of seaweed.

After Christan's birth, when it became more important for Robert to earn money, Mitch gave him a treadle grinding wheel that he had used himself at Big Bay in the days before they had a generator. Robert spent many hours on it carving greenstone, and it was certainly a lot faster than rubbing it by hand on sandstone as he had been doing up to that point.

Whatever was here when the children were babies was taken for granted, like anyone does, so new technology that arrived later was part of the magic of childhood and as wondrous as Catweazle's electrickery. At two, Christan was very proud of his hot-water bottle. Robin had a cover for hers; a teddy bear with its hands sewn together to hang it by, which to her was a sea otter with its hands up on its chest, regardless of the lack of a tail. We called it the otter hotter water bottle.

Visitors were always full of suggestions as to how we could

improve our lives, and electricity was usually at the top of the list: 'What you need is a Ram.' Robert replied that he had been thinking of getting a Pelton wheel. 'Oh, they went out with the horse and cart.' There was a short silence before I pointed out that we didn't have one of them yet, either.

My cousin sent us an electronic Christmas card: *Merry Christmas. I am sending this because I think the kids need a bit of technology.* It was fun for about three playings of 'Jingle Bells', and by then we were all sick of it. They were also given a bear that told the story of 'The Three Bears' in a dreadful American accent as you pressed each toe, and a mouse that sang Christmas carols.

In Queensland staying with Nana and Grandad we weren't very interested in TV, but we did enjoy watching videos of our own choice. We hired *When the Whales Came* and *The Secret of Roan Inish, Storm Boy* and *Blue Fin…*

Christan had a plastic cellphone that had contained bubble gum, and this became his 'radio', like Robert's hand-held VHF. He stood up on the windowsill calling Swag or Elmo as they passed by, crayfishing. After watching *Blue Fin*, in which the fishing boat *Dog Star* goes missing in a storm, it was: 'Gorge River to *Dog Star*: you about there, *Dog Star*?' It didn't work so well after he dropped it into the bath: it started to beep continuously and had to be banished into the workshop until the battery ran out.

Candles cost us a fortune in the first few years, and they often smoked and stank. Our eyes were not getting any younger, either, and instead of reading with a single candle we'd need four or five. The kerosene lantern also stank. For a year or two we used the Tilley lantern which gave much more light and was worth the extra effort of lighting it, but it rarely worked properly and after I realised that the mantle was actually radioactive, I hated it. Thorium is apparently an alpha-emitter; alpha particles are relatively heavy and have to be ingested to do any harm, so I objected to having the Tilley lamp hung over the table. Since that was where the nail was, I tried not to put the food under it, but when Robin threw up after eating too close to it we stopped hanging it there. Smoke alarms also seemed like a great step forward, until we learned that they too contained radioactive americium. They were a bloody nuisance, going off every time I cooked venison steak or opened the stove without first opening the flue, but somehow, once these things are invented, you can no longer do without them.

In a wooden house with the fireplace close to the main doorway, any accident there would probably block the escape route. So Robert built windows without catches that open outwards, so the kids could always push their way out if necessary. He has always insisted on high levels of safety around the fire.

After getting an alternator out of a wrecked Triumph, Robert carved a propeller from a piece of 10 x 10 centimetre rimu. For safety's sake he set it up at the other end of the airstrip, mounted on top of a log off the beach, with ropes attached so that we could pull it away from the wind if necessary. We ran a light for an hour or so each night for a week until the new 12-volt battery started to go flat, whereupon we loaded it onto the trolley to make a grand procession down to the windmill to plug it in for recharging.

We never figured out what went wrong. Perhaps the alternator didn't work or it may not have been wired properly. Maybe the windmill just didn't get up enough revolutions per minute for it to kick in, whereas a generator might have sooner. With no other method of charging it, the battery had to wait until we could send it out with a friend to a battery-charger, by which time it was kaput. One hundred and sixty dollars to run a single light for a week! It must have been the most expensive electricity in the country.

It wasn't much longer before we bought the first solar panel and another battery. As well as having a light at night, Robert could run a small motor and a diamond saw or grinding wheel for working greenstone during the day when the sun was shining. At first the increased opportunity to produce saleable items seemed enormous, but as happens to everyone else, the more you have the more you seem to need. We gradually added four more solar panels, each more efficient than the last as the technology improved, and each time we thought we'd now have enough forever.

Most of the changes happened either in response to the needs of the children or to the things they did themselves. We talked for years about having a small freezer. Christan was growing quickly and we asked for more and more meat on the monthly shopping list, but without refrigeration we'd have to eat it quickly before it went off. Mince or stewing steak could be kept for several days by bringing it to the boil for a few minutes each day. Bacon could be kept until last, but we'd always be eating to a time limit. I have two good pots and two large stainless steel bowls plus sundry smaller things. We were delighted when Mitch sent up a small deer from Big Bay one day. After giving away the front legs, we ate steak for two days, followed by a Sunday roast on Friday. Every bowl and pot in the house was full of meat. I juggled cake mixture into the baking tin, to empty the bowl for the half-cooked roast to sit in while I washed the camp oven to cook the cake, and so on. Both pots had to be boiled each day to keep the stewing meat sterile, while we ate cold roast venison for a couple more days.

Christan was learning about food hygiene at Mt Aspiring College, and his teacher Janet Malloch asked me whether I'd talk to the class about how we preserved food. I declined, thinking that I would probably end up telling them how much we get away with and perhaps that was not quite what she had in mind.

So it was Christan's food requirements that pushed us to buy the freezer. He was 13 and went through three shoe sizes that year.

At the same time we needed a wind generator to fill some of the gap in sunlight hours, particularly during the winter. We could always burn candles when we needed to, but meat in the freezer didn't allow for much downtime. And a few months later when Christan wanted to be able to keep whitebait frozen reliably, he bought a petrol generator himself, for $120.

Staying home for six months at a time meant that changes in the outside world seemed to keep accelerating. In 2007 I wondered for the first time whether I was becoming unable to keep up with the relentless march of technology. As my brother apparently couldn't post letters anymore, he presented me with an email address in case he occasionally felt like communicating.

Collecting our mail in Arrowtown at the end of the same trip, we found the gift of a digital camera from Anne Mitchell. She had also thought to include a battery-charger, which came in handy as the kids hardly put the camera down for the first few weeks except to change the batteries.

Between my complaints about the rapid rate of changing

technology and the fact that I had to wait some time before I got to figure out how to use the camera, the kids, now 15 and 12, were inclined to pat me on the head and strut about in a superior manner, which could have been very irritating if it hadn't been so funny. I certainly did my bit to reinforce it when Christan stuck the camera in front of me with a red light flashing. Thinking he must have set it on the timer, I waited for the flash to explode in my face yet again ... and waited . ... and ... When nothing happened, needless to say, I started pulling faces and sticking out my tongue — unaware that I was being videoed!

Without telephone contact, our main communication was of course by mail. While at school in Wimbledon, my grandmother had written a letter to her parents in China every week, often describing each day in detail. Admittedly, one entry simply stated *Tuesday — washed my hair and dried it by the fire*, but overall her letters, which we still have, are a joy to read and a wonderful record of her teenaged self and the sort of life she led. We also have letters written by my grandfather from China during the Second World War; by my great-grandfather to his father during the siege of the Peking legations in 1900; my great-great-grandfather to his father about his wife and their first two babies, both of whom died in infancy in China; my great-great-great-grandfather to the bishop defending his new translation of the Bible and complaining that 'the Bishop denies to me that liberty of thought which he claims for himself'.

Various other writing has survived in our family, providing glimpses into the lives of those who have gone before us. Written records like these have perhaps come to an abrupt halt, as who today bothers to keep records of email correspondence, much of it only a few words long? No doubt great events still occur, but with instant communicátion we wonder how many detailed records are still kept for posterity.

Mind you, I did find letter-writing a great chore, especially when you have to rewrite so much of it several times over for different recipients. I thought if I had a computer I could type it once and edit it to be sent to different people; press the 'delete swear words' button and send it to my grandmother.

Non-technological forms of communication can be used at times, particularly with those closest to us, although usually not at will.

Aged four, Christan came running by as I hung washing on the line, saying, 'Trampers coming!'

We looked but I couldn't see anyone, and, as one of his favourite games at the time was to pretend that there were trampers staying in the hut next-door, I went back to what I was doing. Christan ran in to tell Robert, who was in the shower washing his hair at the time, and really had him skipping. We all went out for another look, but Christan said that they were way up by the cave — beyond the limit of our vision, but who could say when it came to his?

'They must have stopped for a rest,' he said.

I often had the feeling myself of looking up the beach and knowing that someone would come that day, so we didn't tell him he was wrong.

'So where are these trampers?' we asked three hours later, his credibility at an all-time low.

He went out for another look and there *was* someone coming. As we watched, more and more of them appeared around the nearest point, until we had eight people from the Fiordland Tramping Club hoping to be rowed across the river.

Another time, I had taken Robin to Dunedin when the Correspondence School had chosen her to attend 'Hands on Science' at Otago University in January 2010, and Robert was alone at home when our beloved Chooky became ill and died within 24 hours. The night before he had told me by phone that she was sick, but sitting in a cinema with my sister I missed his call to my cellphone as the ring-tone was drowned out by the opening music of *Avatar*. I didn't recognise the caller's number, either, as he had rung via satellite broadband using Skype, but I'll never forget the feeling of dread that hit me in the pit of my stomach. I'm afraid I didn't enjoy the movie and still had to deliver something to Robin for her fancy dress costume for the '2010; A Space Odyssey' dance that night. She started crying when she saw me, and explained that she had been feeling funny since the night before without understanding why. Although I 'knew', I didn't officially *know* until Robert got hold of me later, so I was able to get through the quick visit without telling her and spoiling her last evening.

In contrast, I was happy to let my grandmother go in peace. Comet McNaught spread across the sky in 2007 while she slept through her last days, only taking sips of water when she occasionally woke. I knew that she was on her way out, but, although I'd thought about her several times throughout the day, I found it impossible to reach her or even to hold her in mind for long.

At about 8.00 or 8.30pm on 26 January, I cooked tea for our tramper friend Ron Miller from Lumsden, and his grandson Ben, while he sat telling us about his friend who had recently died of Parkinson's disease.

'In the end he just slept and didn't wake up to eat.'

'That's what my grandmother is doing at the moment,' I

said, and from that moment she was with me all evening until I went to sleep.

The following morning Ron and Ben headed north to Barn Bay only to get stuck at the Cascade River for three days of rain. Seventeen-year-old Ben was so hungry that he didn't notice the weevils in the WeetBix they found in Maurice Nolan's hut.

I went south, taking a load of food to Ryan's Creek. We planned to fly to Big Bay when our next supply plane landed, for a few days' possum trapping. We'd walk home, spending a night in Robert's bivvy on the way, and if we didn't have to carry so much food it would make the walk more enjoyable. We'd leave the traps at Big Bay to be picked up later, but bring home the fur to be sure that it was kept properly.

I enjoyed my walk that day, and my grandmother was with me all the way as she hadn't been for a very long time. So it was no surprise when a Robinson R22 helicopter landed 15 minutes after I arrived home, and the pilot Brian Adams told me that she had died. I didn't feel there was anything to be sad about that day. She was well and truly ready to go, and I was glad to let her. Although having seen her only three times since coming to New Zealand in 1986, it surprised me how much I missed her presence in my life. Later, Mum told me that my grandmother had been awake for half an hour and talking, and that the last thing she said before going back to sleep was 'Where's Catherine?' It was 3.30pm in Perth, without daylight saving, and 8.30 here, as I was cooking tea for Ron and Ben.

Back at the Big Bay hut I watched Comet McNaught through the window at the end of my bed as it headed towards the South Celestial Pole and my grandmother drifted away with it. The following month the Auckland planetarium announced on the radio that it could no longer be seen with the naked eye, but we could still see it in our dark sky for another week until the waxing moon became too bright.

I was very disappointed when the first mail-drop after my grandmother's death didn't contain a single letter from my family, but when I told them so they got impatient with me and suggested I should keep up with the times. My brother sent an email to the address he'd set up for me with details as to how I should go about receiving them.

'Go down to the nearest Dick Smith's store and buy a laptop . . .' He also managed to answer several of my urgent questions of three months earlier in the first couple of sentences or at least suggested websites where I could try to find out the answers for myself.

'What about a stamped, self-addressed envelope?' I asked, but I gave my new email address to other people in case they also wished to communicate with me that way, promising to check it in five months if I got a chance on our next trip to town.

Just a year after we rejoined the twentieth century by buying a car, we leapt straight into the twenty-first with a laptop computer. Seven months later, before Christan went away to school, we flew Roger Crowe in from Haast to add a satellite dish to the other technology on our roof and — bingo! — we were in touch with the rest of the world by email, Skype and Facebook. I had always accepted my limited means of communication with my family as part of what we were doing here, but neither of us wanted to be out of touch with our son. He'd spent six weeks whitebaiting at Big Bay the previous spring, two of which we spent with him, but for the rest of the time we received only two letters from him, dropped from a low-flying aeroplane! Although he was only 30 kilometres away, to us it seemed that he might just as well have been on the moon, and the fact that my great-granny in China didn't receive the news of her mother's death in England until a month after the event didn't leave us feeling any better about it.

All these new gadgets created an awful lot of work. Christan was hardly ever available to answer the telephone during the day, so we'd have to run the generator at night to drive the 12-volt battery-charger. An inverter then supplied 240 volts to the computer and modem. Robert used a few 240-volt tools, but mostly we felt safer sticking with the 12-volt systems already in place so long as we could charge the batteries. Unfortunately, the $120 generator that Christan had bought with his own pocket money was pretty rough, and it had already blown smoke out of the 240-volt circuit in the freezer and burned out several cheap drill motors, so it wasn't long before it burned out the first battery-charger.

Robert liked to have someone to talk to as he worked through all these problems, and Christan had always been happy to fill this role with his own technical interest. With him away, it fell to me to support Robert in his frustrations. Together we could often reach a conclusion that I couldn't have got to alone, although I lost interest when Robert seemed to be inventing new laws of physics to suit the situation.

In the middle of a long spell of wintry bad weather we had very little solar power, so I was up early in the morning while the easterly wind whistled down the valley driving the windmill. I called Christan's cellphone while he was on his way to school to let him know why we would not be ringing for a while and to ask him to order a new battery-charger for us from a shop in Dunedin. My mum was coming to stay within a couple of weeks, so it arrived on the plane with her. Then, as soon as we'd installed it, the inverter stopped!

I took myself off to bed for a while to knit something and re-establish my presence of mind. Technology, while solving some problems, creates many others. I was still living in the middle of nowhere and had to accept whatever we did or did not have.

Three DOC guys were camped next-door working on the hut, and their generator was a very nice one that ran evenly and could be used with confidence to run delicate electronic equipment. Again we called Christan, and he arrived home for the Easter holidays with a new inverter under his arm. He walked in the door, flicked the switch on the old one and it went! This is a great skill that he has, and the inverter continues to work three years later. Mind you, we'd already tried that particular remedy ourselves several times.

It was a great relief when the generator finally gave up the ghost and we could buy something better. Again, Christan arrived home with it, this time just for the flight in and out with a load of groceries, but he joined in the excitement of starting it up. Our faces lit up as it fired on the second pull of the cord — Robin and I had often taken turns to pull-start the old one 30 or 40 times while the other sat on it — then fell again as fuel pissed out in all directions. Two or three hours and several metres of thread, sealing-tape and chewing gum later, we were back on power.

Having the internet via satellite broadband means that I can check the emails each day or two and know that my family are all well. This has made a big difference and is nice to have, although I managed well enough without it until the kids left home. But I didn't want to go long without hearing from them, when the option was available. Christan is always telling me that I worry about him too much, but I deny it: 'I'm not worrying, but I do like to know when I don't have to.'

For the rest of it, we take it with a large dose of salt whenever people rave to us about how wonderful the internet is and how you can find anything you want to know. Maybe other people are better at it than we are, but we quickly get bored with wading through gigabytes of information about everything you could possibly want to know but probably don't. We much prefer to hear the news on the radio than read it online. You can be doing something useful while you listen, and we really don't have much time to waste in the day. It is understandably very expensive via satellite, so we only have one gigabyte per month, which doesn't go very far when either of the kids are at home, especially as time goes on and we become more accustomed to using it.

And finally, there is the question of power. On a sunny day in summer we have relatively unlimited electricity available, but that is exactly the time when you don't want to be sitting inside looking at a screen. Robert will be carving greenstone, also using the power while it is available, and I probably have something better to do. I prefer to write a letter offline and just get on quickly during the day to send it while checking for incoming messages. Still, with banking and ordering things online to save having to buy them when we get out to town, it can take up a lot of time, and Robert occasionally has to remind me to keep it in balance. Not that letter-writing the old way didn't take up a lot of time, of course.

Anyway, the world out there does seem a little less crazy since 2008 when the recession set in.

Chapter 25

WINGS WEATHERED, FIT TO SOAR

Our friends Cliff and Diane Marchant had five children at Port Gore in the outer Marlborough Sounds. Although they had road access to their farm, it was much easier to jump into their Cessna 185 and pop across to Wellington to collect the mail. Cliff can fly from there to Auckland before piloting Air New Zealand 747s to Los Angeles and London, and back home again the next week. Their children have all chosen careers in aviation: Karen is a flight attendant with Emirates, Paul is a pilot in the Marlborough Sounds and Nelson area since returning from Botswana, Nikki and Chris are aircraft engineers, and Mike is training to be a pilot.

'Not much imagination!' Diane laughed.

Cliff once said to us, 'People used to tell us that we were

depriving our kids by living as we did. Now they ask, "How come they all turned out to be such nice people?" So what is it that we were depriving them of?'

I would have found it harder if Christan and Robin had felt deprived. When Christan was two I met his Long cousins, who are all very well off and have everything that opens and shuts; private-school educations, money to spend on McDonald's hamburgers and Coke. I spent quite a bit of time watching them and wondering whether I was doing the right thing. Christan was five the next time we saw them, and I could see that he didn't think he was missing out on anything, thanks.

Still, at various times the kids would want something, particularly as they progressed through the teenaged years, and various items were added to the shopping trolley that hadn't been there previously. I suspect that many other mothers have the same problem at that age. If mayonnaise and tomato paste had been on the shopping list forever, they would have become ordinary and the kids would have wanted something else instead. Worse still, if you have everything there would be nothing left to wish for! Besides, two or three times a year we came out to town for them to experience all these great things; and every two or three years we spent a month or so on the Sunshine Coast in Queensland with Robert's parents — right in the thick of it with shops, TV and I'm not quite sure what else, on every hand. There was plenty of chance to catch up on anything that might have been missing. So how many kids living in Auckland get to experience what Christan and Robin have? And I bet no one tells their parents, 'You are depriving them!'

When Janet McIntyre was here in 2007 filming for the TV One *Sunday* programme, she tried hard to get the kids to say what they were missing out on, but they couldn't think of anything. Hanging out with kids their own age, certainly, but there is plenty of bad in that as well as good. Whatever situation you are born into has advantages and disadvantages, and overall we have mostly felt confident that the benefits have outweighed anything else.

Travelling out of here alone for the first time, aged 16, Christan stayed with a friend in Christchurch between bus transfers. Dave Hill gave him the remote control for the TV, wondering which of 73 channels he would choose. *Flick, flick, flick.* Finally he stopped, and Dave peeked in to find Christan watching the weather channel.

With kids heading away to school and tertiary education, the pressure mounted on Robert to earn money. He'd always pay for them to fly home and out again whenever they had a chance to get here for a few days. We gave Christan $200 a week on top of all his school expenses: $100 for rent and $100 to live on. I suggested that buying lunch at the school canteen would be reasonable maybe a couple of times a week and he'd be sure of getting a good feed, but that making an effort to bring his own would work out quite a bit cheaper. Only once, in the winter, did he ask for extra — $40 for the power bill. I asked several times how he was managing and whether it was enough to cover everything. His vague answers made me suspect that it was plenty, particularly when I heard that he'd bought lunch for his mate at school. 'But he had no lunch!' was the explanation, and certainly I was glad to hear that my son was generous.

I took him grocery shopping and bought him a good load to get started; tins of food to keep under his bed for a quick meal when necessary, various things in the freezer which we had already stocked with venison and fish. He also needed toilet paper, toothpaste, soap, sunscreen and things to clean his bathroom.

In the sunny corner of his room at Jane Hawkey's house he set up his fur-sewing machine and earned a bit of money during the year sewing possum-skin cushions and scarves.

He had to buy his own toys and had plenty of money in the bank for that. He needed skis, and also bought a lot of climbing and kayaking equipment. I'd offered him a bike for Christmas, but at the time he'd changed his mind about going to school and had opted for a cellphone instead. From Albert Town where he lived it was five kilometres into town, which was a nice ride in the summertime but a bit bleak in winter, particularly in snow. He could take the school bus whenever he chose to, but would only be able to go to school and straight back. To get to the shop for food or to hang out with his friends after school, he needed a bike.

We checked out Wanaka Wastebusters who had plenty of options, but all involved a lot of tools to assemble them which Christan didn't have access to. Next we called in for a cup of tea with a friend, by the end of which Christan had a bike. She said it was nothing flash but would get him around perfectly well until he could find something he really wanted. I bought him a helmet and a visibility vest, and we worked out the best way to ride to school to keep off the main road. Then, with him mobile, I left him to it.

Robin and I spent a week on Stewart Island later that year, tramping and looking for kiwi before visiting Sirocco, the celebrity kakapo on Ulva Island in Paterson Inlet. We caught the boat back to Bluff and collected Christan in Albert Town in the afternoon, as well as my niece Elena, who was coming home with us during his school holidays. She'd been accepted directly into the second year of the Otago Polytech course in Outdoor Leadership and Management on the strength of the university classes she'd taken in the United

States during the exchange year she'd organised for herself, and the summer job she'd had as a rafting guide in Montana. During those holidays, Christan had applied and was also accepted directly into the second year of the same course, and later won a scholarship from Mt Aspiring College to cover $1500 of his fees each year.

But Elena needed some tramping experience before the following February. I blanched slightly when she asked whether there was a shop we could stop at along the way to buy tape to strap up her ankle. This was the first I'd heard about the stress fracture sustained the previous winter when she'd fallen from a climbing wall and twisted an ankle as she landed.

'Do you have any idea where we are going? This is not an afternoon stroll down the beach.'

'The physio said I'll be fine so long as I strap it,' she insisted, but I remained doubtful.

It was already dark by the time we reached the end of the road into the Cascade. The kids organised places to sleep in the hut, and I rigged up the solar panel on the dashboard of the car, connecting it to the battery as it would be sitting there for six weeks until we walked back out.

Elena started vomiting in the night and continued through to the morning before falling asleep at last. Christan, Robin and I discussed the possibilities. I was worried about getting stuck at Barn Bay while the rest of us came down with the bug, perhaps a day apart. Robert was expecting us home by the following afternoon and there would be no way to get a message to him if we continued on. Robin told me that Elena had been feeling sick all weekend without it preventing her kayaking the Nevis stretch of the Kawerau River, so when she woke up I asked, 'You aren't thinking of walking to Barn Bay sick, are you, as well as on a sore ankle?'

'Oh, no way!' she said. 'I don't dare move or I'll be sick again.'

At three, with Elena still sleeping, I made the decision to return to Haast to send Robert a gift of two kids. There was a good chance that Ken Hutchins and Jeremy Arthur would be hunting down our way that evening in their Hughes 500 helicopter and, although I wouldn't ask them to go out of their way, they would possibly be happy to drop Christan and Robin off as they flew past. So it was back up the hill to the car, disconnect the solar panel and reconnect the battery, then drive 50 kilometres up to Haast, where we flagged them down as they passed us, heading to the hangar. They said it would be no problem to do it — but it certainly was for me! I asked Ken to please be extra careful, as this was a precious load he was carrying. I didn't mind so much when I was in the machine with them, but to watch both my kids fly away together was a difficult milestone in my life.

Back at the Cascade four hours later, after the sun had set, I heard a helicopter flying down the Arawhata Valley in the distance, returning to Haast after the hunt, and could assume that everyone was safe.

Robert was disappointed when I didn't appear from the chopper, but he reminded himself that I wasn't due back before the following day anyway. Ken had a job to do in the morning, but he collected Elena and me from the Cascade around noon. After dropping us at home, he and Jeremy carried on south to Yates Point for a hunt. We saw them heading north again later with a load of deer, flying past about a kilometre out to sea, the shortest line between two points. It seemed to us that it could be a long way to swim, but they had two empty fuel containers to hold onto if something stopped working suddenly.

Elena never did get any tramping experience before she and Christan started at Otago Polytech. She had arranged to walk the Heaphy Track with two American friends in January, after spending a week with Christan in Wanaka. Both of them needed to log several more hours of rock-climbing experience including various techniques, and John Hammond, Christan's physics teacher, was an excellent instructor and was keen enough to teach them a lot that week in his own time.

All went well until Wednesday afternoon, when Elena asked for more rope to make a long reach to the last hold at the top of her climb, missed and fell 10 metres. That still would have been OK if she hadn't whacked her ankle against a ledge just before the rope stopped her fall. Some other climbers nearby had a splint, so after immobilising her ankle they lowered her and carried her towards John's vehicle. Christan said that lowering her down the rockface was the easy part, but it was a long way to carry her from the bottom. DOC kept the gate locked, but if John could get a key he could drive in a lot closer to pick her up. When he couldn't get hold of the policeman he tried Search and Rescue, who were very excited and wanted to send a helicopter. Evidently things had been a bit quiet lately and, even when they'd been talked out of that, they insisted on bringing Elena into the Medical Centre in an ambulance.

Chapter 26

HOME IS HOME, WHERE THE HEART IS

When the kids were small I woke up each morning and checked where they were; usually either in their beds or in ours. The sound of the door opening would wake me, and I'd always be aware of their whereabouts. As they grew, of course, we gradually let them go, but during the last couple of weeks before Christan went away to school I realised how entrenched the habit was to wake up in the morning and account for the kids.

Christan flies on a long kite-string. He blasts in and out of home like a cyclone, leaving a big mess and an echoing silence, even if he has spent half the time catching up on sleep. Although reliable, he is also unpredictable, and you can never be sure where he will be by tomorrow. Rosco from Milford Kayaks offered him a guiding job before he'd finished the polytech course in Outdoor Leadership, one of the youngest people to gain the Rock 1 qualification from the New Zealand Outdoors Instructors' Association. At the end of an exciting summer in Milford Sound, which included climbing Mitre Peak alone in sandshoes and bare feet, he took the Tai Poutini Polytech course in ski patrol at Treble Cone skifield, having convinced them to let him onto it despite his marginal skiing ability. At the end of the season he fished for whitebait at Big Bay and trapped possums at home, having had to turn down a job offer as a ski patroller at Big White skifield in British Columbia when he couldn't get a work visa quickly enough.

Four more days passed before he had a job as a cold-galley chef on the last Antarctic voyage of the *Kapitan Khlebnikov*, a Russian icebreaker. When several of their proposed crew were denied entry into New Zealand at the last moment, an urgent call went out for more, and Christan was at home when he received an invitation via my sister's workmate's husband on a Saturday. The ship was sailing from Lyttelton on the following Thursday, 9 November 2011, with over a hundred passengers. Before disembarking in Perth in January, he had an interview with the expedition crew and hopes to go again sometime on another ship. Next he got a job fund-raising for the Red Cross and other charities in Queensland, before coming home to take up a ski patrol position at Porter's Heights for the winter. We were lucky to have him home for a few weeks in between, the longest he has been here since leaving to go to school.

Robin applied for, and was accepted into, the hostel at Mt Aspiring College which runs a busy Outdoor Pursuits programme on weekends, and she makes the most of every possible opportunity. She was elected to the school council and was on the committees for the 40 Hour Famine and Shave for a Cure.

She intends to study zoology and botany at the University of Otago, with the aim of working with endangered birds. Over the past few years she has kept an eye on the local Fiordland crested penguin breeding colony, and we have surveyed them and little blue penguins for the West Coast Penguin Trust. She and I have been out with DOC people to check on transmitters and collect eggs from the Haast tokoeka kiwi and the Okarito brown kiwi, to be hatched and raised on predator-free islands until they are big enough to fight off a stoat and can be released back into their sanctuaries. We were also lucky enough to spend two weeks on Codfish Island volunteering with the Kakapo Recovery Programme in May 2011. Eleven chicks had survived, seven of which were hand-reared in Invercargill after the rimu crop failed. Only four of the mothers had learned to feed their chicks on the supplementary diet, and Robin and I carried food out to feeding stations for them. We also regularly cleaned and topped-up food hoppers for the other breeding females and some of the males, to get them back up to strength after the breeding season, and for many of the juveniles. Robin learnt to use the telemetry equipment to track them, and helped to fit transmitters on three of the chicks before they left the nest at the end of our fortnight.

If Robin says she will do something, it may take a bit of nagging at times but usually it will be done. The house was not much quieter with her going, and her quiet steadfastness feels securely close. She slips back in without much of a stir, and leaves a presence, almost a fragrance, behind such that you don't quite notice that she has gone.

> *On Children*
> ...
>
> *You are the bows from which your children*
> *as living arrows are sent forth.*
> *The archer sees the mark upon the path of the*
> *infinite,*
> *and He bends you with His might*
> *that His arrows may go swift and far.*
> *Let your bending in the archer's hand be for*
> *gladness;*
> *For even as He loves the arrow that flies,*
> *so He loves also the bow that is stable.*

— Kahlil Gibran

Drawing Christan's arrow was a bit like the second day of the target event at the Junior National Championships in Melbourne in 1980. Melbourne is renowned for having all four seasons in one day, but that day we could have done with a bit of the other three. Nor did we have any help from Pat, a member of the Perth club who was a very worldly nun with a wonderful sense of humour. Whenever the weather was discussed with respect to a major tournament, she would offer to 'have a word with the boss upstairs'. And as she lifted her bow and drew it back to aim, everyone else would follow her as the wind always seemed to blow less strongly.

This day it was wet and freezing cold, and we huddled into our tracksuit tops between ends, shedding them for the sake of accuracy whenever it was time to shoot the next three arrows. My coach, Keith Gaisford, hugged me to help me stay warm, as I fought to keep from slipping off the leaders' board that displayed our updated scores after every six arrows.

A traffic-light system told us how much time we had left to shoot three arrows at a time. The green light came on for two minutes when all was clear to start, then changed to orange to warn us that only 30 seconds remained. Any arrow not yet in the air when the lights changed to red was forfeited, and the next two archers at each target stepped forward to take their places on the line.

As I tried to hold steady against the gusting wind with less than 10 seconds remaining, a raindrop hit me right in the eye and all I could see was a blur of orange light pulsing larger and smaller. There was no time left to let down and try again, so all I could do was let go and hope that the arrow would at least hit the target somewhere.

While Robin's event was held in calmer, more tranquil weather, Christan's childhood was a stormy one with many squalls and blustery periods and the occasional gloriously sunny, sandfly-free day. Having released my hold on his arrow, I stand and watch it fly straight and true towards the gold.

I t seemed that we could always go if necessary, perhaps for the kids to go to school. Watching friends from Haast send their children off to board for high school, I wondered how they could bear it, but understood that they were bound to where they lived, whether by a mortgage, a job, other children, or even their family background. I felt that nothing would hold me anywhere more strongly than the bond between us, and it came as a bit of a shock when Christan was ready to go alone. But he needed us here to come home to.

So I'm here for now and can't see anything changing in the near future. Beyond that, I'll see when I get there. I've never made any promises too far ahead, but have always been able to say, 'I'm happy with what I'm doing and mostly satisfied that it is worthwhile.'

At the worst times I'd look up at the dead rata tree on the top of the hill across the river as it held its last branches up in the air, defying the sou'west wind. I always took strength from the sight and promised myself that I, too, could do whatever I had to. So far, I haven't found anything I'd prefer to be doing.

When Christan left I felt that I had suddenly hit middle-age. My eyesight went downhill, I can't work as much as I did, and my memory, which I have always prided myself on, is definitely not what it was. In general women are so much better at multi-tasking than men, and it's just as well that it should be so. If the hunter was distracted every time the baby cried the family would all starve! So long as I only had to cook the food provided, I'd get there sometime with babies intact, and we could always eat it raw at a pinch. It's a scary fact that a menopausal woman, without the same need for those skills, becomes more like a one-track-minded man: 'Don't expect to ask me anything complicated when I'm doing something else, because it just doesn't work anymore. You'd understand that.'

I discovered that having Christan leave wasn't nearly as bad as dreading it had been, and I tried to keep that in mind when it came to Robin. But there were some glaring differences. While I still had her here, I had something to do every morning when I got out of bed. As much as I told myself that other people are worse off — perhaps their child is dying — it doesn't make you *feel* any better. I know that I wouldn't want them to be still at home when they are 40, although I hope they will be close by, and even if you had six kids, you'd miss the absent one and still run out of chicks in the nest eventually.

For 20 years I have written *Mother* in the box marked 'occupation' on immigration forms, and now I felt redundant. What was I supposed to put now? *Redundant mother?* I came here to have kids and grow vegetables, so it seemed that I'd done it, finished the job, and I was left wondering 'What next?'

But life does continue and you don't stop being a mum. There is an enormous pride in watching them fly away. Like the archer, you can draw the arrow, aim carefully, do everything within your ability to send it straight, but once released there is nothing more you can do but watch to see how it flies, and accept, with pride or disillusionment, the results of your effort.

And it is so nice to see how much they enjoy being here when they are. 'Home's home!' So many people have said that to us over the past year or two.

I sat for ages on the beach one day when I should have been collecting firewood — evidently there was enough of a breeze to keep the sandflies away — taking stock of what I had to be thankful for and acknowledging how lucky I am. After all the fights and the hassles, the doubts I had about setting this ratbag loose on society, sure enough, just when they get nice to live with, they leave.

Once upon a time it was a serious crime, a breach of promise, to break off an engagement to be married. Times changed, but it was still difficult to obtain a divorce. Today, people split up left, right and centre, but it is never an easy thing when there are children involved. I have always been extremely grateful that neither Robert nor I had children from a prior relationship, and even more so that, regardless of anything that happened between us, however hard it got at times, neither of us thought for one moment that there was any alternative. The idea of splitting up and sharing the kids every second weekend was simply not an option, no matter what.

It is a great joy to be able to walk out the door and pick a salad for tea. Although I have earned very little money over the past 20 years I've certainly worked, and if Robert bought the sausage, not only did I cook it, I also planted, weeded, harvested, washed, cooked and served the potatoes, parsnip, silverbeet, zucchini and lettuce, rocket, tomato and parsley salad, and collected mushrooms from the airstrip. Spray-free, organic, biodynamic and not genetically modified. I may not earn much, but I figure I'm richer than anyone with a mortgage and an outstanding credit-card bill. What money we have wouldn't go far in the outside world, but it has always earned interest, rather than costing us. And while earning relatively little, we don't pay for petrol to get to and from work, for decent clothes to wear to the office (where you can't wear the same thing every day), for childcare, for a plumber, electrician or roofer when we don't have time to do the job ourselves.

Anyone who knows the feeling you get while driving from Wanaka to the Haast Pass, on first entering the beech forest after Makarora, will understand what I would miss most if I ever have to leave here. In the same way that I feel incomplete when too far away from the ocean, I treasure the serenity I find when I am surrounded by the beautiful, untouched, sub-tropical rainforest that clothes much of the west coast of the South Island of New Zealand. It has been an enormous privilege to make Gorge River my home.

The Flowers

...

Broom behind the windy town, pollen o' the pine —
Bell-bird in the leafy deep where the ratas twine —
Fern above the saddle-bow, flax upon the plain —
Take the flower and turn the hour and kiss your
love again!

— Rudyard Kipling

For more information about our titles visit
www.randomhouse.co.nz